BEYOND HYPOCRISY

Beyond Hypocrisy

Decoding the News in an Age of Propaganda

— *Including* —

A Doublespeak Dictionary for the 1990s

by Edward S. Herman
Illustrations by Matt Wuerker

South End Press   Boston, MA

Cover by Matt Wuerker
Edited, designed and produced by the South End Press collective
Manufactured in the United States of America on acid-free paper

Library of Congress Cataloging-in-Publication Data

Herman, Edward S.
    Beyond hypocrisy : decoding the news in an age of propaganda : including A doublespeak dictionary for the 1990s / by Edward S. Herman; illustrations by Matt Wuerker.
        p.   cm.
    Includes index.
    ISBN 0-89608-436 (cloth : acid-free) : $40.00
    ISBN 0-89608-435-3 (paper : acid-free) : $13.00
    1. Mass media and language—United States.   2. Mass media—Political aspects—United States.   3. Press and propaganda—United States. 4. English language—Terms and phrases.   5. United States—Politics and government—1981-1989.   6. United States—Politics and government—1989-   .   I. Title.
    P96.L342U55   1992   92-2901
    302.23'014–dc20   CIP

South End Press, 116 Saint Botolph Street, Boston, MA 02115

99 98 97 96 95 94 93 92   1 2 3 4 5 6 7 8 9

Table of Contents

The enemy of the moment always represented absolute evil, and it followed that any past or future agreement with him was impossible... He, Winston Smith, knew that Oceania had been in alliance with Eurasia as short a time as four years ago. But where did that knowledge exist?... It was quite simple. All that was needed was an unending series of victories over your own memory. "Reality control," they called it; in Newspeak, "doublethink."

—George Orwell, <u>1984</u>

PREFACE

The Roots of Doublespeak

This book is about doublespeak, the misuse of words by implicit redefinition, selective application of "snarl" and "purr" words, and other forms of verbal manipulation. These usages are integral to language in a world of growing professionalization in advertising, public relations, and news management, and the increasingly urgent demands for these services in business and politics. In the business world, the growth of doublespeak also results from intensifying market pressures, along with the challenge of selling indistinguishable, if not downright noxious, goods as exceptionally worthwhile. In the political sphere, the principles of marketing goods have been extended to the packaging and selling of politicians,[1] with commercial tactics and strategies completely supplanting any sense of obligation to informational substance and the requirements of a genuine democracy.[2]

The large, indeed widening, gap between elite aims and practice and the needs and interests of the underlying population also requires the constant application and refinement of doublespeak. Increased pressure on corporate profits, resulting from intensified international competition and sluggish productivity growth from the late 1960s to the present, led the corporate community to abandon the post-World War II social accord with labor and to roll back wages, working conditions, unionization, and government benefits to workers. This corporate counterrevolution has had its political counterpart in the rightward shift of media and politics, and, in due course, in the Reagan and Bush presidencies which elevated the corporate attack on the working class and social wage to the level of national policy. It is therefore not surprising that the hourly real wage of U.S. workers was lower in 1991 than it was in 1973, and that economic insecurity is endemic. At the same time, the upper classes have been treated solicitously and the structures of federal taxes and expenditures have shifted even further in their favor.

1

The increased grass roots mobilization and activism of the past 25 years
has also threatened elite interests, highlighting the widening gap between
elite and mass aims and perspectives. This sharpened awareness has stimulated efforts at popular participation in government, producing what establishment spokespersons refer to as a "crisis of democracy."*

This kind of "threat" from the masses was anticipated and feared by
the country's leaders from its earliest years. They saw themselves as "natural
leaders" and the non-propertied masses as rabble, unfit for participation in
government and posing a problem of control. In Federalist Paper Number
10, James Madison noted the difference between the "permanent interests"
of society (i.e., property interests) and those of the majority, and the possibility that the majority would use the vote to redistribute wealth and income.
He took heart in the great size of the country and the fragmentation of the
population, which he anticipated would allow the natural leaders to prevent
the interests and desires of the majority from being realized.

An elite-dominated press would also serve to protect the permanent
interests, although, oddly enough, in 1822, an older, perhaps more democratically inclined Madison wrote that "a popular government without popular information, or the means of acquiring it, is but a prologue to a farce or
a tragedy, or perhaps both."[3] The farce *cum* tragedy attained new heights in
the post-World War II era, in which spokespersons for the "permanent
interests" saw the need to "scare hell"[4] out of the masses in order to pursue
their "national security"* concerns to the farthest reaches of the globe (and
into outer space).

In his essay on "Politics and the English Language," George Orwell
observed that political language serves to obfuscate an indefensible reality:[5]
"In our time, political speech and writing are largely the defence of the
indefensible....Thus political language has to consist largely of euphemism,
question-begging and sheer cloudy vagueness....The great enemy of clear
language is insincerity. Where there is a gap between one's real and one's
declared aims, one turns as it were instinctively to long words and exhausted
idioms, like a cuttlefish squirting out ink."

This book describes a world of cuttlefish squirting out ink, explaining
the deliberate enlargement of inequalities under the guises of reducing
"entitlements,"* pruning the "fat"* in social budgets, eliminating "boondoggles"* that sap the incentives of the "undeserving poor,"* and "getting
government off our [sic] backs," while at the same time unleashing junk bond
entrepreneurs, greenmailers, leveraged self-dealers, deregulated savings and

---

* An asterisk means that the word or phrase or a variant of it is included in the
Dictionary that follows. Asterisks are given for its initial occurrence in the text and
thereafter only when the doublespeak aspect of the usage is worthy of special
mention.

loan managers with taxpayer insured deposits, purveyors of "market intelligence,"* Pentagon contractors for Freedom Fighters* and Freedom screw drivers, and other entrepreneurs at home. In the areas of foreign and military policy, we have witnessed the sponsorship by "conservatives"* of a rapidly expanding military establishment to protect the "national security" with "Peacekeeper missiles"* and other instruments of overkill. This enormous buildup of weaponry was explained by the need to provide "bargaining chips"* to allow us to reduce weaponry!

We have also seen a rehabilitation of the threat of "terrorism,"* which is what *they* do, to be dealt with by "counterterrorism"* and retaliation, which is what *we* do. Similarly, there has been much "subversion,"* "aggression,"* and even "naked aggression"* abroad, to which we and our side have responded with "counterinsurgency,"* capital intensive warfare to "save"* the victims, and the displacement of elected governments by military regimes which, after a stint of "pacification,"* hold "free elections."*

In his essay, Orwell stressed deliberate obfuscation as the villain in the perversion of language. Elsewhere in his writings, however, there is a more subtle understanding of the power of self-deception and internalization that can make deception a product of "sincere"* belief. In his novel *1984* he notes the possibility of lying while believing:[6]

> To tell deliberate lies while genuinely believing in them, to forget any fact that has become inconvenient, and then, when it becomes necessary again, to draw it back from oblivion for just so long as it is needed, to deny the existence of objective reality and all the while to take account of the reality which one denies—all this is indispensably necessary.

It was part of the genius of President Ronald Reagan that he was able to internalize and truly believe anything that served his purpose.[7] Others master the art of *apparent* sincerity in telling lies. But disputes over sincerity are essentially red herrings. Sincerity is an unmeasurable quality, and lies quickly become internalized truths when they are convenient and consistent with common belief. What is really important in the construction of a world of doublespeak is the ability to lie, whether knowingly or unconsciously, and to get away with it; and the ability to use lies and choose and shape facts selectively, blocking out those that don't fit an agenda or program. The exercise of these abilities allowed President George Bush to condemn Saddam Hussein and Iraq's invasion and occupation of Kuwait in the forceful terms of a moral and principled opposition to aggression, after the Reagan-Bush administration had steadfastly supported Saddam Hussein's aggression against Iran, and after Bush himself had indulged in a straightforward aggression in Panama one year previously.

In another striking case, in 1984 the Reagan administration denounced the election being held in Nicaragua by the Sandinista government because, in the words of Secretary of State George Shultz, "The important thing is that if there is to be an electoral process, it be observed not only at the moment when people vote, but in all the preliminary aspects that make an election really mean something."[8] Shultz included here a free press and access to the media by all political factions; Sandinista harassment and censorship of the Nicaraguan paper *La Prensa* was therefore of grave concern. On the other hand, in El Salvador's elections of 1982 and 1984, held under U.S. sponsorship to legitimate *de facto* military rule, the Reagan administration paid not the slightest attention to "preliminary conditions," but was entirely satisfied with a successful surface imagery "at the moment when people vote," meaning long lines of smiling voters and a large turnout. The violent destruction of two independent newspapers in San Salvador in 1980 and 1981 was not mentioned by U.S. government officials, nor was the murder of some two dozen journalists. On March 17, 11 days before the 1982 election, four Dutch journalists trying to make contact with the Salvadoran rebels were killed by the "security forces."* Subsequently, their bodies were put on display in the San Salvador morgue and foreign correspondents were shepherded in to see the dead reporters, their mutilated genitals fully exposed for journalistic edification. The U.S. Embassy in San Salvador did not denounce this horrendous case of state terror, nor did it or the State Department suggest that the incident might interfere with journalistic freedom[9] or compromise the integrity of the forthcoming election in El Salvador.

The Role of the Mass Media

More striking is the fact that this story of the mutilation and exhibition of the dead journalists did not appear in the *New York Times, Washington Post*, network news, or in the mainstream media altogether.[10] In fact, in its coverage of the 1982 and 1984 elections in El Salvador, the *New York Times* never once mentioned the killing of journalists or the destruction of the two independent papers.[11] It, the other major papers, and even more enthusiastically the TV networks, featured the surface phenomena of long lines of voters and voter turnout,[12] along with other issues on the government's agenda.

By contrast, in covering the Nicaraguan election of 1984, voter turnout was barely mentioned and no significance was attached to it, but questions were raised repeatedly about the constraints on *La Prensa* and limits on the freedom of the press.[13] In other words, the *Times* and other mainstream media followed a dichotomous agenda for the elections in the two countries, in close accord with the U.S. government's effort to support the one and denigrate the other. This process fits perfectly Orwell's principle of double-think—"to forget a fact" or criterion (here, for El Salvador, a "preliminary condition" like freedom of the press) "that has become inconvenient, and then, when it becomes necessary again [to cast doubts on the Nicaraguan election], to draw it back from oblivion for just so long as it is needed." The internalization of this double standard was so complete that Hedrick Smith of the *Times* was able to apply it in a single article discussing both El Salvador and Nicaragua, apparently unaware of his total capture by doublethink.[14]

Media collaboration with the government in fostering a world of doublespeak is essential to its use and institutionalization, and this collaboration has been regularly forthcoming. As indicated in the example above, an important aspect of the process is simply following the double standard and doublethink implicit in the official agenda. This is done with such assurance and self-righteousness, along with the regular and matter-of-fact use of extremely biased sources—mainly, government officials with a political "spin" to execute—that the public dependent on the corporate media is easily swept along on the tide of doublethink.

A corollary and necessary support for the double standard is the systematic avoidance and suppression of information. If only *Nicaraguan* violations of the "preliminary conditions" of elections are relevant, information on the destruction of newspapers, killing of journalists, and the mass murder of civilians (and exposure of *their* mutilated bodies for public education) in El Salvador is not newsworthy and need not be (and is not) reported.[15] If George Bush's moral revulsion at naked aggression is taken at face value by the mainstream media, his own aggressions and support of aggressions elsewhere need not be reported as context that would give his moral claims deeper meaning (and expose their hypocrisy). Rather, the inconvenient facts disappear into Orwell's black hole, and a new implicit system of definitions of aggression and naked aggression are imposed, without acknowledgement or discussion.

It should also be emphasized that the mainstream media not only allow the agendas of news to be bent in accordance with state demands and criteria of utility,[16] they also accept the presuppositions of the state without question. Most important, they accept the nominal objectives of the state as real, and rarely probe into the actual reasons for state policy and actions. As the state always proclaims benevolent aims and responsive and defensive behavior, if these remain unchallenged, and any evidence to the contrary is either ignored or explained away in terms of miscalculation or "tragic error,"*[17] the groundwork is laid for a world of doublespeak. This would be obvious, for example, if the Soviet press had taken it as a premise that the Soviet Union was always responding to external threats, trying to "contain" the United States, and sought to "protect" Afghanistan in its invasion of 1979 or Czechoslovakia in 1968. That the United States was "protecting South Vietnam" and defending it against somebody else's aggression in the years 1960-1975, was as ludicrous as analogous claims by Soviet apologists in regard to Afghanistan, but these presuppositions were maintained by the mainstream media throughout the Vietnam war.[18]

Another dramatic illustration of the importance of state-supportive premises in generating doublespeak was the U.S. mass media's acceptance of the claim that the Reagan administration sought "democracy" in Nicaragua in its assault on that country in the 1980s. This was truly laughable, as the Reaganites were openly nostalgic for the departed Somoza dictatorship, were using as their vehicles for establishing democracy in Nicaragua an army led by ex-Somoza officers,[19] and during the same period were supporting governments entirely free from any democratic taint on a world-wide basis.[20] There was also an extensive and readily available record of U.S. distrust of popular movements and popular rule and support of terror regimes in Central America; in fact, and simultaneous with the crusade for democracy in Nicaragua, the Reaganites were pressing to resume full support for the murderous military government in Guatemala.[21]

An excellent case can be made that it was precisely the genuinely popular and democratic aspects of the Nicaraguan government that aroused Reaganite fears and hostility.[22] But for the mainstream media, the U.S. government pursues benevolent goals, by definition, so that if it says that it seeks democracy in Nicaragua, that settles the matter.[23] The media failed to provide immediate facts and historical context that would clarify what the United States really aimed at in Nicaragua. They also failed to call attention to the blatant contradictions and hypocrisies, and by accepting them, tacitly or explicitly, sustained or participated actively in a system of doublethink.

In 1991, after Bush had saved Kuwait by destroying it (along with Iraq), he indicated that he would not press democracy on that country because this is not something that can be imposed by force.[24] Except in Nicaragua. The mass media once again failed to make a comparison that would provide meaningful context. Perhaps they saw the difference in the fact that Nicaragua had the advantage of more than a half century of U.S. tutelage, which would make them ready for democracy, but only immediately after the Sandinista ascension to power in July 1979!

Plan of the Book

The preceding examples show that doublespeak is tied closely to ways of looking at the world—to political agendas and frames—that give them authenticity and seeming naturalness and inevitability. They also point up the fact that the national media, as part of the national establishment, play a key role in allowing doublespeak to flourish. It is because of the importance of these contexts in giving words meaning and prominence, no matter how egregiously they may distort reality, that this book has a text, footnotes, and cartoons, as well as a lexicon of doublespeak. The text does not encompass all the words in the dictionary, but it puts many of them into a historical and political context and highlights their role as well as their deceptive and hypocritical qualities. The footnotes show that many of them are quite literally applicable or correspond to a historic reality. The text at certain points also addresses some of the systemic mechanisms that help institutionalize doublespeak, such as the claim that there is a liberal and adversary press by illiberal members of the establishment with excellent access to the liberal-adversary press,[25] and the production of experts closely tied to the government who reiterate and amplify government claims and agendas in the adversary media as "independent" authorities.

The political cartoon has flourished in recent times, and the vast array of bullies, crooks, demagogues, and liars who have swaggered across the Reagan-Bush era stage spouting doublespeak, have provided a cornucopia for the sharp etchings and terse lines of cartoon art. Matt Wuerker came into his own in this era as a political cartoonist for *Z Magazine* and elsewhere, and *Beyond Hypocrisy* is greatly enriched by his cartoons, a number of them appearing here for the first time.

The dictionary covers political, and to a much smaller extent, commercial and cultural language for the entire post-World War II era, with special emphasis on the Cold War, militarization and the arms race, the Vietnam war, and the economics and politics of the years from Lyndon Johnson to George Bush. It represents only a sampling of doublespeak language, but it includes a great many key words and phrases like Aggression (and its variants), Commitment, Containment, Defense, Dole, Entitlement, Force, Free Election, Free World, Independent, Law and Order, Leader, Market, Moderate, National Interest, Quiet Diplomacy, Reform, Responsible, Restraint, and Stability that have been central to the language of doublespeak and that have also been the base on which others have been constructed. A certain coherence may be gathered from the text that puts the words into context and shows their interrelations.

The words and definitions in the dictionary are a mixed bag: some are straightforward descriptions of a distressing reality (Cointelpro, Commercial broadcasting, Free-fire zone, Operation Mongoose, and Pro-life); others are "purr" or "snarl" words that allow a covert expression of approval or disapproval (Adventurism, Coddling, Entitlement, Fledgling democracy, Free World, Leader, Marxist-Leninist, Moderate, Politicize, Pretext, Self-appointed, and Stability). Some of the words are euphemisms that obscure and soften an unpleasant reality (Free World, Interrogation, New Federalism,

Pacification, Peace process, Public diplomacy, and Tragic error). Many of the definitions summarize the implied and selective meanings of a term that has a different conventional and traditional usage (Free flow, Negotiations, Reform, Rejectionism, and Restraint). Quite a few of the definitions are playful while striving to capture some important aspect of reality (Activist, Calculated risk, Conservatism, Conspiracy, Individualism, Infotainment, PAC-men, Quotas, Revolution without borders, and Safety net). Many words and definitions fit more than one of these categories. Obviously, the definitions cannot seize all the important facets of a word—to paraphrase Dr. Samuel Johnson on the aphorism, some degree of truth must be sacrificed in the interest of conciseness and salient imagery. Nevertheless, it is hoped that the entire offering of dictionary, text and cartoons will be found enlightening as well as amusing.

Acknowledgements

The dictionary offered here draws in part from the author's *The Great Society Dictionary* , published in 1968 and long out of print, along with updates of that work published in the Nixon era. Many of the usages of those earlier periods are very much alive today, and they are part of an evolving pattern of manipulative and hypocritical language. Dictionary and text also use materials from the author's columns on Doublespeak that have appeared on a monthly basis in *Z Magazine* from its inception in January 1988.

The author is indebted to many friends for suggestions and comments over the years. Noam Chomsky's political writings have been an ongoing analysis of doublespeak and hypocrisy, and have been an important influence on the doublespeak text and lexicon offered here. Another long-time collaborator, Richard DuBoff, has made many contributions over the years to my arsenal of doublespeak. Mary Herman was an invaluable consultant and editor. Thanks are due to Matt Wuerker for his collaboration, which has added a great deal to this book. Cynthia Peters, Todd Jailer and their colleagues at South End Press have made the production phase of this book plain sailing.

1. The Unfree Flow of Information

Limits on Free Speech

Free speech in the United States certainly exists in the sense that dissent can usually be voiced without threat of violent reprisal by the state, at least in "normal" times. For communities of color, however, the threshold of the normal has been low and the mildest dissent or even attempts to assert citizens' rights have often been met with savage repression in the domestic application of the "mere gook rule."*[1] More generally, freedom of speech has been limited by the fact that the state *does* engage in systematic disruption, harassment, and violent repression when dissent is seen as threatening, as in the Civil Rights/Vietnam war era's "Cointelpro"* and other programs, and in the frequent and sometimes large scale attacks on ethnic, labor, and radical leaders and organizations over the years. Deployment of the local, state and federal police, and national guard to quell labor activism and impede labor organization was an outstanding feature of the U.S. economic and political landscape from the 1860s to the Second World War.[2]

Official and police opposition to labor organization was closely tied to restrictions on freedom of speech. Contrary to ongoing mythology, the First Amendment was largely inoperative and offered little or no protection to dissidents threatening the established order for roughly a century and a half after its incorporation into the Constitution. The Sedition Act of 1798 made it a crime to utter or publish anything that brought high officials "into contempt or disrepute." The Sedition Act was never repealed and was only overturned by the Supreme Court in 1964.[3] Before 1860, statutes in every southern state forbade speech or writing condemning slavery, and these "were uniformly enforced by the courts."[4]

In the post-Civil War era, the labor movement quickly focused on gaining the right to free speech as "peaceful labor demonstrations were regularly and often violently broken up by the police."[5] Harassment, arrests, fines and imprisonments by local and state officials, and the use of police-protected vigilantes as enforcers were common responses to labor organizing and dissident speech. Advocates of women's right to vote, let alone birth

9

control, were regularly attacked by local and federal officials with no obstruction from the courts. "In the early 1900s, Margaret Sanger and Emma Goldman were frequently arrested and sometimes fined or imprisoned for distributing leaflets with information on birth control. Newspapers that offended the postmaster—which included almost anything on the subject of sex or women—were denied the use of the mails."[6] In 1917, women picketing the White House or protesting in a nearby park, seeking support for a constitutional amendment giving women the right to vote, were arrested and jailed for obstructing traffic or disorderly conduct.[7]

The Espionage Act of 1917, an extraordinarily repressive piece of legislation that literally outlawed criticism of World War I, resulted in over 2,000 criminal prosecutions. Despite challenges, none were reversed by the Supreme Court on First Amendment grounds.[8] This almost completely repressive history began to change only in 1919, improving slightly over the next 40 years, and then more rapidly from the early 1960s. Progress came from energetic efforts to expand the scope of civil liberties by social movements, especially during periods of mass mobilization like the 1930s and 1960s. Predictably, these enlargements of democracy were described as "crises of democracy" by spokespersons of the permanent interests. Even in the improved free speech environment of the post-World War II era, however, there were important regressions, most notably in the Truman-McCarthy years, when a new Red Scare caused a quick retreat from the advances of the preceding decades. An important accomplishment of this Red Scare was the purging of many progressives from the communications system and the frightening of those that remained into quiescence or noisy anticommunism.[9] This helped set the stage for global expansion in the name of "anticommunism"* and "containment."*

The Cointelpro activity during the Civil Rights/Vietnam war era and the Reagan administration's multi-leveled "secret war" of "low grade domestic terrorism" against the opposition to its Central American policy showed the continuing ease with which the government can threaten and undermine free speech.[10] Arguably, freedom of speech and organization conditioned on its not being perceived as a threat by the establishment is a very constrained kind of freedom. We are not talking about minor constraints either: the steady attacks on the free speech of labor organizers and striking workers from 1865-1960 had a profound effect on the activities, growth, and ultimate character of unions. Numerous labor organizations were destroyed through state actions and connivance with employers. Many newspapers, journals, and movement organizations were eliminated by advertiser boycotts, by government, or government-supported vigilante intimidation and attacks. The FBI's long and systematic efforts to disrupt and destroy both the civil rights movement[11] and black community activism took a heavy toll: Dr. James

Turner of Cornell University and the African Heritage Studies Association stated in 1974 that the FBI's programs had "serious long-term consequences for black Americans,...[having] created in blacks a sense of depression and hopelessness."[12] The Cointelpro campaigns and the covert war against the Central America antiwar movement were also substantial operations.

As Donna Demac observed in regard to the 1960s,[13]

> The social movements that arose during the period, which sought to make fundamental changes in American society, were not allowed to develop naturally; instead, many either died prematurely or were subverted by infiltrators and provocateurs whose corrupting influence succeeded in discrediting them in the eyes of the public. As a consequence, it is impossible to know in what direction these movements might have gone or what they might have achieved without secret government intervention.

The tendency to stifle serious dissent has been aggravated by a dominant U.S. culture that has never been tolerant of "deviance," as De Tocqueville pointed out back in the early nineteenth century.[14] This gives the state a freedom to repress upon slight and/or fabricated provocation. It means also that informal and less severe forms of reprisal can constrain dissent. Many Americans believe in free speech as a principle, but deeply resent its application in practice; after all, while the Soviet people have had reason to complain, why should we who live in the land of the free and the home of the brave? And as one respondent told the *New York Times,* explaining his shift to Bush (Sept. 20, 1988): "Freedom of speech is very important to me: we should be very proud of this pledge [to the flag], as a nation, and able to take every opportunity to say the pledge." Presumably anybody who doesn't want to make frequent pledges to the flag doesn't believe in freedom of speech. Dissidents who use freedom are abusing freedom.

The Market*

Another very important and greatly underrated constraint on freedom of speech is dissenters' lack of access to the mass media, and thus to the general public. Their freedom is in an important sense only a personal freedom with limited public and social significance. Dissenters may have something important to say that the public would find enlightening, but the "gatekeepers" are free to keep them effectively silent. Of course, they are legally free to start their own newspaper or to buy a TV network as the General Electric Company did in 1985, and it is always possible (and occasionally happens) that a major newspaper or TV station will give oppositional viewpoints fleeting access. But an important feature of the U.S.

system of free speech is the powerful structural limits to access to mass media.

In this *market* system of control, ownership is concentrated in the hands of the wealthy and the agents of the corporate establishment—the gatekeepers. Gatekeeper biases are reinforced by the preferences and biases of advertisers,[15] their natural gravitation to convenient and official sources like the White House, Pentagon, and State Department, and their fear of negative feedback (flak) from bodies and groups that might threaten their position.[16] Dissenters are excluded in the normal sourcing and processing of news, so that freedom of speech is perfectly compatible with systematic barriers to views that jar and threaten.[17] Reporters are forced to work within the limits imposed by the market system in order to survive and prosper in the media organizations.[18]

The market also works in other ways to assure that only proper views can be heard. The General Electric Company not only owns a television network, it funds and promotes "The McLaughlin Group" of dominantly rightwing commentators on the Public Broadcasting System, complementing other monied groups' funding of William Buckley's "Firing Line," thus buying access to their preferred views on a nominally independent network. GE, other corporations, and related foundations also fund the American Enterprise Institute, the Georgetown Center For Strategic and International Studies, the Heritage Foundation, the Hoover Institution, and scores of other allegedly "non-partisan" but ideologically directed research institutes, who finance and publicize the work of approved "experts."* Accredited through these institutional affiliations, these experts can then meet the demands of the media for "non-partisan" and independent sources on subjects like tax policy, poverty, the military budget and arms race, terrorism, and the problems of building democracy in Central America, just as the Advertising Council has provided Public Service ads to fill the gap for mandated "public service" programming on TV with ads nicely fitted to the demands of the powerful.[19]

Market marginalization of dissent has been strengthened by the increased centralization and commercialization of the mass media. The rise of national TV markedly increased mass media concentration, and the almost complete dependence of commercial TV on advertising and its resultant extreme sensitivity to advertiser interests[20] (and the closely related growth and "quality" of audiences and audience expectations) shaped it into an instrument readily mobilized by government propaganda and virtually closed to dissent. The defunding of public radio and TV forced much of this small sector into the commercial nexus and further narrowed avenues of access.

Despite these structural facts, it is frequently asserted and has become a conservative cliché that the mass media, especially network TV and the leading establishment dailies, are both "liberal" and "adversarial" to established authority. To a considerable extent this reflects infighting between the various wings of the establishment, with the hardline right resenting any factual presentations inconvenient to established authority and policy (unless liberals are in power and making gestures toward peaceful accommodation, in which case we are confronted with "subversion"* in *government* rather than in the media and are witnessing "appeasement"*). The business community also generally wants system-supportive materials in the media and business "news" that amounts to press handouts of the relevant business firms. The Pentagon, White House, State Department, local police departments, and conservatives also want the media to serve simply as conduits for government officials.

Neo-conservative Michael Ledeen has complained: "Most journalists these days consider it beneath their dignity to simply report the words of government officials—and let it go at that."[21] Ledeen is wrong: most are quite content to serve as a conduit, but his statement illuminates the neo-conservative view of the role of the press in a free society! Others, like Reed Irvine, openly demand that facts which do not serve their cause be suppressed. During the Gulf war of 1991, Irvine complained bitterly that the media were not serving the Pentagon 100 percent and were reporting facts that, while true, were inconvenient to the war effort.[22] Ledeen and Irvine uphold the tradition of Peter Braestrup's Freedom House study of Vietnam war coverage, which castigated the media for failing to be sufficiently upbeat, whatever the facts.[23]

It is interesting to note that in early 1988 the Soviet press was assailed by Defense Minister Dimitri Yazov for disclosing negative facts about the Soviet war in Afghanistan, which he claimed "played into the hands of the West."[24] The Ledeen-Irvine-Braestrup equivalents in the Soviet Union would surely have supported Yazov's claim that the Soviet press was too liberal and "adversary," as his criticisms of the Soviet press fit their own for the U.S. media with precision. But the "adversary" Soviet press followed the party line on all essentials in 1985, just as the U.S. mass media did in accepting that the United States sought "democracy" in Nicaragua in the 1980s and that it entered a war in the Gulf in 1991 to fight for the principle of non-aggression. The Bush administration wanted to censor the media during the Gulf war, not because they are adversaries, but for the reason implicit in Yazov's critique of the Soviet media: namely, a greedy desire to avoid *anything* inconvenient or negative.

The attacks leveled against the media as liberal and adversary, although often expressing the true beliefs of the business-neocon assailants, have the important effect of driving the media even more closely toward the state party line and away from facts and analyses that would call it into question. Claire Sterling may put forward rhetorical, implausible, and untrue statements on terrorism and the Bulgarian-KGB connection to the plot to shoot the Pope in the *Wall Street Journal, New York Times,* the McNeil-Lehrer News Hour, and CBS,[25] but neither Reed Irvine nor government officials will utter a peep of complaint. An Elliott Abrams on Nicaragua, although representing a party line and a confirmed liar, is safe. Dissidents such as Eqbal Ahmad, Noam Chomsky, Alexander Cockburn, Diana Johnstone or Jane Hunter would elicit cries of outrage on the right; therefore, they are rare participants in public discussions.[26]

At the same time, the continual outcry that the media are liberal and adversarial establishes the claim as fact, so that the very process that constrains the media further gives them added (and totally unjustified) credibility as unbiased.

The Power Laws

The structure of power that shapes media choices and determines who gains access also affects truthfulness in the mass media. Those who have assured access can lie; the more powerful they are, the more easily they can lie and the less likely it is that their lies will be corrected. The higher the rank, the more "credible" the statement; the more credible the speaker, the greater the freedom to lie.

This can be formulated in two laws: a "power law of access" and an "inverse power law of truthfulness." The first law says that the greater your economic and political clout, the easier your access to the mass media; the less your power, the more difficult the access. At a certain point on the declining power scale, access falls to zero. The fall to zero is accelerated if the message is discordant and would offend the powerful. The second law says that the greater your economic and political power—hence, access—the greater your freedom to lie; the smaller your power, the less your freedom to prevaricate. The second law follows in part from the first, as those who would be most eager to refute the lies of the powerful are weak and have limited access, further reduced by their discordant messages. Their messages can be ignored without cost to the mass media (whose biases would incline them toward avoidance anyway).

The media's gullibility and groveling before the powerful occurs despite recognition by media personnel, in principle, that governments lie. But in practice, when dealing with their own government, especially in the area of foreign policy and the military-industrial-complex,* media personnel abandon or shy away from critical analysis and, frequently, common sense.

Propaganda Campaigns

Structurally-based bias and the power laws make the mass media extremely serviceable for system-supportive propaganda campaigns. This all works very naturally as the proprietors, advertisers, and government usually have parallel biases, and their experts and flak machines combine to push the media in the same direction. Thus the great Red Scare of 1919-1920 helped thwart a threatening unionization of major industries;[27] the Red Scare of the Truman-McCarthy years (1948-1955) served to liquidate the old New Deal coalition and clear the ground for an aggressive pursuit of U.S. global interests under the guise of "containment" and protecting "national security"; and the Soviet Threat could be rehabilitated to provide the rationale for the Reagan era stoking of the arms race and a cover for the upward redistribution of income. In the latter period, the terrorist threat, Kadaffi, the KGB-Bulgarian plot to kill the Pope, and the "barbaric" Soviet shooting down of Korean airliner 007 in 1983 could all be brought on line in propaganda campaigns to reinforce the demands of the state.

In all of these cases the mass media collaborated with the government to help engineer consent by means of propaganda outbursts that were built, in whole or in part, on lies.[28] They were also built on Orwellian processes of doublethink: only selected incidents that served the state were subject to propaganda campaigns (Libya and Abu Nidal, not South Africa, Guatemala, Orlando Bosch, or Luís Posada); only politically useful shootdowns of airliners aroused indignation and stimulated concentrated media coverage;[29] and only selected cases of torture, murder, and aggression aroused concern. Crucial to the process was the reliance on the powerful and their accredited experts for information, and the exclusion of contesting viewpoints by dissidents and unaccredited experts.

UNESCO and the "Free Flow of Information"

In 1984 the United States withdrew from United Nations Educational, Scientific, and Cultural Organization (UNESCO), on the ground (among others) of its alleged threat to the "free flow of information." In the standard formulation in the U.S. press, UNESCO was said to be in favor of a New World Information Order (NWIO) whose essence was "government control of the media" and the "licensing of journalists"; whereas the United States and its media were dedicated to unconditional freedom of communications as a matter of high principle. This formulation, a caricature of the real positions of the contending parties,[30] reflected an undisclosed conflict of interest on the part of the western media, as well as remarkable hypocrisy.

For many years western media and news agencies have dominated the international flow of news. Third World spokespersons have long protested the biased portrayals of their countries in western news and called for a two-way and balanced news flow. A more basic Third World concern is the threat to cultural integrity and sovereignty from the flood of western advertising messages and other cultural products, as well as news. A number of Third World (and sympathetic western) analysts contended that true independence and popular mobilization for development are impossible without independent national communications systems.[31] Such concerns were accentuated in the 1960s with the development of satellite communications and remote sensing technologies. The former allows western programmers to transmit news, ads, and entertainment, entirely outside the control of national governments. Remote sensing allows western states to survey the mineral and other resources of lesser powers, again resulting in a loss in control, power, and independence.

The official U.S. position, followed consistently in the U.S. mass media,[32] was that the only issues raised by a NWIO were "freedom of the press" versus "government control."* Freedom of the press meant a commercial press funded by advertising. Might an advertising-based press display a systematic bias based on its restricted revenue source? Might it be affected by proprietary wealth and interest? Might it reflect the national and corporate interests of the home country and its leading multinational organizations? How concentrated could the media become before it should be regarded as "unfree"? These questions were never raised in the U.S. mass media in their frequent reports and discussions of the withdrawal.[33]

A media worried about the effects of the NWIO on the free flow of information should also be deeply concerned about constraints on free flow on their own western turf. It is one of the ironies of the U.S. and British withdrawals from UNESCO, however, that they were engineered by governments notable for increased secrecy, the curtailment of access to information, covert operations, deception, and manipulation of the press. Demac points out that "From its beginnings, the Reagan administration made little attempt to disguise its preference for operating outside congressional and public scrutiny; it quickly adopted an array of secrecy regulations that reached far beyond those of previous administrations."[34] In addition to major restrictions on the free speech rights of government workers and a sharp increase in the surveillance and harassment of those opposed to government policies, the new administration greatly expanded the classification and destruction of documents it deemed sensitive. It even began the reclassification of documents already in the public domain, a policy worthy of a Ministry of Truth and consistent with its systematic lying and rewriting of history.[35]

Demac also notes the increased restrictions on foreign travel of Americans and visits by politically deviant foreigners to the United States, plus substantial efforts to control the flow of messages, electronic and printed, to and from Cuba and other states. Canadian films on acid rain and the effects of nuclear war were forced to bear the label "propaganda."[36] Fulbright fellowships were cut back and politicized, the reduced funds redistributed to straightforward government propaganda.[37] Constitutional lawyer Floyd Abrams remarked that the Reagan administration "acts as if information were in the nature of a potentially disabling disease which must be feared, controlled, and ultimately quarantined."[38]

The Thatcher government was equally or more aggressive in attacking dissident media and whistleblowers. Her government's attitude toward the free flow of information within Britain was described in an off-the-record briefing to U.S. correspondents on Dec. 3, 1986 by Bernard Ingham, the Prime Minister's press spokesman:[39] "There is no freedom of information in this country; there's no public right to know. There's a commonsense idea of how to run a country and Britain is full of commonsense people... Bugger the public's right to know. The game is the security of the state—not the public's right to know."

The U.S. mass media were never very disturbed by the Reagan-Thatcher encroachments on free flow at home, nor did they ever point out during the period of withdrawal from UNESCO the huge contradiction between the Reagan-Thatcher devotion to free flow in UNESCO-related areas and their antithetical policies at home.

Another oddity that might have struck an observer not well indoctrinated with U.S. conceptions of freedom was the rise of authoritarianism in the U.S. sphere of influence over the past several decades. Attacks on the media in these countries went well beyond "licensing" and other alleged evils of the NWIO, and were received by the mass media with virtual silence and lack of indignation. According to the Committee to Protect Journalists, 94 journalists "disappeared" or were murdered in Argentina from 1976-1982, 21 were killed in El Salvador between 1980 and 1984, and 48 were killed in Guatemala between 1978 and 1982, almost all by governments supported by the United States.[40] Numerous papers were closed in these countries, and those that remained open learned a lesson in free flow from the murders. Similar developments occurred in Brazil, Chile, Paraguay, Uruguay, and other states in Latin America in the period coincident with the rising media concern over a NWIO (1973-84).

On the basis of principled concern over a free press and free flow of information, it is hard to explain why the media would be passionately concerned over "licensing" in a NWIO that did not exist, but failed to rouse themselves over the murder of scores of journalists in U.S. client states in the

Third World. The apparent contradiction is resolvable, however, if it is recognized that repressive governments in Brazil, Chile, and Guatemala serve a larger transnational corporate interest and do not interfere with Associated Press and *New York Times* operations and material interests. Thus, what appears to be an unaccountable inconsistency can be explained, but the relevant principle is corporate access and profit, not freedom of information.

Free Flow as Doublespeak

We can see, then, that "free flow"* in western doublespeak is not interfered with by advertising, concentrated ownership and control, or imbalances in economic and technological power among countries. As measured by media expressions of concern, it is not even threatened by systematic reductions in government provision of information, aggressive government news management, manipulation, and lies, or large scale government-organized propaganda operations, so long as these are engaged in by the media's own government and don't directly and seriously threaten media self-interest. The Reagan era witnessed a huge increase in what was officially called "public diplomacy,"* a new doublespeak term for what used to be known as government propaganda. Media attention to and concern with this development was minimal.

The murder of journalists, closing of papers, and censorship in Chile and Guatemala also do not threaten free flow. Free flow is threatened, however, by Third World government efforts to establish news agencies that would compete with the western news oligopoly. Similarly, interference with the flow of western advertising messages and rights to transmit other cultural products into Third World countries, or to enforce standards of responsibility, truthfulness, and public interest on such flows is "government control" and a horrifying violation of the principles of freedom. In doublespeak, free flow is simply the right of the powerful in the communications industry to pursue their material interests without constraint; government control is any threat to such activity, even if it would enhance competition (e.g., new foreign news agencies). Government intervention supportive of such media interests (e.g., subsidies and aid in pursuing satellite opportunities, or helping overthrow democratically elected governments in Brazil or Chile) is not "government control" and does not interfere with "free flow."

2. The Weapons Culture

Defense, Containment, Aggression, and National Security

At the end of World War II, the United States enjoyed a historically unique position of global power. The war had revived its previously depressed economy, teaching a lesson in "Military Keynesianism"* that was quickly incorporated into establishment practice, if not thought. The war had also seriously weakened U.S. rivals: enemies Germany and Japan were defeated and devastated physically, and allies like Great Britain, France, and the Soviet Union were also debilitated. The Soviet Union had been ravaged and suffered enormous casualties. Maintaining a large army, but exhausted and in no position to challenge the United States, the Soviet Union insisted only on preserving a security zone of dominated governments occupied at the end of the war and from which attacks had been launched against it.

In the Third World, the United States was confronted with popular movements threatening to break out of centuries-long subservience, exploitation, and oligarchic-colonial rule. The United States was well positioned to fight against these popular upheavals and to enlarge its own spheres of influence, which it did on a global basis from 1945 onward. In the process, it often displaced its own allies as the dominant power in important colonial areas like Saudi Arabia, Iran, Indochina, Pakistan, Thailand, and Indonesia, among other places.

U.S. leaders were, for the most part, well aware of their power and opportunity, and of Soviet weakness.[1] National Security Council Report 68, prepared just before the beginning of the Korean War in 1950, spelled out a "roll-back" strategy in which a rearmed United States would engage in systematic subversion of the Soviet satellite states, and even of the Soviet Union itself, by means that included the support of armed revolt. The United States was actively involved in roll-back operations in 1949 under a CIA program of organizing guerrilla bands of "former SS men" and CIA-trained Ukrainian operatives within the Soviet Union, parachuting in military sup-

plies.² These operations, along with the reconstruction of the Nazi intelligence apparatus of Reinhard Gehlen as the official espionage corps of the
new West German state, also prior to the Korean war, were not featured in
the U.S. media. The Korean war came along very opportunely to help justify
the desired arms buildup.

NSC-68 was similar to the Reagan era Pentagon "Defense Guidance,
1984-88" report, which also spelled out a program of active destabilization
of the Soviet empire by the deliberately beggaring effects of an arms race as
well as by aid to armed groups within the Soviet bloc.³ The significance of
these documents is that they presume an *offensive* U.S. policy against an
enemy perceived as *vulnerable;* they project U.S. plans to subvert and "bury"
the Soviet Union. NSC-68 does speak of the Soviet design to conquer the
world, but this was an ideological construct that provided the necessary dire
threat to rationalize a forward strategy. NSC-68, like the Reagan era Defense
Guidance statement, rests on the assumption of Soviet weakness and vulnerability, and does not use language suggesting fear of aggression and attack.
This is why these documents have been essentially suppressed in mainstream
media and discourse, which instead gave great play to the rhetorical boast
of Khrushchev that "I am going to bury you."

The national security elite also recognized in NSC-68 that taking
advantage of the positive opportunities open to the United States required a
large military force and mobilized population. Doublespeak embedded in a
convenient matrix of anticommunist ideology was essential, as the U.S.
establishment was obliged to pretend (or internalize the belief) that the huge
global expansion of the U.S. political economy on which they had embarked
was "defensive"* and responsive to some external threat; that we were
"containing" somebody else who was committing "aggression"* and threatening our "national security."

The words and phrases "defense," "containment," "aggression," and
"national security" are core items in the doublespeak lexicon, essential
ingredients of the ink squirted out by the imperial cuttlefish. They deflected
thought from the pro-active and purposeful aspects of U.S. foreign policy,
the locus of the determining initiatives in the arms race and conflict, the source
of the bulk of the killing, and the extent to which the fight was against
indigenous, popular, and democratic movements abroad. Epitomizing the
new world of doublespeak was the change in name of the War Department
to the Defense Department in 1947, just at the historic juncture when the
United States was embarking on a global offensive to reshape the world in
accord with its dominant corporate interests (not in "our image," as in the
common apologetic formulation).⁴

In Greece, where the British, and then even more aggressively, the
United States, reestablished an extreme rightwing regime of former collabo-

rationist elements by terror, fraudulent elections, and a vicious counterinsurgency war in the years 1944-1950, Stalin extended no aid to the communist and other left rebels under siege, and in fact strenuously opposed Yugoslavia's aid to the rebels.[5] Nevertheless, Truman, aided by the "bipartisan"* consensus and mainstream media, successfully made the crushing of the Greek Left and establishment of a rightwing police state by external (U.S.) force a "defensive" action to "contain" Soviet expansionism. This was a model of applied doublespeak that would be repeated often in the years to come.

And from that time till the end of the Reagan era, whenever the United States wanted to intervene to crush some indigenous popular movement or government not to the taste of United Fruit Company or the national security establishment, the search would be on for Reds, the connection would be made to the Soviet Union (along with some lesser devils like Cuba or Libya), and the government would be declared Marxist-Leninist* and a Soviet puppet. The real and massive intervention—by the United States—required an Evil Empire behind the indigenous and popular forces that were the real target. The United States would regularly impose boycotts and escalate threats against the tiny victim, forcing it to buy goods and arms from members of the Soviet bloc. This would then be used to show both the aggressive intent of the victim and its allegiance to the international communist conspiracy.

The U.S. mass media has always swallowed this line of propaganda—even regarding Nicaragua in the 1980s—never allowing that Nicaragua might be getting arms from the Soviet Union in response to a genuine threat or because of the U.S. and allied boycott, and never pointing out that the Sandinista military threat to its neighbors was implausible, unsupported by evidence, and rendered nonsensical by a watchful U.S. military presence.[6] The press has never suggested that the linking of the victim under U.S. attack to the Soviet Union might be a red herring designed to obscure the real reason for opposition to the victim government. The Democratic Loyal Opposition* always jumps into line for fear of being tagged Red sympathizers, and intervention in violation of U.S. and international law proceeds unhampered.

The case of Nicaragua in the 1980s showed that, given the patriotic premises of the mass media and the absence of a political opposition to contest them, lies can be institutionalized and the truth stood on its head. This was shown earlier during the U.S. attack on Guatemala in 1954, alleged to be a response to Soviet aggression, although there were no Soviet troops, advisers, or arms on the scene, and despite the fact that the government of Guatemala had carefully avoided any formal diplomatic relations with Soviet bloc countries out of respect for (and fear of) U.S. sensitivities. It is true that very late in the day, with a U.S.-organized attack in the offing and a U.S. arms boycott long in effect, the Guatemalan government did buy a boatload of arms from Czechoslovakia, the discovery of which created hysteria among

U.S. officials and in the U.S. press. But this is the convenient pathology of imperialism—to bring to life a virus in the hemisphere, to decry its existence, and to mercilessly eradicate it. Soviet control, expansionism, and aggression in the Guatemala case was fiction, on an intellectual par with the claims of the Protocols of the Elders of Zion. But it was taken very seriously in the *New York Times* and media generally, and the uncontested view was that we were behaving defensively, containing the Soviet Union, not committing aggression to enforce our own positive standards of rule in Guatemala.

Behind all these claims and counterclaims was the allegation of a threat to U.S. "national security," the longstanding "Linus blanket" in which the imperial faction and military establishment have regularly wrapped themselves. When tied to the threat of Communism and the Evil Empire, the cry of National Security stills criticism, rationality, and decency. And it is trotted out with abandon. National security is both vague and highly elastic, so that Grenada, Nicaragua, even the entry into the United States of Gabriel García Márquez, Mrs. Salvador Allende, a contingent of mothers of the massacred in El Salvador, or printed matter from Cuba can seriously threaten it. It seems that the national security of the United States, the greatest military power in history, is in constant jeopardy as the country cowers before the threats of popular movements in Nicaragua or Guatemala.

There seems to be a kind of Hoover's Law* at work, in which the threat to National Security increases in direct proportion to the enlargement of the resources available to protect it. Could it be that the "missions" and threats grow to accommodate, justify, and increase the command over resources of the National Security establishment? And is it possible that the alleged "threats" are contrived to rationalize quite different foreign policy goals?[7] Sometimes the cat gets out of the bag, as when Nicaragua suddenly agreed unconditionally to the Contadora group plan of 1984, which would have barred foreign bases and advisers and provided in-country monitoring of any potential threat of mighty Nicaragua to U.S. "national security." At that point the Reagan administration panicked and hurriedly helped its most amenable Central American clients, Honduras and El Salvador, identify previously unseen but overwhelming problems with the agreement, suggesting to rational observers (but not to the U.S. media) that the claim of fears about "national security" was a cover for a hidden counterrevolutionary agenda.

Weapons in Search of Missions

During the period from 1945 to the present, a "weapons culture"[8] developed in the United States to serve the interests dominating the U.S. power structure. These were mainly business interests that benefited from military power projected abroad—the weapons producers themselves; the oil companies that were helped to establish themselves in the Middle East and Venezuela, which benefited from the enforced opening of markets in Europe and elsewhere; other resource-exploiting firms (especially in mining, timber, and agribusiness); and other business and financial firms that were able to take advantage of newly penetrated markets. Wonderful contracts were written for U.S. iron, timber, and other mineral extraction and agribusiness companies following the U.S.-sponsored military coups in Brazil and Indonesia in 1964 and 1965. A large military establishment funded by the taxpayer served these global interests well.

As the weapons culture grew, the industrial interests producing weapons and their Pentagon and congressional allies—a so-called "iron triangle" or "military-industrial complex"* (MIC)—of enormous and partially independent power, gradually emerged.[9] The MIC's ability to command resources rested on its service to the transnational corporate system, as well as its own extraordinary institutional power. It had the further advantage of providing for our "national defense" and protecting our "national security," and what politician would stand against funding defense and national security, especially when the corporate establishment (including the national media) would denounce and defund him for selling his country short?

The MIC is a closed, self-protective, feedback system, loaded with conflicts of interest, but now built into the political economy. It was epitomized in earlier years by the relationship between Representative L. Mendel Rivers of South Carolina (long-time Chair of the House Armed Services Committee), the Pentagon, and the Pentagon's contractors, which carried the iron triangle relationship to an early point of caricature. In 1969, there were nine military installations situated by the Pentagon within Rivers' Charleston, South Carolina district, and the big defense contractors flocked to build plants in the same area, some at his personal request—a Lockheed plant came there, according to Rivers, because "I asked them to put a li'l old plant here." His reciprocal service to these beneficiaries was expressed in 1967 when he told the House that military men "don't have a lobby like some other people. The only lobby they have is the Committee on Armed Services."[10]

Where, as in the case of the military budget and national security, sustaining the necessary level of false consciousness imposes a heavy burden on the powerful, the Big Lies are numerous, audacious, and essentially uncorrectable. And doublespeak proliferates. The lies may be questioned on on the powerful, the Big Lies are numerous, audacious, and essentially uncorrectable. And doublespeak proliferates. The lies may be questioned on a very episodic basis in the mass media, but not in a way that might prevent them from being institutionalized as patriotic truths. They may also be questioned in retrospect, but individually and not as a repetitive and systematic process. This permits *serial* lying, with no lessons learned. In the case of the MIC: dreadnought gaps, bomber gaps, missile gaps, throw-weight gaps, and assorted other "windows of vulnerability" have been brought into existence to justify the production of new weapons systems, in each case based on partial or entirely false evidence.

But in evaluating each successive claim the mass media never review the previous claims and their subsequent collapse. This is crucial to the effectiveness of serial disinformation. As Orwell stressed, doublethink rests on control of the past: "All that was needed was an unending series of victories over your own memory. 'Reality control,' they called it."[11] The continued refusal of the mainstream media to recall the history of the prior "gaps" is an outstanding case in point. This victory over memory reflects the two "power laws" in action. The power behind new weapons systems is too great to be contested seriously in the press, by the leaders of the two major parties, or by political candidates who come near the grasp of the highest office. Relevant historical context therefore cannot surface.

The Soviet military threat and the usual "gaps" were put forward once again by the arms lobby and political rightwing in the 1970s and early 1980s. CIA and other concocted data were adduced to show high rates of growth of Soviet military outlays and Soviet nuclear superiority, and to demonstrate that the United States was engaging in "unilateral disarmament."* Economist Franklyn Holzman's demonstration of the completely spurious methodology used by the CIA ("Are the Soviets Really Outspending the U.S. on Defense?" *International Security,* Spring 1980) was never refuted; it was simply unable to make headway against the imperatives of power. Eventually, after the military buildup had developed its own momentum, it was quietly acknowledged that the CIA had made a little mistake![12] A similar sequence characterized the history of the "window of vulnerability,"* also discovered in the 1970s. It was alleged that the number of Soviet missiles had grown to a point where they could wipe out our land-based missiles in a first strike. In addition to other shortcomings, the "window" analysis simply ignored the existence of our submarines and aircraft in its calculus. The window was quietly shut after it had been exploited[13]—despite its complete absurdity—to justify additional U.S. expenditures on land-based missiles.

It is interesting to note that during the later 1970s and early 1980s, when the gap and window claims were at their peak, estimates by each military service and serious military experts on U.S. versus Soviet advantage indicated that the United States never relinquished its technological lead in weaponry, had a substantial edge resulting from its superior balance among the triad of nuclear forces (land, sea, air), had a better global positioning of forces, and possessed more reliable allies.[14]

The power laws assured that the press never pulled these strands together. Tom Gervasi showed that Reagan's repeated claims of Soviet nuclear superiority and Weinberger's statement that the Soviet nuclear arsenal now exceeded ours in accuracy were not only lies, but *were easily refutable at the time from Pentagon documents and testimony before congressional committees!*[15] He also pointed out that although these lies were the basis on which hundreds of billions of dollars of resources were expended (money thrown at contrived problems), the press could never be bothered to examine these conflicting statements and try to assess their merits.[16] Thus, Reagan, Weinberger, and their allies were even able to brag about U.S. superiority on Memorial Day while decrying the fearsome Soviet edge on TV and before appropriations committees on succeeding days without having to reconcile their statements—a blatant case of doublespeak and doublethink.

Even when a truly lunatic boondoggle certain to intensify the nuclear arms race was put forward, as in the case of the Strategic Defense Initiative (SDI) or Star Wars* program, the power of the MIC was strong enough to preclude anything like adequate criticism. The SDI was supposed to provide a defensive shield in space that would intercept Soviet missiles and thus reduce the threat of war by providing a more-or-less foolproof defense. This extravaganza was based on fantastically complex technologies that did not exist. Its testing as well as deployment would have violated the Anti-Ballistic Missile (ABM) treaty of 1972. It was foisted on Reagan by some of his really far out technical advisers like General Daniel Graham of the World Anticommunist League and the American Security Council, without prior study or approval even from the Pentagon's technical staff. The alternative ways of reducing the threat of nuclear war, like disarmament and a comprehensive test ban (that would have limited the development of new weapons and reduced the reliability of old ones) were ignored in favor of a technological fix pleasing only to the MIC and Armageddon far right, and beyond Rube Goldberg.

There was some criticism of SDI's technical feasibility and probable limits as a defensive system, but it wasn't laughed off the stage as a completely irresponsible proposal, a gigantic waste of resources that would fuel the nuclear arms race, and a further demonstration of Reagan's incapacity for high office. One interesting suppression is worth noting: when the Soviets built a small ABM system for the "defense" of Moscow in the 1960s, a frenzied U.S. establishment declared it to have inherent and terrifying offensive implications.[17] SDI, despite its vastly greater offensive implications, was not treated in this way;

with trivial exceptions in the mainstream press, it was portrayed as a truly defensive system, a "noble dream," although of questionable workability. The power laws precluded an honest discussion of the prior allegations of the terrible threat stemming from "defensive" nuclear systems such as ABM.

Similarly, when Reagan administration officials went to Geneva in the early 1980s to talk about arms control with the Soviets, the press presented this as a serious effort, although numerous statements by Reagan, Weinberger, the Armageddon theorists of the MIC, and the Pentagon's posture statements and Five Year Plan pointed with great clarity to a multi-year buildup aimed at "imposing disproportionate costs" on the Soviet Union and achieving a level of arms superiority that would allow the United States "to exploit political, economic and military weakness within the Warsaw pact and to disrupt enemy rear operations," among other "defensive" efforts.[18] But the mainstream press accepted the nominal claim of the administration that we were arming to the teeth only to "catch up" with the Russians and to provide ourselves with "bargaining chips" to bring the Soviets to the negotiating table so that we could all then jointly reduce arms! When Reagan was finally driven by his own political problems, public pressure, and huge Soviet concessions to agree to some very limited reductions of nuclear weapons, the media read the press release and reported that his sensible approach to arms control had produced these wonderful results. The fact that disarmament was never Reagan's intent was rarely admitted. The lunacy of producing a trillion dollars worth of weapons in order to persuade the enemy to agree to a joint reduction in weapons was not discussed. The unlikelihood of net reductions by this process, which creates corporate and military interests with huge investments in continued and expanded weapons production, was ignored.

Manufacturing and Shifting Missions

A basic feature of the MIC is that it keeps developing weapons that the contractors want to sell. Old weapons are rendered obsolete by newer "follow-on"* versions that are offered for "modernization"* whether newer weapons are needed or not. The point is to command resources, maintain and enlarge profits, and produce jobs. Missions are needed to justify weapons acquisition, and they are usually couched in terms of some threat, some niche that has to be filled to protect our national security. The record shows that such threats will be manufactured or artificially stoked if no real threat is available, and that the mass media will not challenge their basis in reality.

Comical instances abound. I.F. Stone cited a case in which a Secretary of the Air Force explained that we needed a certain bomber to counter a Soviet "follow-on" bomber that did not yet exist, and which the Soviets gave no indication of intending to produce, but which the Air Force thought the Soviets "ought to have."[19] Stone suggested that perhaps the U.S. Air Force should subsidize the Soviet bomber to give more substance to the Air Force's claim.

Another comical but more serious classic of mission creation and switching occurred as a *series* in the 1960s and 1970s in connection with a controversy over ABMs. Because the Soviet Union foolishly deployed a small ABM force around Moscow and a few other places, the MIC and its allies had an irresistible "national security" cover for building ABMs, no matter how pointless militarily.[20] Trying to deflect pressure to develop a full-scale "thick" system, Defense Secretary Robert McNamara announced in 1967 that we would go ahead with a "thin" ABM shield called Sentinel. As the United States had already created a huge missile fleet in response to the nonexistent missile gap proclaimed by Kennedy in his 1960 presidential campaign,[21] and possessed a triad of powerful defenses against the Soviet threat (bombers, submarines, and land-based missiles), there was a problem in justifying the thin deployment. The rationale offered at the time was that it would serve against a possible miscalculation on the part of Red China. In the words of McNamara's colleague, Paul Warnke,[22]

> In a crisis which they had brought on [naturally only the Chinese themselves would have brought on any crisis], if the Chinese came to believe that the United States might attack, they might be tempted to launch a preemptive strike, hoping to bring down at least part of the American house in the face of total destruction, or even only the destruction of their nuclear forces, which at the moment of crisis they feared we were about to wreak on them.

A multibillion dollar investment was thus justified on the supposition of entirely irrational Chinese behavior with a weapon they didn't yet possess! In 1968, Richard Russell, chair of the Senate Armed Services Committee, acknowledged that the rationale was fraudulent and that the "thin" system was only a foot in the door: "It's a base for a system throughout the whole nation. I didn't deceive anybody. When we brought it up they tried to dress it up as being designed to protect us from China. But I stated very frankly on the floor of the Senate that I consider it the foundation of a complete antimissile system..."[23] When the thin system was being deployed, however, the idiocy of the argument of its need for protection against China was hardly raised, nor was the prospect and significance of a "thick" system debated.

The Sentinel was beginning to be deployed in the metropolitan areas of Boston, Chicago, and other cities in 1969 when public opposition forced the interruption of construction. President Richard Nixon soon announced that a new "Safeguard" program was to be launched, to redeploy the missiles that would have been protecting the selected urbanites from a nonexistent Chinese threat to protecting Minutemen missiles against a suddenly discovered Soviet first strike capability. In support of this adjusted mission, Secretary of Defense Melvin Laird disclosed that the Soviet SS-9, a liquid-fueled but large missile, was being built as a first strike weapon. This was only two months after the outgoing Secretary of Defense Clark Clifford had declared our defense deterrent adequate, and not long after his predecessor, Robert McNamara, had boasted of a "numerical superiority over the Soviet Union in reliable, accurate and effective warheads...greater than originally planned, and...in fact more than we require."[24] These contradictions were not analyzed and debated in the media: Laird's "terrifying view of an emerging Soviet 'first strike capability'" easily carried the day, the new mission clearing the ground for producing and deploying weapons the MIC wanted to sell.

Star Wars also went through an evolution in its mission. This ultimate lunatic extravaganza was justified originally on the basis of the threat of a Soviet attack. Even at the height of Reagan era Soviet Threat hysteria, however, SDI could not get full funding, but with the unilateral Soviet withdrawal from the arms race a new funding rationale was sorely needed. The Gulf war helped here, demonstrating the Patriot antimissile missile, and lending credence to a fresh idea then evolving: that Third World upstarts with missiles presented a new and severe problem. As was dutifully transmitted by the *New York Times*, "As the danger of the Soviet military threat faded, the White House grew increasingly worried about the third-world threat."[25] It was also noted that "the missile program has tried to formulate a more limited approach that would address the third world threat while giving a modicum of protection against a small Soviet attack, perhaps begun by accident." The new package, called Global Protection Against Limited Strikes (GPALS*), would include about a thousand land-based missiles and a thousand or more space-based interceptors called "Brilliant Pebbles,"* with the whole system hopefully able to "protect against threats of up to 100 enemy warheads." Brilliant Pebbles have unfortunately not yet been tested, and testing or deploying them would violate the 1972 ABM treaty. But this is an irresistible bargain package—only $30 billion—though it is reminiscent of the Sentinel and Safeguard programs in its opportunistic adjustment of missions. Missions adapt quickly to what the market will bear, the "market" being what the MIC can foist on the taxpayer.

The Civilized Aversion to the Use of Force

A number of doublespeak terms and ideas that the civilized use to characterize themselves and their barbaric enemies involve the process of transference, in which characteristics of the definer are applied to the victim. Barbarians, for example, do not value human life as we do. In Vietnam, as an illustrative case, the enemy was willing to accept heavy casualties and the terrible costs that could be (and were) imposed on a small peasant country by an industrialized power. For western analysts, the failure of the Vietnamese to surrender to superior force showed their lack of value for human life. Our willingness to kill them on a large scale, however, did not demonstrate the low value we place on human life, for reasons never made explicit. The fact is that the Vietnamese were fighting for national independence. The United States was willing to kill millions and destroy a distant country for reasons that its own apologists could never quite clarify.

Another important example of transference is the western pretense that the victims and rebels whom we or our agents are slaughtering are prone to use force,* whereas we and our clients are peace-lovers driven to bullets and bombs by the violent means of our victims. Jeane Kirkpatrick, commenting on the torture-mutilation-murder of the five leaders of the Democratic Front in San Salvador in November 1980, observed that "People who choose to live by the sword can expect to die by it."[26] This observation was made at a time when the Salvadoran government was butchering a thousand civilians a month.

My favorite case, however, was the claim of the U.S. government during the 1960s that we sought peace in Vietnam but were rebuffed by a violent enemy. The truth of the matter is that from our first entry in support of the French, then with our imported "leader" Diem, and up to the time of the Paris Peace Agreement of 1973, we refused to negotiate a political settlement because we had no political base in Vietnam.[27] This was acknowledged in innumerable internal government documents, and official propagandist Douglas Pike conceded that our foe, the NLF, "maintained that its contest with the GVN [the Saigon government] and the United States should be fought out at the political level" and that the use of massed military might was in itself illegitimate, "until forced by the United States and its clients" to use counterforce to survive.[28]

But while the United States had no indigenous support in Vietnam, it had enormous military power, incredibly arrogant and ruthless leaders, and a subservient press. The principle applied in Vietnam, as in many other places, was to refuse to bargain on the basis of the existing distribution of political power; instead, we used our superior military power to enforce our will, no matter the cost to the victimized population. In the early 1960s, U.N. Secretary U Thant, Charles DeGaulle, the Soviets, the Chinese, and all major factions within South Vietnam—the Buddhists, NLF, even much of the elite and many of the generals—wanted to negotiate a settlement, but the United States refused. South Vietnamese governments were installed and overthrown by the United States until it had gotten into place two former French mercenaries, Ky and Thieu, who were willing to fight to the end. As the State

Department's William Bundy asserted at the time, "Our requirements were really very simple...we wanted any government that would continue to fight." In doublespeak, however, as stated by James Reston, the real issue "at stake in Vietnam," was[29]

> that no state shall use military force or the threat of military force to achieve its political objectives. And the companion of this principle has been that the United States would use its power, when necessary and where it could be effective, against any state that defied this principle.

More generally, from the Truman era onward, negotiations with the Soviet Union and its allies were put on hold pending our establishment of "situations of strength" (to use Dean Acheson's memorable phrase) which would induce the enemy "to come to the bargaining table." All through the Vietnam War the Johnson and Nixon administrations were waiting for the enemy to come to the bargaining table. Even Reagan periodically resorted to this tactic in his assault on Nicaragua, but the doublespeak quality of this gambit surfaced when he blurted out that we were waiting for the Sandinistas to "say uncle." This phrase, and the euphemism of coming to the bargaining table, both mean "acceptance of U.S. terms," or surrender. The civilized, in short, have made themselves into devotees of peaceful solutions by identifying their own terms as reasonable and any refusal to accept these terms as the cause of conflict.

It should be recalled that it was the civilized West that dropped atomic bombs on two Japanese cities, and that the country which dropped those bombs steadfastly refuses to commit itself to no first use of atomic weapons. The United States has also been the main propelling force in the arms race. The most telling statement on this point was made by Herbert York, Eisenhower's top adviser on military technology, who asserted that the "rate and scale [of the arms race] have been largely subject to our control. Over the last thirty years we have repeatedly taken unilateral actions that have unnecessarily accelerated the race."[30] The Reagan era burst of rearmament and new boondoggles of enormous magnitude followed in the great tradition of civilized behavior.

Civilized and Barbaric
Shooting Down of Airliners

The western usage of barbarism and civilization rests not only on transference and a refusal to look honestly at history, but also on a mind-boggling double standard. This is dramatically illustrated in the consistently dichotomous western handling of the shooting down of civilian airliners.

When the Soviets shot down Korean airliner 007 in 1983, the Reagan administration orchestrated a huge propaganda campaign of vilification. It is now clearly established that the administration knew that the Soviets did *not* know that 007 was a civilian aircraft,[31] but the Reaganites nevertheless built their campaign on the lie that a civilian plane was deliberately destroyed. The press went along with this propaganda claim, raising an indignant outcry over "cold-blooded murder" and barbarism. Much was made of the messages relayed by the Soviet pilot and ground control honing in on 007 and matter-of-factly asserting that the target had been destroyed. The inhumanity of the act was dramatized by great attention paid to the grieving families of the victims. In the words of Leslie Gelb: "The point, if it needed reaffirmation, was that the leadership of the Soviet Union is different—call it tougher, more brutal or even uncivilized—than most of the rest of the world. President Reagan said the incident was 'horrifying' and cause for 'revulsion,' whatever the exact or possibly extenuating circumstances" (*New York Times,* Sept. 4, 1983). The "savage" act of the Soviet Union, as James Reston pointed out, garnered it "the hatred of the civilized world" (Sept. 4, 1983). The *Times* editorialized on September 2 that "There is no conceivable excuse for any nation shooting down a harmless airliner."

When the United States shot down Iranian airliner 655 killing 290 people in July 1988, Leslie Gelb said nothing about the implications of this act for the quality of the leadership of the responsible country (and Gelb has never said anything in retrospect about the significance for civilization and barbarism of the fact that the original claims by his government on 007 were eventually admitted by the *Times* to have been outright lies). The U.S. media did not relay to the American public the coldblooded messages of those in the act of pulling the trigger on 290 civilians, nor did they focus on the grieving families of the victims, choosing instead to tap the feelings of the U.S. personnel obligated by their duties to kill. And the *New York Times* editorialists found that there *is* a conceivable excuse for shooting down a civilian airliner, namely a "tragic error" and irresponsible behavior of the victim.[32]

Subsequently, in an article in the September 1989 issue of the U.S. Naval Institute's *Proceedings,* David R. Carlson, Commander of the USS Sides, an escort frigate in the vicinity of the Vincennes at the time, wrote that he was disgusted with the apologias for the act, the attempt to blame it on the Iranians, and the idea that the Vincennes was "defending herself against an attack," which he said was based on a series of lies. "When the decision was made to shoot down the Airbus, the airliner was climbing, not diving; it was showing the proper identification friend or foe—IFF (Mode III); and it was in the correct flight corridor from Bandar Abbas to Dubai. The *Vincennes* was never under attack by Iranian aircraft. There was no targeting being done by the Iranian P-3... The conduct of Iranian military forces in the month preceding the incident was pointedly nonthreatening."[33] According to Carlson, well before the shootdown the Vincennes' actions "appeared to be consistently aggressive, and had become a topic of wardroom conversation… 'Robo Cruiser' was the unamusing nickname that someone jokingly came up with for her, and it stuck."

This story would seem sensationally newsworthy: an on-the-scene naval officer suggesting that the shootdown was not a "tragic error" but was based on the trigger-happy characteristics of a Rambo commander, and that all the talk about Iranian errors and provocations was poppycock. The *Washington Post* did have a good back page story on the Carlson report, in which George Wilson suggested that Carlson's statements were "certain to refuel the controversy generated by the shooting."[34] But Wilson was wrong: the *New York Times*, which had accepted the official version of the incident, placing blame on the Iranians as well as tragic error, never touched the story, and no controversy ensued.

A *New York Times* article by Robert Reinhold, entitled "Crew of Cruiser That Downed Iranian Airliner Gets a Warm Homecoming" (October 25, 1988, p. 16), describes the hero's welcome given the naval personnel who shot down the Iranian airliner when they returned to the United States. The captain is shown smiling, a wreath around his neck and his happy wife looking on. The naval personnel had made it to national TV and become celebrities, and in civilized society celebrities receive suitable honors. In April 1990, the commander of the Vincennes was given the Legion of Merit award for "exceptionally meritorious conduct in the performance of outstanding service" and for "the calm and professional atmosphere" under his command. The destruction of the Airbus with 290 civilians was not mentioned explicitly in his citation. The *Washington Post* and *New York Times* both failed to report on this award.

One wonders whether, if the pilot who shot down KAL 007 had been given a triumphant victory parade in Moscow on his return and later received a high Soviet award for meritorious service, the U.S. media would not have considered this in bad taste, even evidence of Soviet barbarism? This applied double standard shows how far beyond hypocrisy we have traveled.

In another instance of a civilized attack on a civilian airliner, the Israeli military shot down a Libyan plane that had gotten lost over the Sinai desert in February 1973, killing 109 people. In this case, the Israelis admitted knowing that it was a civilian airliner, but the U.S. press did not find this of any interest, and the words "cold-blooded," "murder," "savage," or "barbaric" were not used. The Soviet-Israeli contrast provides the ultimate double standard, as the Soviets were declared barbarous on the basis of a western lie, whereas the deliberate Israeli shooting down of a civilian plane aroused not the slightest indignation on the part of U.S. officials, Reston, and the *New York Times* editorial board.

3. The Search for Defensible Frontiers, Globally and in Outer Space

Our Natural Right to Subvert

Imperial powers always have good reasons for expansion and for the repression of the victim nations they conquer and dominate. There is, first of all, the benevolence of the conquering power. Roman general Cerialis explained to conquered tribes in Gaul in the first century A.D. that, in contrast with the Germans, who entered Gaul out of "lust, avarice, and the longing for a new home," the Romans came to provide stability, and by invitation only:[1]

> Roman generals and Emperors entered your territory, as they did the rest of Gaul, with no ambitious purposes, but at the solicitation of your ancestors, who were wearied to the last extremity by intestine [sic] strife... How many battles we have fought against the Cimbri and Teutones, at the cost of what hardships to our armies, and with what result we have waged our German wars is perfectly well known. It was not to defend Italy that we occupied the borders of the Rhine, but to insure that no second Ariovistus should seize the empire of Gaul.

There is, secondly, the need to defend oneself. In the enlargement of the British empire in the eighteenth and nineteenth centuries, the most famous phrase in the lexicon of apologetics was the "search for defensible frontiers." There were always neighboring states from which dissidents and guerrillas could find refuge and from which they could launch attacks. To preempt this required the conquest and subjugation of the neighboring states, thus establishing a more defensible frontier. This could, of course, rationalize continuous expansion as new neighbors harbored guerrillas.

A third good reason, that sometimes overlaps with the previous explanations, is inadvertence. The imperial power, in its blundering efforts to do good, or to protect its borders, expands. This is the heart of Stanley Karnow's explanation of the U.S. takeover of the Philippines and his account of the Vietnam war, both of which constitute the comprehensive abandonment of serious historiography.[2]

Table 1

Forms of Subversion Engaged in by the United States in Eight Countries in Latin America and the Caribbean, 1950-1980
(+ means evidence of use, − means no evidence of use)

Forms of Subversion	Brazil	Chile	Cuba	Dominican Republic	Ecuador	El Salvador	Guatemala	Uruguay
Direct invasion or sponsorship of invasion	−	−	+	+	−	−	+	−
Participation in coups (directing, encouraging, lending support to)	+	+	−	+	+	−	−	−
Assassination or attempted assassination of leaders	−	+	+	+	−	−	−	−
Sabotage (property destruction)	−	−	+	−	−	−	−	−
Destabilization (economic or financial)	+	+	+	+	−	−	+	−
Buying politicians and other officials (including military and security)	+	+	+	+	+	+	+	+
Buying media and media personnel	+	+	−	−	+	−	−	+
Buying intellectuals	+	+	−	−	+	−	−	+
Buying labor leaders	+	+	+	+	+	+	+	+
Black propaganda (lies and rumors dispensed without attribution)	+	+	+	−	+	−	−	+
Subsidizing student, youth, women's organizations	+	+	−	−	+	−	−	+
Providing military forces for occupation or counterinsurgency operations	−	−	−	+	−	−	+	−

Sources: (Principal).

General: Penny Lernoux, *Cry of the People*, Doubleday, 1980; Ronald Radosh, *American Labor and United States Foreign Policy*, Random House, 1969; Philip Agee, *Inside the Company: CIA Diary*, Bantam, 1975; Victor Marchetti and John D. Marks, *The CIA and the Cult of Intelligence*, Dell, 1974; Miles Wolpin, *Military Aid and Counterrevolution in the Third World*, Lexington, 1972; *Alleged Assassination Plots Involving Foreign Leaders*, Senate Select Committee on Intelligence, Rep. No. 94-465, 94th Cong., 1st sess. (1975).

Brazil: Jan K. Black, *United States Penetration of Brazil*, University of Pennsylvania, 1977.

Chile: *Covert Action in Chile 1963-1965*, Staff Report of Senate Select Committee on Intelligence, 1975; James Petras and Morris Morley, *How Allende Fell*, Spokesmen, 1974; Saul Landau, *They Educated the Crows*, IPS, 1978; Fred Landis, *Psychological Warfare and Media Operations in Chile: 1970-1973*, Ph.D. dissertation, University of Illinois, 1975.

Cuba: Warren Hinckle and William Turner, *The Fish Is Red*, Harper and Row, 1981; William Schaap, "New Spate of Terrorism: Key Leaders Unleashed," *Covert Action Information Bulletin*, Dec. 1980.

Dominican Republic: NACLA, *Smouldering Conflict: Dominican Republic 1965-1975*; Carlos Maria Gutierrez, *The Dominican Republic: Rebellion and Repression*, Monthly Review Press, 1972; Norman Gall, "How Trujillo Died," *New Republic*, April 13, 1963.

Ecuador: Agee, *Inside the Company*.

El Salvador: NACLA, *Guatemala*, 1974; Stephen Kinzer and Stephen Schlesinger, *Bitter Fruit*, Doubleday, 1981; Blanche Wiesen Cook, *The Declassified Eisenhower*, Doubleday, 1981.

Uruguay: Agee, *Inside the Company*; A.J. Langguth, *Hidden Terrors*, Pantheon, 1978.

A final good reason for expansion is the natural superiority of the expanding country or race. Savages do not put resources to the best use—they do not make deserts bloom (nor do they make forests into deserts). They stand in the way of *über menschen.*

Modern imperial powers often conquer neighbors in the old imperial fashion, but they usually leave after a stint of pacification, leaving the neighbor in "friendly hands." Modern empires also put relatively greater weight on destabilization and subversion of offending governments and the exercise of indirect control. The United States occasionally invades countries directly, usually to shore up a discredited puppet regime about to fall to indigenous but radical or reformist rule (Vietnam, the Dominican Republic, Lebanon). The invasion of Grenada in 1983 appears to have had a double motive: to "stand tall" in the wake of the loss of 241 marines in Beirut, which occurred only days before the incursion; and to take advantage of the disarray following the murder of head-of-state Maurice Bishop to oust a radical regime. Panama was invaded in 1989 in order to remove Manuel Noriega and reassert U.S. control, and to allow *George Bush* to stand tall. Indirect control of these two former clients was quickly arranged, aided by a modest pacification effort.[3]

But the United States has enlarged and protected its domains mainly through subversion; i.e., the undermining of disfavored governments by open and covert hostile actions that weaken their authority and strengthen the power of their enemies. This covers a wide range of activities: boycotts and other forms of economic warfare; bribery and subsidization of politicians, journalists, and intellectuals; hostile propaganda; sabotage and terror, direct and through proxies; and the encouragement and support of coups. A very important form of subversion has been the wooing, bribing, and brainwashing of foreign police and military personnel, who are brought to U.S. facilities in Washington, D.C., Ft. Benning, GA, etc., where they are treated lavishly, taught to distrust their own people, and made into *de facto* agents of U.S. power, frequently proving their worth in the vanguard of subsequent coups.[4]

The United States has used these methods regularly against governments of which its elite and leadership disapprove. Table 1, reproduced from *The Real Terror Network*, shows the enormous scope of U.S. subversive activity for eight Latin American countries up to the early 1980s. The table is surely an understatement as many of these subversive operations, like bribing journalists, politicians, and military leaders, are hidden from public view and only disclosed on a sporadic and partial basis. Only by reading relatively obscure books would it be possible to find out that in the period leading up to the Brazilian coup of 1964, hundreds of Brazilian politicians had been secretly funded by the U.S. government;[5] or that in the early 1960s, the Vice President, Minister of Labor, son and physician of the President, and numerous police and intelligence officials and political leaders in Ecuador were on the CIA payroll, among a vast array of equally subversive operations.[6]

All these activities would be clearly identified as subversion and furiously denounced if engaged in by an alien power, but since they were done by us, different responses follow. First, the word subversion is inapplicable, by semantic agreement that no such invidious word could apply to ourselves. Second, the media do a fine job of suppressing or muting evidence of our subversive actions, especially those that are less easily rationalized, such as organizing assassinations, bribing foreign politicians, and sponsoring coups against freely elected governments.

But the media's greatest achievement lies in *normalizing* such activities and even giving them a high moral tone. In the trial of Manuel Noriega, the prosecution finally acknowledged that the U.S. government had paid him at least $300,000 for services rendered.[7] But the prosecution claimed that this was not to support his drug dealing, it was merely a payoff for his services as a spy against his own government. This separation is hypocritical, as even if Noriega was paid for spying, his patrons knew about his drug dealing and protection was part of the package. Most importantly, the media reported this admission of bribery of a high officer of a nearby client state very matter-of-factly, essentially reproducing the way the information was conveyed by government authorities—there was no indignation[8] at the use and protection of an important agent in the drug trade. By contrast, press reports of the arrest of Soviet spies in the United States, Canada, or elsewhere in the Free World can barely conceal their indignation, the implication being that employing spies is reprehensible. Our hiring spies, even when we have seduced high officials of friendly neighboring countries to betray their own governments, is passed through the prism of doublethink and treated as differently as is our and their shooting down of civilian airliners.

A 1976 Senate report disclosed that the United States had been involved in at least a dozen attempts to murder Fidel Castro.[9] There is also substantial evidence that we engaged in or sponsored a large number of acts of sabotage against Cuban property, that our Cuban refugee proxies committed numerous acts of terrorist violence against Cuba, including the blowing up of a civilian airliner, and that we have even employed chemical and biological agents against Cuban crops and farm animals.[10] If Castro had done similar things, they would be cited regularly as definitive proof of his terroristic and subversive proclivities. And if he (or Kadaffi) had printed a terrorist manual such as the CIA wrote for the contras in Nicaragua, the government, media, and "experts" would have had a field day with such solid evidence confirming his (or Kadaffi's) terrorist qualities. As it is, the western experts never cite the contra manual and its applications as a case study in terrorist process, although it provides an outstanding model. The mainstream media mainly ignored these major acts of terror or treated them antiseptically, as isolated incidents or "blunders," not as evidence of criminal and terrorist activity. There was also a generous dollop of apologetics in uncritical reporting of official denials, alleged provocations, and references to security threats. Castro and Kadaffi reveal their true natures by questionable acts; the United States is provoked or at most errs and gives its enemies grist for propaganda!

The Search for Honest Quislings

Because the U.S. role in the Third World has been primarily to shore up the old order, preserving the huge traditional inequalities of wealth and foreign privilege in the face of challenges from below, it has regularly aligned itself with local oligarchs and military leaders of an unsavory character, who organize what the National Liberation Front of Vietnam called "country-selling governments." In South Vietnam, in order to find leaders willing to front for a foreign invader and preside over the U.S. destruction of their land and people, the United States eventually had to resort to mercenaries who had fought for the French, were somewhat dim in intelligence, and were thieves and drug dealers.[11]

In country after country over the past half-century, the United States has organized governments run by scoundrels who would do the necessary dirty work. The list is impressive: the old Chiang-Kai-Shek clique, the rapacious and former collaborationist military leaders of Thailand, Argentine and Chilean generals, the Shah of Iran, the Indonesian generals, Ferdinand Marcos in the Philippines, Stroessner in Paraguay, the Guatemalan generals, Mobutu in Zaire. Our favorite collaborationists tend to be crooks as well as murderers, and because of the corruption endemic in these U.S.-sponsored governments they have been called "shakedown states."[12]

This has led numerous establishment intellectuals and pundits to remark on the moral deficiencies of backward peoples and to trace the roots of the problem to Asian, African, and Latin American "human nature." The idea that there could be a pernicious selectivity at work, that the West sought out the dregs by preference, and that western influence was itself corrupting, was, of course, an unacceptable line of thought. In regard to South Vietnam, Malcolm Browne regretfully observed in 1964: "Unfortunately, most of the really intelligent, dedicated and patriotic men and women who form the stuff of sound leadership stayed with the Viet Minh."[13] Most of them, however, were eventually killed by U.S. military forces, or by local mercenaries in Operation Phoenix* or similar death squad operations. No generalizations based on such information about the aborting or crippling of alternative paths of development can be found in the western media.[14]

Moderates and Extremists

The "leaders"* put in place to serve U.S. power are invariably labeled "moderates"* by the U.S. mass media. This follows by definition from the fact that they are supported by the U.S. government and serve U.S. interests. U.S. officials treat them as reasonable people we can "work with," and suggest that any little unpleasantnesses in which they may have recently indulged are under review and will be corrected soon, under our tutelage. That is, they will do our bidding, kill only the right people, and allow foreign investment and sales, even if at a heavy price in a "corruption drain."*

Indonesian head of state, General Subandrio Suharto, for example, came into power on the wave of an outburst of terrorism that involved the slaughter of between 500,000 and a million people, mostly landless peasants. He and his coterie are also contenders for honors as the greatest thieves in history.[15] But Suharto terminated any populist or radical threat to control of Indonesia and he has maintained an open door to U.S. investment and served as a staunch U.S. ally. Despite the mass slaughter he has therefore been treated by the U.S. political and corporate leadership as a fine fellow, as has the media and intellectual community. Thus, the *Christian Science Monitor* of February 6, 1987 referred to Suharto as a "moderate leader," and Michael Leifer, writing in the liberal *World Policy Journal,* featured the "stability" that Suharto brought to Indonesia, acknowledging extreme corruption and serious human rights violations only in passing.[16] Generals Videla and Viola, Argentinean leaders during the holocaust of 1976-83, were regularly referred to by the *New York Times* as "moderates" with "democratic leanings."[17] In 1933, the U.S. *chargé d'affaires* in Berlin communicated to Washington that hope for U.S. interests lay in "the more moderate section of the [Nazi] party, headed by Hitler himself...which appeals to all civilized and reasonable people" and appeared to have the upper hand over violent extremists.[18]

The tone employed in treating these client state killers is always low-keyed, and their motives are seen as benevolent—the London *Economist* described Suharto as "at heart benign"[19]; the *New York Times* wrote, "What is in doubt is not General Videla's good intentions but..." These publications never impute benign hearts nor good intentions to leaders of enemy states such as Daniel Ortega or Fidel Castro—such individuals are invariably treated with sarcasm and sneers, their motives suspect.[20] The difference is based completely on political bias, sustained by selective reporting.[21]

Following the propaganda lead of their government, the media commonly establish the moderateness of client state leaders by claiming that the "moderates" in high office are regrettably unable to control the extremists under and affiliated with them, who seem to be doing a great deal of killing. This violence is ascribed to a tragic battle between extreme leftists and extreme rightists, with our friendly government officials in the middle. The extreme rightists may be government agents—either members of the armed forces or of death squads often composed of past or present members of the armed forces[22]—but in the government-media version, the moderates in the government do not condone these murders and are striving to improve things. We must therefore support them in their struggle to control their subordinates and agents!

This droll exercise in apologetics was evident in the *Times'* editorials and news reports on Argentina: in the editorial cited above, "General Videla and the officers who surround him held out for a more moderate course...There is no evidence that he and the other members of the ruling junta condone the recent military excesses. What is in doubt is not General Videla's good intentions but his ability to control military men driven by obsessions..."[23] This apologetic for state terror, which is repeated in other editorials and is manifest in the "news" coverage, was never supported by evidence; it resulted from taking at face value the self-serving statements of Argentine and U.S. officials, just as a Soviet journalist might have reported without question a claim by Stalin that the ongoing killings and torture grieved him and were carried out by subordinates out of control and obsessed with the fascist and western imperialist threat.

A 1980 Amnesty International report exposing the 60 Argentinean detention centers in which torture was carried out, and which linked the death squads to the military establishment, was never found newsworthy by the *New York Times*.[24] News selection and suppression complement and service the acceptance of propaganda for friendly terror.

The government and media employed this same apologetic frame for state terror in El Salvador in the 1980s.[25] Here, José Napoleon Duarte was the "moderate" head of a moderate junta, unable to contain the extremes of right and left. The death squads were rightists "out of control," like the Argentinean army. This was once again implausible and fraudulent, as most of the killing was done by the Salvadoran army, and the death squads were a controlled and protected affiliate of the army.[26] Duarte was a powerless figleaf who gave the impression of moderateness by an earlier history that was irrelevant to his performance and role in the 1980s, but which was reported without question by the mainstream media. Subsequently, Alfredo Cristiani played the same role as front man for the extreme rightwing ARENA party, founded by Roberto D'Aubuisson. As he served U.S. power, the nominal power and figleaf role were once again ignored—Cristiani was a moderate by the fact of his service and acceptability to U.S. officials.

The long record of media apologetics that has made any servant of U.S. power a moderate has left only one question remaining: is there any limit to

scoundrelism that would cause an individual supported by the U.S. government to fail to be identified as a moderate in the U.S. press? No limit is
observable as yet. When Roberto D'Aubuisson came near to becoming
president of El Salvador in 1982, U.S. officials began to stress the "variety"
within the ARENA party, the doctrine of "changing course,"* and the importance of giving people a chance. Ambassador Hinton said that "Anyone who
believes in the Democratic system should give him [D'Aubuisson] the benefit
of the doubt." The press began to accommodate as well. A 1982 interview in
the Mexican paper *El Día* in which D'Aubuisson lauded the Germans for
their efficiency in handling the Jewish problem was suppressed. An article
by Warren Hoge in the *Times* of April 1, 1982 captures the new look of a
fascist in process of becoming a moderate. "Rightist Flag Bearer" is accompanied by a flatteringly thoughtful picture of D'Aubuisson, and the article
criticizes him gently for his "impulsiveness and desire for confrontation" and
the fact that his "behavior was uneven."

Staged Elections As A Control Device

The United States has mastered the art of staging elections in Third
World client states as a means of assuring the home populace that a U.S.
interventionary process is meritorious and serves a higher purpose. These
"demonstration elections"* are fraudulent in their very essence, for the
following reasons: (1) They are organized by a foreign power as a public
relations effort to ratify the rule of local authorities satisfactory to the foreign
power. Where elections will not yield the desired results, perhaps because
the local environment cannot be controlled, as in Vietnam in 1956, the United
States avoids them. (2) They are usually held after a stint of military occupation and pacification and under conditions of ongoing state terror, which
weakens and decimates the oppositional forces, leaves the voting population
fearful and traumatized,[27] and allows the "loyalists"* to control the machinery
of elections. (3) Put otherwise, the main conditions of a free election—freedom of speech, assembly and press; freedom of intermediate organizations
to mobilize people; freedom of all factions to put up candidates; and the
absence of fear and terror among the populace—have never been even
approximated in U.S.-staged demonstration elections in Vietnam, the Dominican
Republic, and El Salvador. (4) Even beyond these considerations, the intervention of a powerful outsider by its very nature alters the parameters of an election
by the biasing effects of massive deployments of foreign money and propaganda
and by the need of indigenous parties and the populace to placate the intruder.[28]

Although these points are quite obvious, the U.S. demonstration
elections in South Vietnam in 1966-67, in the Dominican Republic in 1966,

and in El Salvador in 1982 and later, and the Guatemalan elections of 1984-1985[29] were extraordinarily successful because the U.S. mass media handled them like a propaganda agency of the government.[30] The government said, in effect, "focus on long lines of voters and smiling faces, stress the size of turnout, and *don't* discuss freedom of the press, free speech, the decimation of dissident organizations, the inability of the rebels to participate, and state terror and fear. Emphasize procedural fairness and avoid substance." In accord with this call by the government, Stephen Kinzer quoted the independent observers of the International Human Rights Law Group on the Guatemala election of 1984 to the effect that the election was "procedurally fair," but ignored their repeated observation that the population was in a state of "permanent fear."[31]

It was pointed out in the Preface that in connection with the Nicaraguan election of 1984, the mass media, again following the lead of their government, simply reversed agendas, forgot about procedural fairness, and concerned themselves with freedom of the press, the ability of an opposition to run, and the like. As we noted, this pushes us to the limits of doublethink and doublespeak: using different criteria for demonstration elections and those opposed by their own government, and even misrepresenting facts within the framework of double standards.[32]

The mass media duplicated this feat in their coverage of the Nicaraguan election of 1990. Their view, without exception, was that Mrs. Chamorro and UNO beat Ortega and the Sandinistas in a free and fair election, marred only by Sandinista abuses. It was repeatedly stated that this was the first free election in Nicaraguan history, the basis for the claim being that the Reagan administration had declared the 1984 election a "sham," which was therefore an established truth for the Free Press. The fact that the Latin American Studies Association observer team described the 1984 election as a model of fairness by Latin American standards,[33] and that Lord Chitnis representing the British Parliamentary Group had found it superior to the Salvadoran election of the same year,[34] had no impact on the mainstream media. These authorities came to the wrong conclusions, and their messages were therefore simply not reported.

For David Binder, the Chamorro victory in the 1990 election was a payoff for US "patience" in pursuing the electoral option.[35] The decade-long U.S.-sponsored terror and economic warfare was written out of history and was not mentioned by him as the primary area in which the United States had displayed both diligence and "patience." In the real world, the U.S. attacks which devastated the Nicaraguan economy were certainly the primary contributor to a fall in *per capita* income of over 50 percent between 1980 and 1990. It seems obvious, therefore, that the United States had purposefully tilted the playing field in a direction unfavorable to the ruling party.[36] It is a cliché of U.S. politics that parties in power are punished by the voters for poor economic performance.[37]

The U.S. media never assessed this deliberate creation of an unlevel playing field and its bearing on the outcome and "fairness" of the elections. The massive intervention of the United States in funding opposition groups and parties and engaging in numerous manipulative activities in Nicaragua was mentioned only briefly if at all, and it was never suggested that this was a gross infringement on Nicaraguan sovereignty or affected the election results. The fact that similar interventions by foreigners in a U.S. election would be illegal was never mentioned.[38] The only suggestions of possible unfairness were found in the Sandinista control of the army and election machinery, which for the *New York Times* made the Sandinistas a "Goliath" in relation to the U.S. supported coalition.[39]

Finally, the failure of the United States to dismantle the contra army in accord with the Tela Agreement[40] left that terrorist force in place to resume operations if Mrs. Chamorro lost. President Bush told Mrs. Chamorro publicly that the boycotts would end if UNO was victorious. There was thus every reason to believe that if "Goliath" triumphed, economic and proxy terrorist warfare would continue. Nicaraguan voters therefore cast ballots under conditions of blackmail: vote for Chamorro and UNO or suffer further superpower attack. This point was never made in the mainstream media.

The Nicaraguan people finally said "uncle" after a decade of terrorism and boycott, an over 50 percent reduction of income, and a blackmail threat at the moment of voting in 1990. That the U.S. media could trumpet this as a triumph of democracy is beyond hypocrisy.

Terrorism and Retaliation

One of the most potent weapons of the western establishment designed to justify beating up smaller countries is the need for defense against "terrorism." The terrorist is a fearsome symbol, conjuring up visions of a bewhiskered, foreign-featured bomb thrower threatening western (white) innocents. Like National Security, terrorism is a fuzzy notion that can be employed with great indignation against selected enemies while ignoring, supporting, and carrying out similar actions by ourselves and allies. This can be accomplished only if a cooperative media will not look closely, ask questions, and challenge double standards and propagandistic usage. And the U.S. mass media have been more than cooperative.[41]

The use of this propaganda weapon has been greatly aided by the rise of an industry devoted to producing and disseminating the West's selective version of terrorism. The industry consists of government officials, terrorism experts housed in and funded by government related and corporate funded thinktanks, and private security firms. These experts and security firm personnel work for governments and corporations who have their own narrow views of terrorists. Salvadoran peasants, Chilean workers, and South African blacks would have a different view, but they don't have the resources to fund thinktanks, experts, and data bases listing "terrorist incidents." The funded experts respond to their funders' demands—and not surprisingly, it turns out that the West is defending against terrorism, not terrorizing; that Libya and North Korea are terrorist states, not El Salvador, South Africa, or Israel.

On February 2, 1988, FBI chief William Sessions told the press that the surveillance of CISPES had been legitimate because it had possibly given support to a "terrorist" organization, namely, the FMLN rebels of El Salvador. In any rebellion, force is used; by Sessions' logic, George Washington's army was a terrorist organization. If we consider, as we obviously should, who initiated the violence, whether the rebels had explored political options before resorting to arms, and the forms and levels of violence and intimidation, the evidence is clear that in El Salvador state terror came first and on a large scale, and that political options were entirely foreclosed before the armed rebellion developed. As Archbishop Romero told President Carter in 1980, the people's organizations are "fighting to defend their most fundamental human rights"; and in his diary he noted that the opposition forces were being subjected to "a general program of annihilation" to which they were responding. Given these considerations, the FMLN should not be regarded as a terrorist organization at all; it is more reasonably described as engaged in "self-defense" and "counterterrorism" against the Salvadoran state and its external (U.S.) managers, who are the real terrorists.

How does the propaganda system obscure the evidence that the Salvadoran state terrorizes and that the United States, as the organizer, protector, and supplier of this regime, is an international terrorist state? Partly by arbitrary and highly political word manipulation, and partly by brazen government-media doctoring of evidence.

An important element of word manipulation is the confinement of "terrorism" to acts of violence and intimidation carried out by individuals and small groups. Dictionary definitions have always extended the reach of the word to governments, and in years gone by, terrorism was associated primarily with governments. This was based on the quantity and quality of violence carried out by state and non-state actors, as only states use systematic torture as a method of intimidation, and the scale of their acts of violence makes the terrorism of individuals and small groups look relatively insignificant. The concepts of "retail" and "wholesale" terrorism capture the fact that individual and rebel group violence is on a small (retail) scale, whereas state violence is on a large (wholesale) scale.

The shift to using "terrorism" only for small-scale violence was a highly political choice of word use, corresponding to an identifiable political agenda. In 1981 President Reagan and Secretary of State Alexander Haig announced that they were shifting U.S. priorities from "human rights" to "terrorism." "Human rights" policies were concerned with the abusive activities of states like Argentina, Chile, Guatemala, and South Africa. These countries were already receiving muted attention, given their client status, but Reagan was actually entering into alliances with these agents of wholesale terrorism (all of whom greeted his accession to the presidency with enthusiasm). The point of the newly invigorated concern over retail terrorism was partly to divert attention from the now "constructively engaged" state terrorists, who were unleashed to invade and kill on a larger scale in Lebanon, South Africa, and Central America, and partly to justify other Reagan era policies (rearmament, the upward redistribution of income, etc.), which required a patriotic, confused and thereby more manageable public. The media went along with these new priorities and the related system of doublespeak and propaganda about terrorism without notable dissent.

Confining "terrorism" to the acts of retail terrorists is sometimes rationalized on the ground that they attack innocent civilians, whereas state terrorists are presumably more discriminating. While this stance is made plausible by airline hijackings and airport bombings, it is a false generalization. Retail terrorists are often highly selective, and state terrorists frequently engage in deliberate intimidation by murder of large civilian populations. The National Liberation Front (NLF) of South Vietnam, for example, punished cadres who victimized untargeted civilians. On the other hand, B-52 bombing raids in Vietnam, and Israeli bombing attacks on heavily populated areas, were (and are) well understood as efforts to victimize noncombatants. After Israeli Prime Minister Menahem Begin had criticized earlier labor governments for indiscriminate attacks on Arab civilians (in response to attacks on his own policies), Labor Party spokesperson Abba Eban defended the earlier bombings on the grounds that "there was a rational prospect, ultimately fulfilled, that afflicted populations [i.e., innocent civilians deliberately bombed] would exert pressure for the cessation of hostilities." In other words, the intent of Israeli bombing had been to intimidate the civilian population into pressing their leaders to alter their policy. This is a confession of planned indiscriminate murder of civilians.

Another important doublespeak device for rationalizing one's own and friendly terrorism is to describe it as "retaliation" and "counter-terror." The trick here is arbitrary word assignment: that is, any violence engaged in by ourselves or our friends is *ipso facto* retaliation and counter-terrorism; whatever the enemy does is terrorism, irrespective of facts. Of course the enemy always says that his violence was provoked by prior acts of ours or our clients, that he designates as terrorist, but the enemy claims are never allowed; our claims and those of our allies are never questioned. When the Israelis bombed Tunis on October 1, 1985, killing some 55 Palestinians and 20 Tunisian bystanders, the Reagan administration and western press found that this was "retaliation" for prior PLO actions, but the PLO's explanation that its acts were based on earlier Israeli acts was inadmissible. Word assignment based purely on political preference is doublespeak in action.

The Orwellian quality of this selective assignment of the words "terrorism" and "retaliation" is highlighted by the 1982 Israeli invasion of Lebanon in the sequence of violence, and by the factual background of that invasion. The official Israeli-U.S. and western media formulation is that the invasion was designed to eliminate "pockets of terrorism." But the invasion took place after a period in which the PLO had successfully maintained a cease-fire on the borders of Israel for 11 months, despite Israeli provocation. This caused consternation among the Israeli leadership because it made it hard for them to use the claim of "terrorism" to refuse to negotiate a political settlement. On June 25, 1982, the Israeli analyst of the PLO, Yehoshua Porath, wrote in *Ha'aretz*, that "the decision of the government (or more precisely, its two leaders), [to invade Lebanon] flowed from the very fact that the cease-fire had been observed." He went on to say:

> The government's hope is that [following the invasion] the stricken PLO, lacking a logistical and territorial base, will return to its earlier terrorism: it will carry out bombings throughout the world, hijack airplanes, and murder many Israelis. In this way, the PLO will lose part of the political legitimacy that it has gained...undercutting the danger that elements will develop among the Palestinians that might become a legitimate negotiating partner for future political accommodations.

In short, the Israeli leadership wanted and deliberately provoked PLO "terrorism" to justify a refusal to negotiate. This makes the Israeli invasion a major act of terrorism, the later PLO acts responsive and induced by the plan. But in western ideology and the western media, this does not alter the rule: Israel only retaliates; the PLO engages in terrorism.

We can see that the use of doublespeak by arbitrary word assignment is bolstered by — and even requires — a refusal to look at current and historical facts. Fact suppression is extremely important to doublespeak in general.

Israel and the Palestinians

The Middle East, and especially the conflict between Israel and the Palestinians, has yielded a cornucopia of doublespeak usage. This is a result of the huge gap between western pretensions and nominal values, on the one hand, and western interests and policies, on the other. Israeli governments have absolutely refused to do any political business with the Palestinians for decades, and have carried out policies toward Palestinians in Israel that have been regularly compared in the Israeli and world (but not U.S.) press with those of South Africa.[42]

Doublespeak on the Middle East is also greatly affected by the power of the pro-Israeli lobby in the United States. In addition to its virtually unconditional support for Israeli actions, the Jewish establishment has abused and threatened retaliation against intellectuals, journalists, and politicians who voice criticism of Israeli policy or who support any kind of challenge, penalty, or restriction on aid to the Israeli state. Although the Jewish lobby is not a large one, its resources and connections, the commitment of its supporters, and its ties to the military-industrial complex make it potent, and political candidates vie with one another in vows of fealty to Israel.[43] For the Jewish establishment itself, there appears to be no limits to Israeli violence against unarmed civilians that will not be rationalized by alleged "provocations." And if beatings and the cracking of the bones of women and children are acceptable, what next for the "two-legged animals" and "grasshoppers"?

With the effective cowing of many of the politicians, intellectuals, journalists, and editors who are not already true believers, the stage is set for the institutionalization of myths, big lies, and doublespeak. Many of the myths center in the origins of the Israeli state and the basis for the exodus of Palestinians that followed, which are beyond the scope of this discussion.[44] The concept of "terrorism," which has been central to the Israeli effort to dehumanize the Palestinians and provide the basis for a refusal to negotiate a political settlement, has been discussed in the previous section.

Rejectionism and Superrejectionism

In parallel with the usage on terrorism, in western doublespeak the Israeli state and United States never "reject," only the enemy does. The treatment is humorous, given the facts of the case: The *New York Times* asks whether the PLO can step into the diplomatic breach as "an acceptable negotiating partner with Israel," and answers: Yes, if it renounces terror and its "sterile rejectionism." Otherwise, Israel would "not find the courage to go to the negotiating table with an organization formally [sic] dedicated to its destruction" (Editorial, August 19, 1988). If we ask why the stronger party should lack courage, but the weaker one, whose existence is not even recognized by the stronger, should be obliged to muster up the courage, the

Times offers no answer. Note the *Times'* mention of the Palestinians' "formal" dedication to Israel's destruction, which permits it to avoid addressing the fact that in January 1976 (and periodically thereafter) the PLO accepted a "practical" proposal for a two-state settlement that amounted to *de facto* recognition and guarantees of Israel's security and sovereignty.

In an editorial a month later, the *Times* again berated Mr. Arafat for persevering in his rejectionism, noting, however, that "Heading to a Nov. 1 election, Israeli politicians seem lost in a wilderness of slogans" (editorial, Sept. 9, 1988). On one side, straightforward rejectionism; on the other, simple confusion! In the same editorial the *Times* acknowledges that Shamir has said that he will never even talk to the PLO and that Peres engages in his own evasive doubletalk. As noted earlier, Israeli analysts even explain the 1982 Lebanon invasion in terms of the Israeli leadership's fear that Arafat's control over "terrorism" would force unwanted negotiations.

The Israeli leadership has also shown exceptional hostility to Israelis and Palestinians who hint at the possibility and desirability of mutual recognition. But for some unexplained reason, Israeli "super-rejectionism" is never designated "sterile rejectionism" and the burden of successfully opening a diplomatic track is always on the PLO. The insufficiency of the hesitant feelers of the weaker party in the face of super-rejectionism is the entire focus of attention as "rejectionism." This is beyond hypocrisy.

The "Peace Process"

The Camp David accords introduced, at least for the western media, something called a "peace process."* This endearing phrase tells us that in the western view the agreements were "a good thing." In fact, the Camp David agreements successfully pulled Egypt out of effective opposition to Israeli policies, thereby giving Israel a freer hand, but without resolving in any way the underlying Palestinian-Israeli conflict. Furthermore, while the accords called for negotiations among Israel, Egypt, Jordan, and representatives of the Palestinians on the status of the Israeli-held territories, the Israeli Knesset quickly voted that after the transition period it would "act to fulfil its rights to sovereignty over Judea, Samaria and the Gaza district," thus negating the agreement to negotiate. The ensuing settlement program in the Occupied Territories, internal repression, and continuous warfare indicates that the "peace process" actually facilitated a more efficient "war process." The clear failure of the accords to advance peace has not interfered in any way with the western usage—a good thing deserves a warm phrase: "peace process."

Antisemitism

With Israel's increased power and aggressiveness, its enlarged role as western enforcer against the lesser breeds of the Middle East, and its utility as a surrogate arms supplier of South Africa, Somoza, the Nicaraguan contras, Guatemala, Honduras, and pre-Alfonsin Argentina, the attitude of traditional antisemites toward Israel has changed. In 1967 Xavier Vallat, who was responsible for thousands of Jewish deportations to the death camps as the Minister of Jewish Affairs under the Vichy regime, wrote an article in the rightwing French newspaper *Aspects de la France,* explaining that he was now a Zionist ("Mes raisons d'être sioniste," June 15, 1967), and expressing his support for Israel in its struggle against the Arabs. This fascist was effusive over the Jewish people's discovery of its nationality and their ethnic-religious tendency to domination ("à tendance dominatrice"). Many other leaders of the radical right have flocked to the support of Israel. Arguably, this is because the dominant Israeli "semites" are westernized and are keeping in their place more backward and troublesome semites. The Israelis merit approval in the same way that Duarte, Sadat, Generals Thieu and Ky, Savimbi, and their cadres, armies, and police do for their service to western interests. A shift in attitudes toward "semites" has accompanied these new relationships, and western contempt and hatred has been largely displaced from the former victims to the more threatening "semites" (the latest set of victims).

This change is hardly recognized in the West. "Antisemitism" is a word applied only to attitudes toward the *former* victims, now integrated into western power structures. The hostility in the West to Arab semites is never described as antisemitism. And many of the rightwing friends of Israel haven't sloughed off their traditional antisemitism and dislike of Jews. Thus, Jerry Falwell mouths traditional antisemitic sentiments easily and frequently, but loves and supports Israel and is honored and feted there. Is he an "antisemite"? In the transvaluation of values of the Jewish establishment in the United States, certainly for its large rightwing contingent, the usage of the word antisemitism has subtly shifted from hostility, hatred, and steretyped attitudes toward Jews to criticism of and hostility toward Israel. Nixon's classic antisemitic utterances revealed on his tapes, Reagan's incredible performance at the Nazi cemetery at Bitberg, Argentine state antisemitism, the antisemitism of the Christian and radical right, and even the revelation of U.S. official protection and patronage of Nazi murderers after World War II—all are treated benignly by the media because these traditional manifestations of antisemitism are combined with "support for Israel." Meanwhile, Jesse Jackson's referrence to Jewish areas as "Hymie" towns is serious business—because Jackson is not a "supporter of Israel." In the world of establishment doublespeak, antisemitism has become, first and foremost, criticism of and hostility to Israel. Traditional antisemitism is of lesser importance, used strategically to denigrate those who display the really important failing.

4. Repelling Naked Aggression and Upholding the Sanctity of International Law in the Persian Gulf

President George Bush and his administration have devoted primary attention to external matters, first in Panama, then for a more extended period and with vastly greater attention and resources, to the Gulf war and its aftermath. Interestingly, at the same time as Bush was proving in daily headlines that he could stand as tall as his great mentor, there were also daily headlines describing terrible and worsening problems in the United States. New York State and City suffer acute fiscal crises, Philadelphia is struggling to avoid bankruptcy, and while these and numerous other cities and states are forced to make drastic cutbacks in services, urban poverty, decay, crime, and drug crises continue unabated or worsen. The Bush administration's neglect of education and infrastructure, while diverting capital and technology into warmaking, continued Reagan era policies that seemed deliberately designed to undermine long-term productivity and competitiveness.[1]

Bush's preoccupation with the Gulf brings to mind Mrs. Jellyby in Charles Dickens' novel *Bleak House*. Mrs. Jellyby spent her greatest energies organizing other do-gooders to help and straighten out the poor natives of Borrioboola-Gha in Africa, while her own family was neglected, resentful, and pathetic. A difference between Mrs. Jellyby and George Bush as models of misplaced priorities, however, is that Mrs. Jellyby meant well and at least did not seriously harm the recipients of her ill-conceived charity.

The contradiction between domestic conditions and the diversion of leadership attention and material resources to warmaking was occasionally noted in the mainstream media in the immediate aftermath of the war. Some liberal pundits boldly suggested that,if we could mobilize so exhaustively to contain naked aggression, we might also do the same for domestic problems. But generally, the political success of the bi-partisan war and the power of the war party kept such views muted. We were number one again, and what more could a free people ask? It took the better part of a year after

49

the end of the war for U.S. politics to be reoriented toward its massive domestic problems, which included a recession that had begun in July 1990 and showed no signs of terminating by the end of 1991.

"Another Hitler"

Whenever the U. S. establishment pushes somebody to the top of its hit list and wishes to mobilize the public for a program of destabilization and aggression, a demonization campaign is unleashed. For the Reagan replacement of concern over "human rights" with "terrorism" as the heart and soul of U.S. foreign policy in 1981, Kadaffi was brought on line. He was a perfect foil—dark-skinned, Arab, anti-Israel, supporter of national liberation movements, inclined to rhetorical excesses, and a sponsor of terrorists (although hardly competitive with the United States and South Africa in this respect)— and his emergence as a symbol of evil is a classic case of government-press collaboration for larger state interests. But each successive designated enemy has been demonized—even Daniel Ortega in the 1980s, Iran's Dr. Mohammed Mossadegh in 1953, and Dr. Salvador Allende in the early 1970s.

There is a remarkable flexibility in this process. A leader like Cambodia's Pol Pot, "another Hitler" and sometimes allegedly "worse than Hitler" in the years 1975-1980 when the U.S. establishment was first trying to overcome the Vietnam Syndrome, suddenly became a shadowy figure when the United States quietly began supporting him and the Khmer Rouge after their ouster by Vietnam in 1979.[2] It would not have been helpful to the U.S. policy of bleeding Vietnam for the Free Press to have called attention to U.S. support for a man furiously assailed as a mass murderer a few years back; always accommodating, the Free Press remained silent.

The history of Manuel Noriega displays the reverse pattern. This thief, murderer, and long-time collaborator with the drug cartel served as a paid CIA agent and was tolerated and used by the U.S. leadership for years—during which he was accorded minimal attention by the media—until he began to drag his feet on supporting the contras and displayed other signs of inadequate subservience to his former Washington masters. Although his involvement with the drug trade had diminished over the years, in 1985 he suddenly became a very bad man, the kind that the United States can't abide, and the government-Free Press propaganda mill got us ready for his ouster.

Saddam Hussein fits the Noriega pattern. A brutal dictator from the very beginning of his rule, he was referred to by Evans and Novak as "handsome and toughly [sic] elegant" and saluted by the *New York Times* for his "personal strength" and "more pragmatic, cooperative line" when his policies were in accord with U.S. interests in the mid-1970s. In the 1980s, he was quietly supported and supplied with arms by the West, and his shipping in the Gulf was protected against attack, while he was committing aggression against Iran. Western support didn't flag when evidence surfaced that Hussein was using chemical weapons against the Kurds at home and in the war against Iran. The *New York Times* even commended the United States and Soviet Union for having jointly supported Hussein in his war against Iran, apparently regarding this evidence of collective action as more important than the fact that it contributed to a major blood bath.[3]

The United States even provided vast quantities of grain to Hussein with $5 billion of U.S. government loan guarantees from 1983-1990. The Government Accounting Office, noting the prospective loss of $2 billion in these guaranteed credits, commented that "It seems that the U.S. desire to build a strategic and agricultural trade relationship with Iraq outweighed the apparent financial risks involved and discounted evidence of Iraq's human rights violations."[4]

With Iraq's occupation of Kuwait, however, U.S. officials and the compliant Free Press once again reversed course and began to focus on and wax indignant over Saddam Hussein's long-obvious ugly features and military capabilities. Suddenly, with Hussein elevated to the top of the U.S. hit list, he was "another Hitler."

Naked Versus Properly Attired Aggression

Hussein's occupation, looting and absorption of Kuwait was a case of "naked aggression."* Aggression is a bad business, but calling it naked aggression means that we intend to do something about it. Our own aggressions in Grenada, Panama, the Dominican Republic, and Indochina were of course properly clothed in a cloud of justifying rhetoric, and given our power and propaganda muscle, they were not even designated aggression by the western intelligentsia and press.

Similarly, when states invade and occupy countries with our tacit approval and under our auspices, an invidious word like aggression, let alone naked aggression, is not applied. Indonesia's invasion of East Timor in 1975 occurred only hours after a visit by President Gerald Ford and Secretary of State Henry Kissinger, and was carried out with their tacit approval. UN actions to counter this aggression were nullified by U.S. lobbying and votes,[5] and the Free Press has always paid minimal attention to this occupation and slaughter. Israel's invasion of Lebanon in 1982 was also not naked aggression—it was another Operation Just Cause, by rule of affiliation.

South Africa's occupation of Namibia was condemned by the UN Security Council, General Assembly, and International Court between 1968 and 1971. South Africa simply ignored their orders to leave. This did not disturb the West's good relations with South Africa, and the United States actively collaborated with it in supporting Savimbi and destabilizing Angola. The imposition of an apartheid system in Namibia, the accompanying seizure of assets and looting, and the extensive repression and killing were of no concern to the West. And when the South-West African Peoples Organization (SWAPO), a national liberation movement, emerged in Namibia, it was not viewed as legitimate and given support; like the ANC it was treated as a terrorist organization.

With naked aggression, no compromises are possible. The aggressor must be removed, quickly and without retention of any ill-gotten gains. Otherwise, how will naked aggressors of the future be deterred? And only naked aggressors *need* to be deterred. We will not even allow a naked aggressor to save face, so that he must accept humiliation as well as total defeat. The merit of this insistence on humiliation, beyond the deterrence factor, is that he may not be willing to accept this, in which case we can smash him on the basis of higher principle.

"Properly attired aggression"* is a different matter. South Africa's illegal occupation of Namibia was the basis of quiet diplomacy and constructive engagement over many years. The imposition of the system of apartheid on the black population of Namibia was not intolerable, and U.N. Security Council condemnations of its attacks on Angola were vetoed by the United States. Mrs. Thatcher, the "Iron Lady," eager to oppose Iraq's naked aggression by immediate force of arms, was the "Mush Lady" in response to South Africa's invasions, occupations, and extensive state terrorism, consistently opposed even to mild sanctions.

In the 1980s, U.S. negotiations with South Africa and Angola directed toward a Namibia-Angola war settlement put great weight on South Africa's "security interests" and fears of Cubans in Angola. The Reagan-Bush era position was never that the illegal occupation of Namibia should be terminated forthwith and without conditions. The larger framework of relations was taken into consideration, South Africa was able to maintain control of a strategic bay, and the economic interests of its nationals, although obtained under a system of illegal occupation and coercion, were protected. But South Africa's was not naked aggression—it was properly attired.

Snow White and the 150 Dwarves

During the Gulf war the U.S. establishment and mainstream media were indignant that once again the United States was having trouble getting its allies, with the exception of the Iron Lady, to join enthusiastically in "burden-sharing"* and support of military action against Iraq. They forgot how much they owed us for past police services and protection against the long threat of Soviet attack, and they seemed unaware that we operate in the interest of the world community, not self-interest. Thus, what is good in the perception of U.S. leaders is good for the world, not just for ourselves.

Those who join us in our international crusades recognize these truths. The view that Bush engineered the war to serve his own and other parochial U.S. interests, and that the war was damaging to the welfare of countries like Germany and Japan, is not even suggested, let alone debated. That the countries other than our Gulf protectorates joined us either because of threats, bribery, or to try to exercise some constraint over the world's foremost "loose cannon" is a cynical canard.

Goals in Daily Transition

Although the real goals of the Bush administration in the Gulf were submerged in a welter of public relations claims, it was sometimes acknowledged by officials and commentators that we were there to protect access to and control over major oil reserves. The related threat of Saddam Hussein to oil supplies and prices, and thus to the U.S. consumer, also received considerable play. Some have called this the "life style rationale" for war. Of course, the Bush policy itself led to a substantial elevation in oil and gasoline prices, which later receded. It is not at all obvious that Saddam Hussein would have wanted, or been able, to elevate prices as high as OPEC pushed them in the 1970s, but he was less easily controlled than the authoritarians hitherto in charge, and he represented a growing independent force in the control of Arabian oil. He also threatened the military domination of Israel, the U.S. surrogate standing alone since the fall of the Shah.

The occupation of Kuwait provided the Bush-CIA-military-industrial complex allies with an opportunity to reassert U.S. leadership of the western world, to firm up U.S. domination of the Gulf and control over oil revenues, and to justify the imperial military deployments and budget imperilled by the disappearance of the Soviet Threat. It was also designed to help Bush recoup his personal political fortunes. The banking, oil, pro-Israel, and military industrial complex constituencies could be mobilized to support this new thrust, but in my view this was a "presidential war"* *par excellence*, with the causes to be found in the parochial and self-serving calculations of Bush and his security state coterie. The secondary effects of a major war in the Gulf, like large numbers dead, starving, and made refugees in still another part of the world ravaged by western military force, and even the substantial costs to the United States, were of little interest to them.

Aside from the threat to friendly control of oil sources, the real U.S. goals were rarely mentioned or debated. Nominal goals were featured heavily and evolved on an almost daily basis according to public relations assessments. Obviously, democracy in the Gulf could not be stressed as an objective. Rather, naked aggression ranked high. The "life style" rationale for war was mentioned, but it seemed a little mundane, one administration official telling the press that it was important "that people not see this as a battle over oil." In spite of this admonition, James Baker at one point suggested an even more mundane objective: jobs. This lead balloon was greeted with derision, and cartoonists had a field day (Tony Auth, in the *Philadelphia Inquirer,* showed an Iwo Jima flag-raising, the flag reading "Help Wanted," the heart-rending quote on the side reading: "It's About Jobs."—James Baker). The threat that Iraq might soon have nuclear weapons was also raised, and being found to arouse public concern more than other objectives, was heavily stressed. In short, nominal objectives were *ex post,* fluid, and opportunistic; real objectives were rarely examined or considered in depth.

"The Mere Gook Rule"

During the Vietnam War it was reported that cynical U.S. lawyers working in that country had coined the phrase "the mere gook rule,"* to describe the very lenient treatment given U.S. military personnel who killed Vietnamese civilians.[6] This was a minor manifestation of a U.S. contempt for the poor, yellow-skinned people we were allegedly "saving." The racist element in that war of salvation added to another extremely important factor influencing U.S. policy: the Vietnamese were voiceless in the United States and their pain and material and human losses were politically irrelevant and largely unreported here (and only slightly less so in our Free World allied and client states). The only politically relevant casualties were those of U.S. military personnel.

We can express the foregoing in economics lingo by saying that Vietnamese casualties were "externalities" and the marginal cost of dead Vietnamese was zero from the perspective of the important players in the U.S. political system. This made it feasible to employ capital-intensive methods of warfare in Vietnam, with a lavish use of air and artillery firepower, and extremely destructive weaponry, in order to keep U.S. casualties down. The rule was, when in doubt, bring in the bombers to level what would automatically be called "a suspected Vietcong base."* It is an interesting fact that napalm was used far more heavily in southern Vietnam than in the north, the reason being that North Vietnam, as an independent country, had some access to the world media, whereas the South Vietnamese peasantry was being "pacified" by the United States in connivance with a local puppet military government, so that the people being saved were voiceless.

Thus, the reverse side of the coin of policies to reduce U.S. casualties was enormous casualties and devastation for the Vietnamese civilian population and land. This connection was never discussed in the mainstream media, and Vietnamese slaughter and destruction were politically costless to U.S. political and military leaders. These were mere gooks. When the war ended, the United States didn't have to spend a dime to help the Indochinese societies that the napalm, fragmentation bombs, B-52 raids, and Rome plows had devastated and shattered. Even today, the U.S. establishment, when it deigns to mention Vietnam, focuses on unaccounted-for U.S. casualties, not the millions of mere gooks killed, injured, and beggared in our capital-intensive war of aggression.

Apart from its failure to produce a clear "win," a major problem with the Vietnam War from the standpoint of leaders of the U.S. national security establishment was that it lasted too long and produced too many U.S. casualties (even if only a tiny fraction of Indochinese casualties). One avenue pursued in subsequent actions to avoid this problem was to pick on tiny victims that we could easily overwhelm. Another was to employ even more capital-intensive methods of fighting to get our casualties down to acceptable levels.

These are matters that George Bush understands. He watched the Grenada experience, where a brief operation with few U.S. casualties was a resounding political success. He saw that the lies, the discrepancy in size of contestants (the "bully factor"*), and the violations of international law were of no concern to the patriotic press. Bush's Panama invasion was a notable success, in the Grenada mold. There was a brief embarrassment at not capturing Noriega in the first assault, but he eventually surfaced and was apprehended and brought to this country for trial. The press once again served the state with enthusiasm, swallowing the shifting rationale and downplaying the brazen illegalities.

In the "mere gook rule" tradition, the press focused heavily on the lightness of U.S. casualties, and barely noted in passing that substantial numbers of Panamanians also died. Only 23 U.S. military personnel killed—what a triumph! In the first week of Operation Just Cause, estimates of Panamanian casualties were sparse, and pictures of Panamanian victims and areas of devastation were rare. The media tended to accept Pentagon estimates of 202 civilians killed and its inflation of Panamanian *military* casualties, ignoring evidence of Pentagon destruction of medical records and cover-ups of mass killings and mass graves. Serious evidence points to thousands of civilian deaths and massive destruction.[7]

Once again, the United States shattered a poor society, and as in the case of the triumph over mighty Grenada, it was a success story—that is, there was a "win," minimal U.S. casualties, and virtual suppression of what happened to the "mere Panamanians" during the war. The media also quickly dropped Panama from the news, so that the U.S. failure to pick up the pieces of yet another victim we had "saved" did not cost Bush votes.*

It should be understood that our "little brown brothers"* always bring self-destruction on themselves. It works this way: we lay down the law, saying that you must accept our terms, without concession or qualification. In the case of Vietnam, the Vietnamese had to agree that our puppet regime would retain control of South Vietnam, or they would be bombed back to the Stone Age. Saddam Hussein had to get out of Kuwait "with his tail between his legs" (Cheney), in abject submission, or be blown up. If our opponents do not submit and we are obliged to blow them up, clearly this is their responsibility.

The kinder, gentler America has never been visible to foreigners who stand in our way. And discussions of the costs of the Gulf War in this country, both in planning and in retrospective assessment, once again featured *U.S.* casualties in a brazenly exclusive way; the cost to mere Arabs as sentient human beings was virtually ignored. This, despite our alleged service as global policeman in a New World Order, and despite the supposed applicability in the West of a humane value system based on the Judeo-Christian ethic.

Super-Lies

Superpower leaders can engage in super-lying and get away with it. I recall vividly President Lyndon Johnson and Secretary of State Dean Rusk intoning repeatedly in the mid-1960s that North Vietnam should "leave its neighbors alone," Reagan and Shultz in the mid-1980s denouncing Nicaragua's "revolution without borders," and Johnson stating that he was aching for negotiations with the Vietnamese but simply couldn't find anybody to negotiate with. On the last point, we have a perfect analogy with George Bush and James Baker, who allegedly tried "diplomacy" in the Middle East but were obliged to fight because the enemy failed to respond.

Johnson's ploy was to pretend to be interested in negotiations, while secretly warning the North Vietnamese that only surrender was acceptable. It was well known in 1965 that Johnson had fended off all independent and indigenous Vietnamese attempts at a negotiated settlement, and had put in place a puppet military regime in South Vietnam designed strictly to fight, but he had to clear the ground for war at home by a public relations gesture.

That his peace moves were phoney and designed to manipulate consent at home was obvious to anyone who followed the unfolding events and had a vestige of sense and integrity. But the mainstream media hewed to the administration's propaganda line and played dumb. In response to an early PR effort, James Reston stated in the *New York Times* (Oct. 18, 1965) that "The problem of peace lies now not in Washington but in Hanoi..." Getting this core piece of disinformation accepted by the media was essential to freeing the Johnson administration to fight a war in Vietnam.

George Bush aborted and fended off any and all attempts at a diplomatic resolution of the Middle East crisis, and the belated Baker trip to Geneva to meet Iraqi leaders was openly a PR operation. In an exact follow-on to Johnson's secret messages to Hanoi, Bush sent a private message to Hussein with an ultimatum demanding that he leave Kuwait unconditionally and promising to arrest and try him as a war criminal. Nevertheless, Bush and Baker repeatedly spoke of "diplomatic" options having been exhausted, and Bush, in his speech before the National Association of Religious Broadcasters on January 28, 1991, stated that the war in the Gulf was a "last resort" after "extraordinary" diplomatic efforts had been tried and failed.

This truly Big Lie was not contested in the U.S. mass media. Paralleling James Reston's performance of 1965, Thomas Friedman wrote in the *New York Times* on January 20, 1991, "Now that *diplomacy has failed* [emphasis added] and it has come to war..." Just as in 1965, it was essential to engineering support for war that the image be conveyed that the United States was prepared to engage in serious diplomacy. And just as in 1965, the mainstream press helped to convey that image.

This propagation of big lies does not require Pentagon censorship; the mass media do it freely and naturally. Censorship deals with the little lies (whether a plane was shot down, or 10 rather than 6 body bags were shipped off today), not the big ones that portray our country as benevolent, fighting aggression, and eager for diplomatic solutions.

The "Allies"

One of the droller features of the U.S. assault on Iraq was the regular news reporting of attacks carried out by the "allies," and under "United Nations" auspices, not by the United States. Of course, the United States organized the allies, using extensive arm-twisting, bribery, threats, and misrepresentation of U.S. goals, with only Great Britain gung-ho in support (apart from the sheikdoms); it pushed the earliest possible use of force on the members of this "coalition"; it alone decided when the war would start; and 90+ percent of the bombs dropped by the "allies" were of U.S. origin.

The flow of information and disinformation about the allied effort was also controlled by U.S. officials.

The practice of a great power covering up its aggressive and violent strategies under the guise of collective action goes back a long way. In the first volume of his *A History of the Ancient World,* in a chapter on "The Athenian Empire," Michael Rostovtzeff described how Athens bullied and manipulated client states in the fifth century B.C. as it carried out "her ambitious foreign policy," and that "all this was exceedingly displeasing to the 'allies,' as the subjects of the Athenian Empire were still officially called..." (p. 270). During the Vietnam war, the United States mobilized fighting units from "allies" like Australia, Thailand, and Korea, which were essentially mercenary forces, obtained by threats and generous "revenue sharing" for which the kinder, gentler United States always finds resources. So the Vietnam war too was fought by "allies"! And the murderous Korean war, in which the United States almost completely leveled North and central Korea, with the systematic bombing of dikes and destruction of food and water supplies, the massive use of napalm "splashed" (Winston Churchill's phrase) over houses, people, and animals, and coming close to precipitating a war with China and using nuclear weapons, was fought under the UN cover. It must have been consoling to the world to know that this was done by "allies" under UN auspices, rather than by the United States alone.

Super-Aggression as Fighting Naked Aggression

The war with Iraq was the third major direct U.S. assault on a Third World area in the last 40 years (I am not counting the attacks on Central America and numerous lesser but deadly interventions). In each case, the United States acted in the name of fighting aggression, transforming complex local events into rationales for embarking on campaigns of truly massive destruction. In the case of the Korean War, the question of who started it remains controversial,[8] but the United States quickly steered consensus to a North Korean invasion without provocation, and mobilized its "allies" and the UN as cover for the virtual destruction of North Korea.

In the case of Vietnam, also, the U.S. official position, accepted by the mainstream media, was that we were countering "aggression from the North," as well as "internal aggression" by the South Vietnamese who had the audacity to resist the rule of our chosen proxies. In reality, the aggressors were the French, who tried to reestablish their colonial rule (with U.S. and British assistance) from 1945-53, and then the United States through 1975. The United States killed millions and left the Indochinese peninsula shattered. While it did not succeed in keeping puppet governments in power, it successfully set back and badly damaged the revolutionary process in Southeast Asia through extreme violence: a super-aggression* in the name of fighting a fabricated aggression.

In Iraq, the United States again fought in the name of countering aggression, as it proceeded to smash a smaller power and lay waste another Third World area. In this case, in contrast with Korea and Vietnam, there was a definite aggression by Iraq. But several points should be noted. First, the choice of aggressor to be smashed was highly selective, and the resistance to this aggression was organized by a country still occupying its previous victim (Panama).[9] Second, the Iraq aggressor aggressed against Iran from 1980-1988, with support from the United States and the "allies," with nary a moral issue nor need to teach a lesson arising. Third, the United States virtually enticed Iraq to enter Kuwait, reassuring Saddam Hussein publicly and privately that the conflict was strictly an Arab problem and that we had no agreement to defend Kuwait. Such information was even given to Congress on July 31, 1990, *after* the CIA had informed the Bush administration that an Iraqi army was poised for an attack on Kuwait, and only two days before the invasion.[10]

This failure to try to constrain Hussein by diplomatic means, and *de facto* invitation to invade, reflects either staggering incompetence or a remarkably sophisticated conspiracy to entrap. The failure of the U.S. mass media to consider this set of facts and issues as worthy of front page reporting and intense debate is prime evidence of their irresponsibility to the public and service to the state. My own view is that the Bush team invited Hussein into Kuwait through sheer incompetence, but not only were they deeply annoyed when he did invade, they also saw that he could usefully be set up as a naked aggressor who must be taught a lesson. This would allow the Bush team to serve its own ends (see above, Goals in Daily Transition).

The main point here, however, is that the lesser and invited aggression by Iraq allowed a really massive aggression, "principle" being employed with extraordinary hypocrisy and opportunism. With its enormous resources, connections, pliable and purchasable allies and clients, and patriotic press, the United States can get away with this. Its own aggressions disappear from view, its support of allied and client state aggressions are ignored, its earlier support of Hussein and virtual invitation to him to invade Kuwait is not newsworthy, its complete refusal to allow the invited aggression to be resolved by diplomacy is referred to as "failed diplomacy," and its own plans for super-aggression are treated as in its own propaganda—as a defensive response of the "allies" to naked aggression.

Operations Just Cause and Desert Shield

The Pentagon, CIA, and FBI never fail to produce code names for their various aggressive and subversive operations at home and abroad, often positive sounding when for public consumption, but frequently cynical and even sinister when for internal use—Operation Alpha, Bootstrap, Brotherhood, Camelot, Chaos,* Djakarta, Minaret, Phoenix,* Rat-Killer,* Veritas, Vulture, etc. Their selections of names would make an interesting study in values and propaganda strategies.

The contrast between Operation Just Cause* (Panama) and Operation Desert Shield* (the Gulf) is perhaps a reflection of the fact that the invasion of Panama was a "plain vanilla" aggression in violation of international law. Rationalized in terms of the need to depose a very bad man, we justifiably took the law into our own hands. (For outsiders, this might look like lynch mob law; for properly brought up U.S. citizens and press, this was High Noon justice.) But in this case, our legal position being extremely flimsy, we needed a name for the operation that would put it in a good and proper light. We did not require such verbal support for our occupation of Saudi Arabia and the Emirates—Operation Desert Shield would do—although the accompanying moral indignation over Iraq's aggression contained the usual breathtaking level of hypocrisy.

Let me make a constructive suggestion, however, in the interest of alleviating our budget crisis. As all our operations are "just causes," why don't we simply call them OJC-1, OJC-2,...OJC-n, and save a lot of money on public relations?

Censorship and Disinformation

The U.S. mass media did a marvelous job of helping George Bush engineer consent for his presidential war. One of their greatest achievements was transmuting Bush's skillful design, manipulation, and mobilization for war into a triumph of collective security and "internationalism." Once the war was under way, the media moved even more aggressively into a "we-they/winner-loser" frame of reference as if describing an exciting game, energetically rooting for the home team and ignoring alternative perspectives and inconvenient information.

In the light of the mass media's performance up to January 17, 1991, the imposition of censorship by the Pentagon would seem as superfluous as bringing additional radioactive wastes to Hanford, Washington. The cooperative media were even reluctant to call the Pentagon's rules for news reporting "censorship" or to accuse the Bush administration and Pentagon of using "disinformation."[11] News reports from Iraq were regularly labelled as censored and state-produced, but this was not done for Pentagon releases and information through "reporting pools." The networks and the *Times* and *Washington Post* not only failed to join in a suit against the Pentagon protesting this censorship, they did not even report the suit as news.

The Pentagon censors news because it is greedy. It wants rooters who never criticize a misplay or boo a bungling quarterback—it likes a completely subservient claque. There is no doubt that the press would like details on casualties—even Iraqi casualties—that the war-makers want kept under the rug. The media would surely stress *our* casualties more than enemy victims, but the Pentagon would prefer that neither be discussed. However, as even the Soviet military establishment harshly attacked the Soviet press for disclosures undermining the war effort in Afghanistan,[12] unless we accept that the Soviet Union had an "adversary press," the desire of the Pentagon to control the flow of information hardly proves the existence of an adversary press here.

From Vittorio Mussolini to Tom Brokaw

In earlier years, the statements of Italian dictator Benito Mussolini's son Vittorio, a bomber pilot in Italy's attacks on Ethiopia in the years before World War II, were held up as the epitome of the inhumanity and degeneracy of fascism. In his book *Voli sulla ambe,* published in Florence in 1937, Vittorio referred to war as "The most beautiful and complete of all sports." His most famous line was "It was diverting to watch a group of Galli [Ethiopian tribesmen] bursting out like a rose after I landed a bomb in the middle of them."

The word "beautiful" appeared regularly in U.S. network TV coverage of the U.S. ("allied") bombing of Iraq on January 16th and in the days that followed. Tom Brokaw bubbled with enthusiasm at "the threatening beauty of it" and a CNN reporter in Saudi Arabia spoke of "the most beautiful sight" of the bombers taking off on their missions of glory. As Brent Sadler saw it on ITN, "The night sky was filled with the star-spangled display of threatening force." Jim Stewart of CBS News referred to "two days of almost picture-perfect assaults," and Charles Osgood of CBS found the bombing of Iraq "a marvel." Like Vittorio, the Free World establishment reporters uniformly exalted bombing attacks as exhilarating and aesthetically pleasing. They also uniformly failed to call attention to the fact that there might be human agony and death under the surface of their observations.

In his science fiction novel *Fahrenheit 451,* Ray Bradbury described a future in which people would be holed up with wall-to-wall TV, from which they would be treated to spectacles of the actual search for and execution of terrorists. U.S. TV coverage of the war in Iraq offered a bowdlerized infotainment variant, covering the war in a game and propaganda format. The propaganda format was designed to show the war in a good light from the standpoint of the administration, Pentagon, and weapons manufacturers, keeping casualties and "collateral damage" as far out of sight and mind as possible. In keeping with a culture of sports and games, it provided a controlled video-game and sport exhibition of a high-tech war, managed by the Pentagon and media to show good colors, high-tech successes over the enemy, excitement, and interspersed patriotic images (flags, pictures of our leaders past and present, patriotic scenes). It was "picture-perfect" as CBS's Jim Stewart said because it was carefully selected and well managed. Vittorio Mussolini would have been impressed.

Warspeak

The doublespeak component of official and media messages reached new heights with the coming of war in the Gulf, and some elements of the media even called attention to the development of choice Orwellisms, like "collateral damage." It is interesting, however, that the media paid no attention to the ultimate Orwellism perpetrated by Bush and some of his supporters (including the editors of the *New York Times*) in obtaining congressional approval to fight.

The classic illustration of an Orwellism has always been that "War is Peace." In addressing Congress, Bush told it that a vote to give him war powers offers the best chance for peace, and many of his supporters made the same point. Following his success in obtaining congressional sanction to go to war, the newspaper of record editorialized that "Congress has armed the President, first and foremost, for peace." There it was—a vote for war, which began within a week, was a vote for peace! The phrase "peace-keeping mission" was also used by officials and the press to describe the Bush team's efforts. Big Brother triumphs in the Free Society and Free Press via free market processes.

In straight warspeak, the aim is to soften language that might suggest unpleasant happenings and to lend support to our claims of benevolence and decency. Thus, after Desert Shield had served its role in the pretense that we were only "defending" our Gulf clients, Desert Storm* was coined by the Defense Department for what others had called Desert Sword. Storm suggests natural forces, not a human instrumentality that applies a cutting instrument to human flesh. War in the Gulf became an "operation." Military forces were referred to as "assets."* Bombs, which suggest things that kill and which are used by terrorists, were "ordnance." Bombing raids were "sorties" and "visits" or "revisits."

The fact that we were killing people demanded linguistic adjustments. First, we had "smart"* or "precision" bombs that could pinpoint military targets. This was done with surgical precision in "surgical strikes," suggesting the careful removal of diseased tissue. The concept of a surgical strike was developed during the Vietnam War to assert that we were aiming accurately at military targets, and implying that we were able to avoid killing civilians. In reality, massive firepower was used to reduce U.S. casualties, civilians were considered an ocean in which guerrilla fish swam, and inducing them to flee the countryside by indiscriminate firepower was part of U.S. policy. Vast numbers of Indochinese peasants were killed in "surgical strikes." It may be recalled that the "neutron bomb" was touted for *only* killing people and sparing structures, etc., so that combined with smart bombs, everything can be taken care of by Free World arsenals.

During the Gulf war the U.S. media were completely taken in by "smart bombs." In the early weeks of the fighting, with the Pentagon only offering visuals of bombs on target, the media conveyed the impression that few if any civilians were being damaged by the unprecedentedly intense bombing raids. Eventually it was revealed that the smart bombs were missing their targets about 40 percent of their time, and that only some 5 percent of the bombs dropped were smart.[13] The media's deceptions were compounded by their failure to pursue aggressively the question of the nature of targets, their proximity to civilian habitations and workplaces, and the on-the-ground results of the bombings. If the national water supplies, electric power stations, roads and bridges, and sewage facilities were legitimate targets, this posed a threat to water and food supplies and health that would be catastrophic to the civilian population. There was a further question of whether the civilian society had to be destroyed to get the aggressor out of Kuwait, or whether the scope of the devastation indicated a hidden agenda—points not raised in the mainstream media. In keeping with the national values on relevant casualties, the U.S. mass media gave these questions about zero attention during the fighting and minimal attention thereafter (except for the suffering of the Kurds, under attack by an official enemy).

The concept of "collateral damage" derives from nukespeak, and refers to allegedly unintended killing and destruction arising out of a nuclear attack. It was used in the Gulf war as a complement to "smart bombs" and "surgical strikes," acknowledging that despite all our precautions and precision some civilians may have been killed and nonmilitary targets destroyed. The difference between us and them is that they *intend* that their missiles and bombs hit civilian targets. This is terrorism. Our killings of civilians are inadvertent and tragic errors, although with two thousand sorties a day, they might be regrettably frequent.

The attempt to preserve the image of Uncle Sam as Mr. Clean who used civilian-friendly smart weapons and didn't kill people continued after the war as an established truth, maintained by a reluctance to report uncongenial information,[14] and by keeping eyes and benevolent concern firmly focused on the Kurds. The word "slaughter" was used with some indignation—but only in regard to Iraq's "appalling" attacks on the Kurds, not in reference to U.S. attacks on Iraqis. Both the *Times* and *Post* charted "Iraqi losses" and the "toll" of the war, but only in regard to Iraqi weapons losses and *without mentioning Iraq's human casualties*.[15] These Iraqis are "mere Arabs," and as victims of U.S. violence it is natural that they be "disappeared" by a patriotic media committed to protecting the image of U.S. benevolence. The self-censorship was really impressive. The propaganda line was captured in the headline of Patrick Tyler's article in the *Times* of March 31, 1991: "'Clean Win' in the War With Iraq Drifts into Bloody Aftermath." That the win was not bloody is a Big Lie, but one now institutionalized.

Murder by Immobility

There still remained the uncomfortable problem of the "turkey shoot," in which a completely helpless army in retreat from Kuwait was mercilessly slaughtered, many by weapons of doubtful legality such as fuel air bombs. This has been handled in the mainstream media largely by eye aversion. However, Paul Berman in the May 27, 1991 *New Republic,* offered another approach to apologetics for the turkey shoot, and provided a pathbreaking innovation in doublespeak as well. He first directed attention to Saddam Hussein's and other Arabs' declaring the retreat a great Iraqi victory, and railed indignantly at the perversity of their refusal to admit utter defeat, although in the end he found the entire business quite "laughable." Further:

> The reluctance to retreat, the too-long delay before a life-saving panic set in, in short, the strange and horrifying immobility that littered the desert with Iraqi corpses, was the very thing that constituted the Iraqi triumph—if not in the present, then as a "prelude," in Saddam's word, to the future. We laughed when these victory claims were broadcast to the world.

The blame associated with the reluctance and delay in retreating is followed later by an explanation of "why we were unable to negotiate peacefully with the Baathists," which it turns out is based on the contrast between those "ultimately oriented...toward natural reality" (us) and "something else" (the Baathists). Appropriately, Berman compares this realism-irrationality contrast in the Gulf with the difference between the "conquering Spaniards and the Aztecs in 1519-21"! No sentimental nonsense from realist

Paul Berman, although there is some remarkable idiocy as well as self-deception in the reference to the "life-saving panic" that hit the Iraqi soldiers. But the *pièce de résistance* arises from Berman's inability to name the agent generating the corpses—he therefore describes it as "the strange and horrifying immobility" that littered the desert with corpses, not the turkey shooters from the United States. I guess those other-worldly Aztecs who, like the Iraqi conscript soldiers, lacked the reality principle—Berman does not mention the Judeo-Christian ethic—also died of a horrifying immobility.

War Crimes

During the Persian Gulf war the U.S. media were once again indignant at enemy war crimes, while full of admiration for the restraint and cleanliness of our warmakers. The premise seemed to be that as we are good, by definition, serving as the world's volunteer global policeman in another Operation Just Cause (Number 17 or thereabouts), the enemy had no right to fight back. It is reprehensible to shoot a cop on his beat. The U.S. media and Democrats had earlier accepted the Reaganite premises that even the Nicaraguans had no right to self-defense once the global cop had decided that their government must be removed; hence, any arms the Nicaraguans obtained from abroad were by definition illicit and menacing. In the Gulf war, where there was naked aggression and where the cop was not beating up some small villain on its own and in the face of a toothless international consensus of disapproval, any actions taken in self-defense were doubly illicit.

As usual, the media paid no attention whatever to possible U.S. war crimes, such as the attacks on nuclear reactors, which violate international law,[16] and the use of fuel air bombs—which the media pointed to as an ominous threat of chemical weaponry when it was alleged (apparently falsely) that the Iraqis had them, but which they simply refused to discuss or investigate when it turned out that the United States had and used these murderous weapons.[17] The massacre of tens of thousands of completely demoralized retreating Iraqi soldiers in the "turkey shoot" also raised questions of war crimes, but not in the patriotic media.

During the Vietnam war, as well, the press got quite angry over rebel attacks on U.S. military forces; the enemy simply wouldn't stand still and fight on our terms. Our use of defoliants on a massive scale, the deliberate and systematic destruction of food crops by chemicals, the use of napalm, phosphorus and fragmentation bombs, and the employment of B-52s for the bombing of peasant villages ("enemy base camps") was given minimal attention and was never described in indignant language. It was never suggested that the use of "free-fire zones"* and "skunk hunting"* (a bit of country boy fun and games, shooting from helicopters any Vietnamese that came in sight) was criminal.

During the Vietnam war, the press repeatedly regurgitated the assertions of U.S. officials and pilots that U.S. forces were bending over backwards to avoid harming civilians, a huge misrepresentation of fact. In 1991, Ted Koppel asserted (Jan. 17th) that "indeed the point needs to be made that great effort is taken, sometimes at great personal cost to American pilots, that civilian targets are not hit." This statement is based solely on official statements. The record of official lying during Koppel's stint as an ABC newsperson has been massive. The test of an independent journalist, as opposed to a state propagandist, is that serial lying by his sources causes him to doubt the next self-interested statement. Koppel fails this test resoundingly, but in ample company.

Pride in Genocide

Bush managed us into a war of super-aggression, with the aid of the Democrats (see the new book by John Crawl, *Studies in Spinelessness*), press, corporate establishment, and general populace. Senator George Mitchell, in calling for us to get behind the President, noted that we have had our "debate," so now we must rally round our boys, flag, God and country, etc. Funny, I don't remember any debate in Congress or the press *while the key decisions were being made*—I recall some posturing after the mobilization of troops and UN consent for war was already obtained, but no debate, except in a Pickwickian sense.

We must give some credit here to the population at large, so easily mobilized by hack politician-demagogues who wrap themselves in the flag, lie incessantly, and ooze insincerity and hypocrisy. Both Lyndon Johnson and George Bush, after having maneuvered us into war, called for "prayers for peace"* and were not jeered out of office. This is a populace that can revel in beating up Grenada, in winning a 1984 Olympics from which the only serious rival had been bullied into withdrawal, that applauds rival team quarterback injuries and systematically produces noise so that quarterback signals can not be heard by enemy teams. This is a populace whose enthusiasm for war escalates upon seeing the bombs soaring through the air. B-52s and smart bombs raining down on another relatively defenseless country brings out the flags and pride. This is a people that could elect and re-elect Richard Nixon and Ronald Reagan, and vote in the unspeakable Bush-Quayle team. This is a people for whom the Southern Strategy* works, and who could wax enthusiastic about the swaggering bully, liar, and sycophant Ollie North.

Normalizing the Unthinkable

Doing terrible things in an organized and systematic way rests on "normalization." This is the process whereby ugly, degrading, murderous, and unspeakable acts become routine and are accepted as "the way things are done." There is usually a division of labor in doing and rationalizing the unthinkable, with the direct brutalizing and killing done by one set of individuals; others keeping the machinery of death (sanitation, food supply) in order; still others producing the implements of killing, or working on improving technology (a better crematory gas, a longer burning and more adhesive napalm, bomb fragments that penetrate flesh in hard-to-trace patterns). It is the function of defense intellectuals and other experts, and the mainstream media, to normalize the unthinkable for the general public.[18] The late Herman Kahn* spent a lifetime making nuclear war palatable (*On Thermonuclear War*, *Thinking About the Unthinkable*), and this Strangelovian phoney got a very good press.

Normalizing Shooting Human Fish in the Gulf Barrel

During the Gulf war Uncle Sam was an Equal Opportunity Employer, and our boys and girls over there were doing their assigned jobs, repelling naked aggression in another Operation Just Cause. The war was forced upon us by Hussein's rejection of the UN's and "allies'" insistence that he disgorge Kuwait, much as Bush "plainly" did not want war (Anthony Lewis).

Having made it Operation Just Cause No. 17, a game with winners and losers, we could reasonably root for us—the moral force—to win. We were also defending Kuwait, and if once again the party being "saved" was "destroyed," this was not our fault—besides which, there was the "principle" of non-aggression to which we are utterly devoted.

The media could thus focus on our brave boys, girls, generals, and officials to tell us all about their plans, moves, reactions, and miscellaneous thoughts. We could watch them in action as they take off, land, eat, joke, and express their feelings on the enemy, weather, and folks back home in the Big PX.[19] They were part of an extended family, doing a dirty job, but with clean bombs and with the moral certainty of a just cause.

The point was not often made that the enemy was relatively defenseless, in somewhat the same position as the natives colonized, exterminated, and enslaved by the West in past centuries by virtue of muskets and machine guns (see John Ellis' *The Social History of the Machine Gun*). Our technical superiority reflects our moral superiority. If it all *seems* like shooting human fish in a barrel, one must keep in mind that we are dealing with lesser creatures (grasshoppers, two-legged animals, cockroaches), people who don't value life as much as we do, who allowed "another Hitler" to rule over them, and who stand in our way. Only the voiceless could express the view that "this was the most cowardly war in history."[20]

One of the effects of high-tech warfare, as well as the systemic focus on "our" casualties, plus censorship (official and self) is that the public is spared the sight of burning flesh. That enemy casualties were given great prominence during the Vietnam War is one of the great, and now institutionalized, myths of our era. Morley Safer's showing a GI applying a cigarette lighter to a Vietnamese thatched hut is used repeatedly to illustrate media boldness at that time because it was so extraordinary. It caused Safer and CBS a lot of trouble (and he has been trying to make up for his sin ever since). Enormous government pressure and flak from other sources caused the media to provide grisly photos of enemy victims only with the greatest caution, and very infrequently, especially in light of the grisly reality. Capital intensive warfare in itself makes for distancing the public from the slaughter of mere gooks and Arabs. This is key to normalizing the unspeakable and unthinkable.

On February 5, 1991, the *Philadelphia Inquirer* carried an AP dispatch by Alexander Higgins, "Marriage finds new expression in gulf: Honey, pass the bombs." It is a little romance, of a newly married couple, located at an airbase in Saudi Arabia, and therefore regrettably obliged to sleep in separate tents, whose function is to load bombs on A-10 attack jets. It is a personal interest story, of two people and their relationship, with a job to do in an unromantic setting. A fine study in the routinization of violence, of the banality of evil and the ways it is impressed on the public.

The UN and International Law

The United States has displayed great flexibility* in its concern with and relation to the UN and international law. The rules are: when these can be used to meet our ends, we are their dedicated advocates; but when the votes are going the wrong way, or international law interferes with our plans, the UN and international law are treated with disdain or are blithely ignored. And the establishment experts and media fall into line without a peep.

The brazenness in this dichotomized treatment and behavior, carried out with considerable self-righteousness, is remarkable. The United States can invade country after country in violation of both national and international law, accompanied by a demonization process that pits the United States against Satan. Law is irrelevant when one is in conflict with Satan. It helps here that the mainstream media gloss over, if they mention at all, that Satan was our ally or paid agent until yesterday. The UN Charter or OAS agreements may be violated, but the press is reliably uninterested. The UN may vote condemnations of our invasions by large majorities, with only the United States and its closest allies and most dependent clients in opposition, but only a very careful reader of the papers will discover this occasionally on the back pages.[21] When U.S. allies invade other countries, as Israel did Lebanon in 1982 and South Africa did Angola in 1981 (among other occasions), the U.S. will veto UN Security Council condemnations. These matters, also, are not featured in the press.

When the United States is running roughshod over international law and the UN is voting against us by huge majorities, U.S. officials can rely on the fact that nobody is able to enforce the law against the dominant superpower and its wealthy allies and clients. No sanctions, let alone applications of force against the violator, are even proposed because of their obvious unenforceability. Not only can the abusing power violate the law without penalty, its leaders and press complain bitterly that the UN and International Court of Justice are "hostile forums"* and have ceased to be useful institutions as they were when the United States had an automatic majority at the UN.

But when we are confronted with "naked aggression," as in Iraq's invasion of Kuwait in August 1990, where what the U.S. administration wants to do may be coordinated with UN approval and the sanction of international law, the United States is suddenly a passionate devotee of both. The media can be counted on, first, to avoid stressing, or even noting, the transformation from contempt and cynical violation when the UN and law aren't going our way—or even the contemporaneous double standard, as in simultaneously ignoring Israel's refusals to obey UN resolutions as a regular and ongoing affair.[22] Second, the media can also be counted on to avoid looking closely at how a great power like the United States uses bribery and coercion to mobilize its supportive constituency for the selective enforcement of international law.[23] Attending to the aggressive pressure employed, the rewards granted and penalties inflicted, would suggest the use of raw power rather than mobilization by moral force for a highly moral enterprise.

The U.S. manipulation of the UN and international law in the case of the Gulf war had many other facets. The UN resolution finally extracted by the United States giving it the right to go to war did not *require* war—that was an option to be used if needed to get Iraq out of Kuwait. The UN Charter itself makes force a last resort, requires that the Security Council find that peaceful means of resolution have failed, and assigns responsibility for the use of force to the Council, not to the U.S. president. An excellent case can therefore be made that the U.S. attack on Iraq violated both the UN Charter and the UN implementing resolution. A Soviet agreement with Iraq, summarily rejected by the United States (and the "allies") would have fulfilled the primary UN resolution without the killing of 50-100,000 Iraqi soldiers (mainly young conscripts) and causing massive destruction to Iraq and Kuwait. The Bush administration's refusal to accept, or even consider, this proposal was a *de facto* violation of international law and the UN resolution. The urge to assert power and kill was too strong in the U.S. leadership. On the rare occasions where the point was mentioned in the U.S. mass media, there was not the slightest expression of regret and indignation. These were "mere Arabs."

While Bush was prating about the sacredness of international law, and while he and other establishment figures were threatening that Iraq would have to pay damages for its acts of vandalism in Kuwait, the Bush administration had a due bill for its own "unlawful use of force" against Nicaragua to the tune of $17 billion. The administration was reportedly twisting the arm of the Chamorro government to drop this claim in order to receive the puny $300 million that the United States had voted for its victim, but was holding back in this further exercise of blackmail. In another illustration of doublethink, the U.S. mass media allowed Bush and company to pontificate and moralize about law and Iraq's bill for damages, without saying a word about the contemporaneous U.S. bill due for damages. The impression was conveyed that the United States was being generous to Nicaragua; the question of international law in the inconvenient case was consigned to the black hole.

The experts conformed to this doublethink schema very well. There were many Op Ed columns on the proper mechanism for bringing Saddam Hussein to justice, none of which mentioned the problem of the U.S. debt to Nicaragua and the difficulty in bringing a superpower to abide by the rule of law. The *Times* reported on April 19, 1991 that Thomas M. Franck, a Professor of International Law at NYU, thought that the United States should seek new authority from the UN before establishing refugee bases in Iraqi territory. These things, he said, should be done collectively "and not unilaterally," as the United States had been especially careful to do up to this point, because if a nation's sovereignty were so violated "it could be a recipe for chaos."

In connection with the 1986 decision of the International Court of Justice that the United States should cease its "unlawful use of force" against Nicaragua, the same Franck, in an Op Ed column in the *Times* of July 17, 1986, contended that the United States should ignore the World Court, because "America—acting alone or with its allies—still needs the freedom to protect freedom." So when the United States is able to mobilize international bodies to do its bidding, when acting lawfully is consistent with attaining its objectives, Franck sanctimoniously urges our meticulous adherence to the niceties of the law. When the rule of law stands in our way, he allows that as the always righteous party we may disregard it. This is truly "responsible" and, if not "politically correct," certainly "really correct" expertise in action.

5. The Crisis of Democracy at Home

The Privatization of Government

Private power and the incessant demands of capital as the main engine of the economy have always influenced, and for long periods completely dominated, the U.S. political system. Modest change can be effected, however, when things get bad enough and when the interests of the fragmented majority coalesce, usually briefly. These circumstances bring moderate reforms that alleviate pressures from below. But they arouse great anxiety among the dominant elites, who denounce the extremism of "special interests" and their spokespersons in these periods of "crisis of democracy" and "democratic excess" (i.e., approaches to actual democracy).

The processes by which the excesses are contained, although they may make democracy a formal affair without much democratic substance, are institutionalized and made to seem natural by the established institutions. Their seamier features are glossed over or suppressed. The civics texts in schools and the mainstream media focus on the nominally democratic forms, the wonderful system of checks and balances, and the superficial elements of the electoral horse races. As is the case in demonstration elections in El Salvador and other client states, the media stress personalities and the positive, while avoiding a critical look at whether the fundamental requirements of free elections are met, such as reasonable equality of funding and access to the mass media by representatives of all major classes and constituencies. The possibility that important options which might serve the interests of large numbers are systematically excluded from the political arena, because any candidate espousing them would be defunded by the main sources of money in politics—as well as vilified as an extremist by the mass media—is itself excluded from discussion. As only "moderate" positions can be adequately financed and treated respectfully and as "serious" by the mainstream media, the severely circumscribed options are made to seem natural and normal, like the competition among the "moderate" parties in El Salvador and Guatemala.

The belief by a considerable proportion of the population that elections in and of themselves represent genuine democracy in action, and give sovereignty and free choice to the public at large, is a tremendous achievement of the western system of governance. It legitimates elite control and weakens the force of criticism of western governments and institutions. The public is rendered quiescent because "it" has spoken, and significant numbers are impressed with the argument that protest is improper because the government represents the popular will, validated by a democratic election. In the classic phrase of William Penn: "Let the People think they Govern and they will be Governed."

A further factor contributing to quiescence is the belief that, given the freedom and opportunity for personal achievement in the United States, failure is a result of individual inadequacies (or bad luck), not defects in institutions. We need more "moral fiber,"* which will only be weakened by coddling the lazy and ne'er-do-wells.

Of course the system must produce some minimal payoff for the underlying population—or at least for a significant fraction of that population—in order to keep the excesses under control. In the provinces, where this has been more difficult, the U.S. establishment has often actively colluded with and even helped organize National Security States to keep the masses apathetic and passive by means of state terror (always called, however, counterinsurgency, pacification, the restoration of stability, or even counterterrorism). While this has not been necessary on such a grand scale at home as yet, it is clear from the support of so many terror states abroad that it remains a viable option if needed. The record of the state in the Wilson-Palmer raids and Truman-McCarthy and Cointelpro eras demonstrates how quickly gross violations of civil liberties—from simple harassment to outright murder—can be instituted when it serves establishment interests.

The Business of Politics

The mainstream media have recently displayed a surge of interest in and concern over "money in politics" and possible abuses associated with political action committees (PACs)* and other anomalies. This was precipitated by a number of developments, including the savings and loan scandals and the involvement of five U.S. Senators with the unsavory S&L executive Charles Keating, the departure of Democratic Party leaders Tony Coelho and Jim Wright from Congress under clouds of impropriety, the discomfiture of the Democrats as they fall still further behind in the endless quest for campaign funding, and a host of complaints by politicians and critics that money is subverting democracy. A stream of books has conveyed the same message: Elizabeth Drew's *Politics and Money*, Philip Stern's *The Best Congress Money Can Buy*, Brooks Jackson's *Honest Graft*, and many others.

While the press and liberal critics touch on the diversion of politicians' attention from substantive issues to raising money, and the growing influence of funders on candidate selection and success, the main focus of the press has been on corruption, a dramatic matter that allows a great deal of moralizing and a minimum of serious analysis of the workings of the system. The *New York Times,* for example, published a series on money in politics in March and April 1990 that addressed all of these matters in a superficial way. What it failed to do was examine the class skewing of politics by money and its detrimental impact on democratic substance.

The *Times* did not attempt, for example, to assess the validity of the "investment theory" of politics spelled out by Thomas Ferguson and Joel Rogers in their book *Right Turn.* This theory shows how the dominant parties and their major candidates shape their programs to the demands of the business "investors" in the electoral process, with the result that the non-investing majority of the population is effectively unrepresented and thus disenfranchised in the political process.

The Democrats' Search for Investors

According to the "investment theory" analysis, in the environment of the 1970s and 1980s the Democratic Party was abandoned by many of its traditional business supporters who shifted to the party (Republican) and candidate (Reagan) they believed would better serve their changing and urgent interests. The leaders of the Democratic Party responded to this development by abandoning populism and the traditional Democratic appeal to a mass base, which put off business investors, in favor of a frantic competition for funds from the military-industrial complex and other business interests. It chose to go for the money first, the voters as an afterthought. This explains Mondale's suicidal stress on balancing the budget and tax increases (but not tax reform), Dukakis' similarly unappealing program, and the ongoing efforts of the Nunn-Robb-Strauss group to slough off the New Deal-populist tradition entirely in favor of "moderation" (i.e., policies that appeal to monied interests).

In fact, the efforts of the Democratic "moderates" to raise money has provided a textbook case of systematic subversion of politics by money—Brooks Jackson's book *Honest Graft* is largely an account of the struggle of Tony Coelho and his fellow moderate Democrats to increase the Party's competitiveness by virtually unrestrained pursuit of corporate support. The book is valuable in showing Coelho's remarkable powers of rationalizing this groveling for money as well as the policy compromises that ensued. Policy was regularly bent in accordance with the exigencies of money-raising. This pursuit of and accommodation to investors may be read as a more thorough-going integration of politics and government with "the market," meeting the "effective demand" of investors but removing the interests of the unmonied majority from even the nominal pitches of the dominant contesting parties. It is true that, previously, the populist pitches and promises were seldom fulfilled, but at least they were on the agenda to be discussed and fought over. In the era of moderation they are rarely even debated.

The abandonment of a populist agenda in favor of investor service should be front page news on a regular basis. The catch, of course, is that the mainstream media are also dominated by investors, and their proprietors and advertisers don't like populism, progressive taxes, etc. We may note the parallel of this process with the operations of commercial television, where the networks and cable entrepreneurs are wealthy people who solicit advertisers by selling them access to audiences. And just as political investors place constraints on what politicians can support (if they are to get the funding necessary to run), so media entrepreneurs and commercial advertisers sharply limit the programs that TV may offer (and command the ad revenue necessary to broadcast).[1] Not surprisingly, the "investment theory" and its devastating implications are omitted in the *New York Times* articles, and the entire structure of news accommodates to the privatization of politics and government. Robb-Strauss-Coelho and company are portrayed as "moderates," and the view disseminated by the media generally is that the trouble with the Democratic Party is the undue influence of "special interests"[*] (in its recently refurbished definition), not its perversion by the quest for money from "investors" and unwillingness to serve a mass base.

A front page article by Richard L. Berke in the *New York Times* of July 17, 1989 is entitled "Democrats Trail in Fund Raising, And Many Blame New Chairman." The article does not focus on the effect of fund raising on constituency representation and democratic substance, it frames the issue in terms of "investors'" complaints about Ron Brown's excessive liberalism and ties to Jesse Jackson. The subordination of party programs and government to investor demands is simply part of the natural background, and the problem is seen as the poor service rendered by the "too liberal" party to the investor community.

Moderates and Extremists; National and Special Interests

Opinion polls from the late 1970s into the 1980s indicated that the public wanted a more equal distribution of income, less foreign intervention, strong environmental protection, and, except for the period of the Iran hostage crisis and the huge pro-arms propaganda campaign of the late 1970s and early 1980s, smaller military expenditures and greater social welfare outlays.[2] "Consensus" programs approximated those espoused by Jesse Jackson. In the mass media, however, Jackson was portrayed as an extremist, explicitly or by implication; the moderates were the mainstream Democrats like Gore, Robb, and Babbitt who stressed their commitment to a strong defense, interventionism, and "realism" on welfare budgets and income distribution. The public seemed to want the populist program which the moderates had abandoned. But what the Democratic moderates proposed and what the investment community wanted were well correlated.

Similarly, the phrases "national interest"* and "special interests"* were transmogrified. In earlier years, special interests meant narrow, mainly business groups who sought political privilege by lobbying and bribery. More recently, special interests has come to mean substantially larger citizen and popular constituencies, like blacks, women, farmers, Hispanics, labor, environmentalists, and others who comprise a substantial numerical majority of the population. At the same time, business interests (except farmers) have disappeared from this category—and by an unspoken new premise, their interests have become synonymous with the national interest.

This identification of the national interest with business interests rests in part on the fact that many politicians cannot imagine a solution to economic problems other than making things more attractive for business investment, plus the realization that if they did propose alternative solutions, their campaign funding would dry up. The "moderation" of Robb, Babbitt, Nunn and company is well attuned to the corporate-investor consensus rather than the public consensus, and thus, in the new semantics, to the national interest, as opposed to those of "special interests."

Capture and Life Cycle
Theories of Political Investment

In times of great pressure, the business community mobilizes its forces to alter the political climate in its favor. Its command of resources and power is such that when it presents a fairly solid political phalanx, it can put in place a government that will serve its interests without compromise, and which may even indulge in outright class warfare as the Reagan administration did in the 1980s. In these periods of business-sponsored counterrevolution, businesspeople take over a host of important government positions, conflict of interest becomes blatant, and government operations are corrupted, dismantled, and manipulated with abandon. Teapot Dome had nothing on the operations of James Watt, who was a hero to and an excellent fund raiser among the beneficiaries of Interior Department largess.[3]

When scandals become rampant under a full-fledged business regime and substantial segments of the population (including some sectors of business) are severely damaged, the mainstream press eventually rouses itself, "reform" may become credible, and an opportunity is carved out again for the party more moderate in its obsequiousness and service to the business community. We may move into the reform phase of the political cycle, although this is not a certainty. The New Deal came into existence only after an economic collapse in the 1930s. The Reagan counterrevolution, however, did not result in a collapse, and instead of a victory for "reform," a consolidator of the counterrevolution triumphed. It may be that effective national macro-stabilization policies combined with the advancing power of technology and growing importance of large sums of money for electoral success have so elevated the role of investors as the dominant constituency of the major parties that reformism has been permanently stalemated.

The Crisis of Democracy

The 1960s produced a "crisis of democracy"* in the minds of U.S. elites. Neither before nor after this period did they see a crisis, despite the decline in voter participation (now below nineteenth century levels), the plutocratization of politics, the diminished substantive content of electoral campaigns, and the increased importance of demagoguery and news management. The fact that nobody can compete seriously for national political office who poses a serious challenge to the security state and MIC, or takes a strongly populist position on tax-expenditure policy, is not seen as a problem. This is the way things ought to be: the permanent interests in firm control, the "business" of politics making the two parties into branches of a single property party, and the "transaction costs" too high to make organizing the effectively disenfranchised masses worthwhile. The financial requirements of plutocratic politics gives the property party an effective monopoly.

Some establishment spokespersons make no bones about the fact that the characteristic of the 1960s that merited the designation "crisis" was the arousing of the masses and their organization into groups that could lobby and protest. Some establishment commentators and analysts were openly nostalgic for the times when a quiescent public allowed the government to be run by a small clique of Wall Street lawyers and bankers.[4] In consonance with this vision of the 1960s as an era of threat and irrational upheaval, the mainstream media in recent years has portrayed the period as one of violent protest and mindlessness.[5]

In short, for the dominant elite, democracy *means* rule by themselves without challenge from or participation by ordinary citizens. This parallels usage, and even more, practice, in dealing with the Third World, where, for example, a crisis in Nicaragua that arouses the U.S. leadership to action, to see a need for free elections and "democracy," is the overthrow of the Somoza dictatorship and the coming into power of a group pursuing "the logic of the majority." Somoza's mode of governance was acceptable, not challenged for any electoral or democratic deficiencies. The U.S. mass media did not actually call Somoza's rule democratic, but neither did they call attention to its failings or U.S. support of highly undemocratic rule. Our alliance with the terror state was rationalized and protected in many ways—people not ready, "traditional" modes of rule, Central American human nature, moving toward democracy under our tutelage, and, of course, eye aversion. Where elections were held under conditions of massive state terror, as in El Salvador and Guatemala in the 1980s, but with power in the hands of groups pursuing the logic of the *minority,* the media rushed to applaud the "fledgling democracies" with "elected" leaders.[6]

Red Scares

The U.S. establishment has regularly used Red Scares to counter any serious reformist threats at home or opposition to the enlargement of military budgets and interventionism abroad. In the nineteenth century and in the years immediately after World War I, the Red threat was used primarily to attack unionization, as it provided an excellent moral and political cover for anti-strike and anti-organizing intervention.[7] The great Red Scare of 1919-1920 rested on the complete cooperation of the mainstream media in a frenzied outburst and attack on a non-existent threat of communist subversion, which served well the corporate establishment's fight against the *real* threat of union organization.[8]

In the Truman-McCarthy era, the hysteria over an internal communist threat was highly serviceable to an expanding corporate system's interest in dismantling the New Deal reformist coalition and clearing the ground for large scale weapons acquisitions and an aggressive external stance ("containment"). The propaganda agents and political servants of the corporate establishment succeeded in making informer allegations of Soviet invasion plans and penetration into government, the Hiss trial, etc., into high visibility issues.[9] Instead of focusing on the fraudulence and hidden purpose of the claims, and the sinister role of J. Edgar Hoover and the political police, the media and liberal establishment accepted the McCarthyite premises, thereby giving up the game in advance. The counterattack of many liberals was that the charges failed to distinguish between good (anticommunist) and bad liberals and that the Nixon-McCarthy campaign was "playing into the hands of" communism.[10]

The red scares of the Carter-Reagan era focused heavily on the external Soviet threat, which provided the basis for a serious assault on freedom of information and an increase in domestic surveillance and harassment.[11] As discussed earlier, the alleged Soviet "strategic superiority" was based on plain vanilla lies, once more allowed to go unchallenged by mainstream media and which provided the moral environment for the Reagan-Bush era "defense" buildup. Again, the doublespeak component of this revitalized Red Menace was impressive.

With the crippling of the Soviet threat by unilateral Soviet actions and subsequent dissolution, red scares might appear harder to produce in the future. But if the past is any guide, when the establishment needs a threat, one will be forthcoming, and it need not be real, or even moderately plausible, to be effective. Perhaps a series of Little Satans, like Kadaffi, Noriega, and Saddam Hussein, requiring air strikes, invasions, and pacification programs to protect our national security and provide stability, will suffice to keep the weapons culture's preferred investments and production lines operating in the New World Order.

Black Scares and the "Southern Strategy"

The manipulation of racial fears and hatred has been another long-standing technique of elite leadership management. Pitting poor whites against blacks in the South after the Civil War was a prime mechanism of control. It was revived in parallel with the civil rights movement and advance of blacks out of third class into second class citizenship, following *Brown versus Board of Education of Topeka* (1954), the civil rights legislation of the 1950s and 1960s, and the rise of movements like those first led by Martin Luther King, Jr. and Malcolm X.

In the 1964 presidential election, Barry Goldwater used what was termed the "Southern Strategy"* in an attempt to win votes. This technique of deliberately appealing to white racism by the use of code words became a central weapon in the Republican Party's arsenal, as it could be used to pull white working class voters away from the Democrats while obfuscating coalition building issues like who gets taxed. Under Nixon, Reagan, and Bush, deployment of the Southern Strategy won significant support from white workers while the administrations pursued economic policies seriously adverse to worker interests.

The new polarization strategies necessitated a major advance in doublespeak. Nixon, Reagan, and Bush each proclaimed the dawn of a new spirit of national unity, togetherness, gentleness, and kindness while deliberately pitting races against one another and encouraging group enmity. The Southern Strategy has relied heavily on code words and phrases, like "busing,"* "crime in the streets,"* "law and order,"* "welfare,"* "Willie Horton,"* "drugs," and "quotas"* to communicate the barely-hidden messages designed to arouse racial fears and anger.

Because the Southern Strategy has been used by representatives of the powerful, it is treated very gently by establishment media. Gary Hart's infidelities aroused much comment about "character,"* but George Bush's aggressive use of the New Polarization in the 1988 election, with Willie Horton as his symbol, and his return to this strategy with his denunciations of "quotas" and vetoes of civil rights bills in 1991, led to no reflections on his "character" or morality in the mainstream media. It is as if the German press in 1928 gave assiduous attention to the marital infidelities of a Social Democrat, while finding Hitler's attacks on the Jews of little interest.

Law and Order

Conservative governments focus heavily on "law and order" (L&O) and its doublespeak partner, "crime in the streets." These code phrases signify the purported threat posed by poor blacks and other minorities to white safety and jobs. Conservative policies *generate* disorder, crime, and job scarcity by increasing unemployment, withdrawing the safety net from the weak, unleashing greed, encouraging corporate abandonments, and returning society to the law of the jungle. The conservative "solution" to increased crime and violence is more police, prisons, and an end to "coddling."* This is a feedback process, in which basic policies and attitudes encourage alienation, hopelessness, and crime, which the conservatives then attack only at the level of symptoms while exploiting the other social results of their policies with the Southern Strategy.

This interaction is replicated in the Third World, where church spokespersons have pointed out for years that the "development model" imposed by National Security State leaders (with generous transnational corporate and IMF assistance), by its inhumanity, creates a revolution that previously did not exist.[12] The misery and induced revolution can only be contained by police state terror, instruction in which has been provided by the School of Coups in Panama and in Fort Benning, Georgia.[13] By these means the L&O regimes service the requirements of corporate capital, domestic and foreign, providing a favorable investment climate. These linkages are not featured in the mainstream press.

It is notable that the two recent U.S. presidents who most strongly expressed their concern with L&O, Nixon and Reagan, closed out their terms enmeshed in scandals. Nixon barely avoided impeachment; Reagan was immune only because of his administration's remarkable success in taming the press and Democrats, as well as an apparently prosperous economy. Nixon's Attorney-General, John Mitchell, served time in prison. Reagan's Attorney-General, Edwin Meese, left office under a cloud. Numerous other high officials and advisers were prosecuted, although few served jail terms. It is rarely noted in the mainstream media that the present L&O Supreme Court majority was chosen by officials who went—or should have gone—to jail for blatant disregard of the law. The exposures of massive influence peddling in the Housing and Urban Development Administration (HUD), the Pentagon scandals, and the protection given drug dealers willing to support the contras are probably only the tip of a large Reagan era iceberg. The "sleaze" factor was also becoming increasingly prominent in the Bush administration in 1991,[14] which could hardly be otherwise given the great overlap in personnel and spiritual affinities with the Reagan cohort.

In brief, there seems to be an inverse relationship between the trumpeting of a concern for L&O and actual adherence to the rule of law. L&O governments—invariably rightwing—are exceptionally unprincipled in their willingness to ignore the law and manipulate public fears to achieve, maintain, and exercise power. Their aim and role is to serve the governing class (including themselves), weaken labor and welfare measures, and advance the interests of the national security establishment. These are aims of the dominant class as a whole, although some elements would pursue them less aggressively and in a more compromising spirit, and an even smaller minority has a broader vision of the national interest. For the dominant majority, however, protest marches and strikes in pursuit of lower class benefits or in opposition to state imperial ventures are readily seen as "disorder" and, if large-scale, a "crisis of democracy." This world view was formalized in Sir Frank Kitson's 1972 book *Low Intensity Operations,* where "subversion" is identified as any kind of pressure designed to force the governing class "to do things which they would not want to do" (p. 3). The function of L&O is to assure that the majority do not so pressure the governing class.

Class Application of the Law

L&O regimes simultaneously weaken the law in its application to the elite and government agents, while intensifying its application to the majority. They come into office like an army occupying hostile territory, including in their cadres carpetbaggers and crooks who want to take advantage of the new opportunities to loot. Both Reagan and Nixon were fond of distancing themselves from "the government" and "Washington bureaucrats," except when wrapping themselves in the flag to justify an assault on some foreign target. Part of the very design of such regimes is to bring government into disrepute while weakening and dismantling many of its civil functions. Much of the corruption under Reagan was assured by putting into office administrators who opposed the laws under whose authority they served and refused to enforce them (e.g., the EPA, OSHA, Department of Justice civil rights division). Given the intimate relationship of the regime with vested interests, HUD and Pentagon contracting inevitably attained new levels of corruption.

It is a long Republican tradition, also, to suspend or weaken the antitrust laws in response to the interests of the Party's corporate constituency. As admitted by business consultant Charles Stevenson in 1934:[15]

> Practically, under the Harding, Coolidge, and Hoover Administrations industry enjoyed, to all intents and purposes, a moratorium from the Sherman Act, and through the more or less effective trade associations which were developed in most of our industries, competition was, to a very considerable extent, controlled. The Department of Justice acted with great restraint and intelligence and only enforced the Sherman Act against those industries who violated the law in a flagrant and unreasonable manner.

The antitrust laws of the 1920s were also weakened by a Supreme Court which interpreted the Section 7 anti-merger provision of the Clayton Act out of existence. In the 1926 decision *Thatcher Manufacturing v. FTC,* the court held that if a company illegally acquired controlling stock in another company, but used its control to merge the acquired firm's assets into itself before the FTC could act, the FTC couldn't do anything about it. There is nothing like a well selected court to adjust the law in accord with the demands of the vested interests!

One of Ronald Reagan's earliest presidential acts was to pardon two FBI agents who had been convicted for illegally burglarizing the office of a legal political organization. In another important symbolic action, in 1983 Richard Helms, the former CIA director who had been convicted of perjury, was given what Reagan called a "long overdue" National Security Medal. Stealing and lying in the service of the state is not a crime for an L&O regime, even when established as a crime in a court of law. Logically, violations of the law by state agents should be considered especially serious crimes by true believers in the law, but as noted, L&O regimes are run by individuals for whom the law is merely an instrument for private or ideological service. For them, the end justifies the means, although these same individuals often pontificate that one of the sinister features of communism is the belief of its leaders that the end justifies the means. Frequently, L&O personnel don't see their own operations in terms of ends/means relationships; rather they regard the law as applicable only to others, as they man the barricades as guardians of the "really correct" and social order. The FBI officials in charge of Cointelpro violated the law continuously and blatantly, and when asked about their concern over the program's legality, answered: "We never gave it a thought."[16]

The power of the L&O regime and the interests of the security state are reflected in the media and courts, which help exempt their operatives from the rule of law. Virtually the only basis on which Iran-Contra law violators were obligated to pay fines, and in a few cases spend a brief period in jail, was for their failure to pay income taxes on the hidden fees paid them for serious legal violations.[17] Judge Gerhard Gesell decided against sending Oliver North to jail on the alleged ground that a jail term would not make North a better man[18]—a standard not often applied to ordinary criminals. But in fact, Gesell was almost surely reflecting the "election returns" or attitude of the community, reinforced by the power of the security state, on crimes of patriots claiming to serve the state.

How are we to explain the numerous indictments of Reagan officials, the Levine-Boesky prosecutions, and the pursuit of Watergate criminals if L&O governments and the corporate system are virtually freed of the encumbrance of the law under such regimes? One reason is that many of them are not in the L&O business. A second is that abuses escalate on such a scale that even minimal enforcement must address the more blatant cases, which often enter public consciousness through investigative reporting, lawsuits, and confessions of disenchanted ex-officials. A third reason is that the elite and government agents who quickly take advantage of the relaxation of legal constraints get cocky and push too far, threatening other members of the elite and the credibility and viability of major institutions. Boesky, Levine, and their associates were hurting important corporate interests while making their inside-information-based killings, and insider abuses make ordinary investors leery of participating in an unfair game. Nixon and company were attacking the Democratic Party and the prerogatives of Congress. Reagan was also running roughshod over Congress. These aggressors had to be curbed, although not too harshly.

Getting Tough on the Underlying Population

Harsher treatment is meted out to the classes being pacified under an L&O regime. Analyses of trends of law and court decisions under L&O governments show that they gradually enlarge the rights of the state and the powers of the police, increase the severity of penalties for lower class crimes, and fill up the prisons.[19] Considerable court discretion exists for many crimes, and under a L&O judicial system "terrorists" get long prison terms and brutal treatment—a Japanese radical, apprehended before committing any crime, was recently given 30 years;[20] radicals Alejandrina Torres, Silvia Baraldini, and Susan Rosenberg, consigned to the Female High Security Unit in Lexington, Kentucky in 1986, were kept in subterranean cells, under constant TV surveillance, and were handcuffed and manacled by chains around their waist when requiring medical visits. Whether petty drug users and dealers get probation or long sentences depends on judicial "judgment."

Prison populations grow under L&O regimes partly because of the economic policies which they institute. Planned recessions, union-busting, the collapse of low-income housing programs and economic supports for the poor, all increase pressures on the lower classes, pushing them toward anger, protest, and crime. Recognition of government unconcern and even active hostility toward them, lavish displays of wealth, and evidence of blatant favoritism in economic policy and application of the law have similar effects.

As noted earlier, as "crime in the streets" increases, middle and upper class fears grow and L&O policies are justified in a self-reinforcing system. Crime in the streets thus serves the interests of the L&O regime, strengthening its political power and justifying militarization at home and abroad.

Fascist and Third World L&O Regimes

Fascist regimes stress L&O, and they have served functions similar to those of L&O governments in countries like the United States and Britain, which have maintained electoral forms. It is understandable, therefore, that western elites have tended to be sympathetic to fascism, although regretting its occasional excesses. They have become hostile mainly where fascist regimes posed real political challenges to their interests. Thus in the 1920s Mussolini was treated with great warmth by the U.S. elite: Judge Elbert Gary, head of U.S. Steel, stating in 1923 that "a master hand has, indeed, strongly grasped the helm of the Italian state"; Republican Party statesman Elihu Root remarking before the Council on Foreign Relations in 1926 that "Italy has a revival of prosperity, contentment and happiness…"[21] Spanish fascist General Francisco Franco had a steadfast protector and ally in the United States, from the time of Harry Truman onward. As noted earlier, the U.S. *chargé d'affaires* in Berlin in 1933 considered Hitler a "moderate," and he continued to be favored as a bulwark against the left until he was seen as threatening our interests.[22]

The same of course applies to L&O regimes in the Third World, many of them organized under U.S. sponsorship to contain restive majorities. These regimes have exhibited in intensified form the characteristics of the sponsoring L&O governments in the developed countries. Money for the police and army is greatly increased, corruption becomes more systematic and large scale, and economic policies that immiserate the majority and generate "communists" are pursued, thus justifying an investment in L&O. As in the United States, the leaders who run these states also frequently call for a return to "traditional morality." The mercenary generals installed by the United States in Vietnam imposed regulations against long hair while running a system of organized prostitution, theft, torture, and murder. The generals in Latin America are also very keen on "morality."

6. The Struggle for Incentives and Against Boondoggles, with Compassion

One of the most notable features of Reagan-Bush era policy has been the incessant bullying of the weak. On the international plane, the Reagan administration launched direct and indirect attacks against Iran, Libya, Nicaragua, and Grenada, not exactly heavyweights. The ratio of U.S.-to-victim GNP in the four cases was roughly: 40/1, 120/1, 1,500/1, and 36,000/1. In the Bush era, major attacks were made against Panama and Iraq, with GNP ratios of 9,700/1 and 40/1. Traditionally, assaults on extremely small opponents were considered to be the mark of a bully and reprehensible, but not in the United States when our country does it. We know that Green Bay Packers' coach Vince Lombardi said that "winning is not the most important thing, it is everything"; but would Vince, his players, and fans have been proud to smash a high school football team? You've come a long way, baby!

Class Warfare as Economic Policy

On the home front, the bullying of the weak has been the very essence and function of Reagan-Bush economic and social policy—class warfare under the guise of national policy. Reagan's election was the culmination of the corporate campaign of the 1970s to "get the government off our backs," which, translated from doublespeak, meant get the government to reduce the social wage by dismantling the welfare state and redistributing tax and expenditure benefits from the poor to the rich. It also called for "deregulation," which, again translating from doublespeak, means, among other things,[1] that the government should reduce or eliminate attempts to protect the public from price-gouging, misrepresentation, and threats to worker, consumer, and environmental safety. That is, the "our" in the phrase "our backs" is the corporate community, and government gets off the corporate back by reducing benefits to the weak and not interfering with business' freedom to inflict damage on the community at large.

85

The cliché does *not* mean that the government should become less secretive, encourage freedom of expression, or reduce its use of covert and manipulative operations in the news and informational spheres.[2] It also does not imply any reduction in the size of the military establishment, required to protect "our" security. In short, the corporate agenda for the United States captured in the phrase "getting government off our backs" is identical with its agenda for Third World countries—freedom means economic freedom for the business community and a "favorable climate of investment," not political freedom. In fact, a reduction in political freedom has often been helpful in improving "freedom" in its primary sense, the one operational in shaping U.S. foreign policy, and the freedom underlying the very concept of the "Free World."* This is why Marcos (until he could no longer deliver a favorable investment climate) and Suharto have been entirely acceptable "leaders" and "moderates," and why Reagan's attacks on the First Amendment were not seriously troubling to the corporate establishment (and the mass media).

Reaganomics* and the Reagan counterrevolution, which George Bush has been striving to consolidate, translated the corporate agenda into economic policy. This required an intellectual and doublespeak apparatus to justify it in terms of general theories of work incentives, inducements to save and invest, and the beneficence of trickle-down. Lying and obfuscation were needed as well because, as New Right leader Paul Weyrich observed, "The rural people in West Virginia don't understand Reaganomics, and frankly, if they did, they wouldn't like it." Thus, President Reagan could claim that his program was "equitable" and would require "sacrifices from us all," and James Reston dutifully reported in the *New York Times* that the Reagan economic program represents a "serious attempt...to spread the sacrifices equally across all segments of society."[3] Furthermore, given that "we" are a caring people, as President Reagan frequently assured his audiences, we would not harm the "truly needy," only the shirking "employables." For the former, our caring government, truly representing our caring people, would provide a "safety net."*

David Stockman stated in 1981, "We are interested in curtailing weak claims rather than weak clients."[4] Although it was clearly the weak clients whose claims were curtailed, this turns out to be a coincidence grounded in ancient principles refurbished to rationalize the corporate agenda in the 1980s ("supply-side economics," Friedmanite *laissez-faire*). If the main goal of the tax cuts of 1981 was, as Stockman acknowledged, "dropping the top rate from 70 to 50 per cent," this wasn't based on mere greed of the beneficiaries; it was necessary to stimulate saving, investment, and harder effort. But while the rich needed the carrot of higher after-tax income and lower marginal tax rates to save, invest, and work harder, the poor needed the stick of reduced government benefits to make *them* work.

This dichotomous view of the incentives appropriate to the rich and poor goes back a long way. William Temple wrote in 1770 that the poor need the whip of hunger because the lower classes "are naturally so fond of ease and indolence that they will not labor while they have the Means of idleness in their power." In his failed presidential run of 1964, Senator Barry Goldwater made essentially the same point, and with a vigor that merited its designation as "Goldwater's Law."* (Having also resorted to the Southern Strategy and urged a reinvigorated arms race and more aggressive foreign policy, Goldwater anticipated all the main themes of his victorious Republican successors. Poor Goldwater was a "premature neo-reactionary," but he also lacked deviousness and an impressive television presence.)

In the same tradition, Charles Murray rushed into the fray in the 1980s, arguing in *Losing Ground* that the mistaken generosity of the liberals and government had once again damaged the poor, and concluding that reduced benefits were imperative in order to increase their incentives and well-being. Similar sentiments have been expressed by many writers in the United States and Great Britain over the past two decades as the intellectual community responded to the new market demand and ideological currents emanating from the business community.[5] Murray himself was given a $100,000 grant by Richard Mellon Scaife, who quickly recognized the superior quality of Murray's research.[6]

Actual policy in the Reagan era was not based on any well-thought-out analysis or plan—it was merely a reflection of business demands and a translation of business' search for short-term gain into economic policy. It was the economics of "grab and run" or "immediate gratification" (corporate version). The economic analysis underpinning "supply side economics" was both foolish and incompatible with empirical evidence of the effects of tax rate changes on work effort, saving, and investment.[7] But this did not affect its acceptability, or at least toleration, in the mainstream media, because it rationalized what the powerful wanted. At the time, no unrelenting questioning or major investigative reporting or analyses were directed to the blatant and highly vulnerable economics of the rich. And as William Greider has shown, during the election of 1984 the major media failed to recognize that structural deficits had been built into the budget by the Reagan programs, and the media did not question Reagan's claim that no tax increase would be necessary.[8]

Stockman himself pointed out—implicitly contradicting his own statement that only weak claims were targeted—that the "hogs" really indulged themselves at the now open trough: "The hogs were really feeding. The greed level, the level of opportunism, just got out of control."[9] And he acknowledged a thorough-going loss of control over the military budget based on the strength of its clients. Cuts to weak clients were carried out in area after area without regard to the success or failure of programs or the possible negative long run effects of their elimination. Education, training, and preventive medicine programs that might reduce future dependency and increase economic efficiency were slashed across the board. Thus, major cuts were made in community health centers and migrant health programs, despite findings of high effectiveness in reducing infant mortality and improving health status, reductions in required hospital use, and 80 percent or more poor or near-poor users.[10] On the other hand, the military budget was increased sharply even before plans were formulated on how the money could be used. Walter Mossberg wrote in the *Wall Street Journal* (June 9, 1981) that the new Reagan military budgets "are just costlier versions of those drawn up by the departed Democrats...the Reagan plans reflect no major changes in military strategy or tactics; they simply provide more money." As noted earlier, this was "throwing money at *non-existent* problems," based on ideology and interest group pressure, as well as the new pugnacity.

For the wealthy and business community, tax sheltering was encouraged and handouts were lavishly made, creating open-ended drains on the treasury with no intellectual justification but the philosophy of trickle-down. In one case, 534 wealthy investors bought Metromedia's entire stock of billboards, which they agreed to sell back five years later, after they had "depreciated" the $485 million asset as a tax shelter. This type of transaction was carried out on a large scale, most notably in the buying and selling of buildings. The large tax credits available to business in 1981 were unusable by firms that had little or no taxable income; the law and treasury interpretation therefore generously allowed these firms to sell their credits to other companies that could use them. This violated the economic efficiency logic of the tax credits, but this flagrant loophole, referred to as a "safe harbor" provision of the tax code, was preserved for several years. A company like General Electric, well positioned to take advantage of this opportunity as it was both highly profitable and owned a large finance company that specialized in lease financing, not only avoided all federal taxes in 1981-83 but even received a tax rebate of $283 million for those years.

Under Reaganomics, "Unto everyone that hath shall be given...but from him that hath not shall be taken away." It would even be taken away with petty vindictiveness, as in the proposal (quoting Norman Miller in the *Wall Street Journal* of Feb. 8, 1982) "to take pennies from jobless people by rounding weekly unemployment compensation checks 'down to the next lowest dollar.'" But generally the poor were stripped of benefits with a carelessness that matched the ease with which largess was thrown at "savers" (i.e., the affluent) and the military establishment.

The stripping of benefits from the weak was largely a function of the power to protest and resist. For example, Reaganite class warriors found Social Security invulnerable to "load shedding"* because of the breadth and energy of middle class support. However, as Michael Katz has pointed out, "the administration did succeed in trimming one aspect of social insurance whose constituency seemed, incorrectly as it turned out, incapable of mounting a sustained protest: namely, the disabled."[11] The Reaganites used administrative regulation to lop some 200,000 disabled off the rolls between March 1981 and April 1982. The procedures employed were so crude that a majority of the challenged cases were later reversed in court. Furthermore, the House Government Operations subcommittee found in 1986 that in its zeal to knock a half million people off the disability rolls between 1981 and 1984, the Social Security administration had created "a new industry of multimillion-dollar examination mills" that overbilled for examinations, inflated laboratory fees, and wasted millions on unneeded exams. Representative Ted Weiss noted that "The federal government was unforgiving in its review of America's disabled people but looked the other way while some doctors gouged the government."

During the Reagan and early Bush years of counterrevolution, the tax burden shifted sharply away from corporations and the wealthy to the middle and lower classes. Between 1980 and 1990, the bottom 20 percent of income recipients had a federal tax rate increase of 16.2 percent; the top 20 percent had a federal tax reduction of 5.5 percent; and the rate for the top 5 percent fell 9.5 percent.[12] The 59 percent of the population in the lower and middle income ranges had a larger federal tax obligation in 1990 than in 1980, despite the Reagan tax cuts, mainly because of the regressive Social Security tax increases. Going back to a 1977 base, 90 percent of U.S. families paid more federal taxes in 1990; federal tax changes since 1977 cost this 90 percent $25.6 billion, while the richest 10 percent saved $93.1 billion.[13] According to the Congressional Budget Office, the bottom 20 percent, with an average family income of $7,725 before taxes, saw their incomes drop 3.2 percent between 1980 and 1990, while the top 20 percent, with an average family income of $105,209, enjoyed an increase of 31.7 percent, the top 5 percent rising by 46.1 percent.

The Economic Recovery Act,
Recession, and Spiralling Deficits

Although the large tax cuts of 1981 were carried out under a law called "The Economic Recovery Act of 1981" and were supposed to increase saving and investment and bring economic recovery, they failed to achieve these effects. The Fed had to adopt an even tighter monetary policy to control inflation given the expansionary character of the tax cuts. A major recession followed. In spite of the huge tax breaks given to business and the wealthy, business investment fell during the recession and recovered only to its pre-Reagan levels (relative to GNP) in the post-recession years (1984-1990). The huge federal deficits—produced by the tax cuts plus military budget increases, which more than offset the cuts in the social budget—were financed by *foreign* saving. These deficits, along with higher interest rates, raised interest payments on the debt so much that the increase alone equalled the Reaganite cuts in the social budget.

The title of the basic 1981 tax law and its "capital cost recovery provisions" are themselves fine illustrations of doublespeak. "Capital cost recovery" sounds so worthy and innocent. Who would deny a pitiful giant like GE the right to recover the cost of its capital? Of course, the actual legislation allowed GE to recover it considerably faster than the rate of real depreciation of their facilities, so it was really a tax subsidy. The ability to purchase other firms' depreciation to further reduce tax liability obviously has nothing to do with recovering capital. As the Economic Recovery Act was followed immediately by a major recession and the onset of massive deficits, a more accurate title would have been: The Fat Cat Enhancement Act of 1981, or The Deficit-Maker.

Consumerism, Saving, and Investment

There is an obvious contradiction between the ancient virtues of saving and hard work and the world of heavily advertised, expensive, and non-essential consumer goods that "you owe to yourself." Consumerism and easy credit are not conducive to saving, and while consumption opportunities may cause some to work harder, low-income families may experience a sense of hopelessness, frustration, and outrage at the insistent advertising presentation of a good life clearly out of their reach. They may even develop anti-social pathologies and display a lack of "moral fiber"* in the face of serious abuse and injustice.

It is evidence of the genius of the system that these pathologies and rejection of the work ethic are not attributed to the market system, consumerism, and a consequent breakdown of family and community; they are allocated instead to a "culture of poverty,"* loose morals, and the excessive generosity of the state under the influence of egg-heads and do-gooders.[14] This remarkable achievement in causality reversal, making the victims (and those wishing to provide them with modest assistance) the villains and agents of disorder, is, once again, reflective of the power of money to define agendas and elicit rationalizing theories, as well as to fix the meaning of words.

Reagan and the supply-siders proclaimed that their policies of tax cuts favoring the wealthy and corporations, cutbacks in the social budget, and deregulation would unleash a frenzy of work effort, saving, and investment. Common sense, on the other hand, suggested that given the accompanying tight money, excess business capacity,[15] increased military spending, and the empirical evidence on incentive effects of tax changes, the major effects of their policies would be to redistribute income upward and produce large deficits. In fact, personal saving fell to a historic low of 3.9 percent in 1986, partly because the beleaguered middle and lower classes were forced to borrow (dissave) to make ends meet under the new conditions of class warfare. The increasingly affluent upper classes, meanwhile, went on a buying binge in the Potlatch years, instead of putting their huge income increments into saving.

Harvard economist Benjamin Friedman has pointed out that from the 1950s through the 1970s net business investment came to 4.1 percent of national income, but was 2.7 percent in the years 1980-1987.[16] The net investment rate from 1979 through 1989 (2.6 percent) was even below that of the immediately preceding period of oil shock and the vilified Carter government (3.5 percent during the years 1973-1979).[17] Reagan's fiscal policy, the resultant tight money and high interest rates, and an overvalued dollar "delivered not more capital formation but less, not faster growth in productivity but slower, and an economy that is not a stronger but a weaker competitor."[18] Overall investment fell sharply during the recession of 1982-1983, and then recovered only to the levels of the prior few decades.

Acceptable and Unacceptable Deficits

Although saving was stressed in the Reagan rhetoric and the business community usually takes a dim view of unbalanced budgets, Reagan more than doubled the national debt in his first five years in office without eliciting more than modest protest. The business community did not like the large ·deficits, but it appreciated the things Reagan did in producing them—building up the arms budget, imposing regressive tax cuts, dismantling the welfare state, and generally catering to the needs of corporate capital. Furthermore, part of the reason the Reaganites were willing to produce large deficits was their desire to reduce the size of civilian government and keep it down, the theory being that with taxes cut and deficits in place it would be hard for the liberals to rehabilitate those functions of government serving the majority (as opposed to the corporate community and military-industrial complex). This valuable service of the deficit was clearly evident in the budget debates and compromises of the Bush years.

It is ironic that earlier deficits only a fraction of the size of those produced by Reagan and Bush were found unacceptable by the business community, and its representatives and the media became quite vocal over the threat of the large deficits to "stability." As an illustration of the double standard, chair of Citicorp Walter Wriston stated in 1978 that federal deficits were "diverting available capital from productive private investments to finance public expenditures. Only a reduction in the federal deficit would reverse this trend."[19] That was in the Carter years. Speaking before the Business Council in the Reagan era, Wriston pooh-poohed the·threat of deficits, stressing the difference between capital and operating budgets, which he had not mentioned in connection with the Carter budgets; for the latter, all types of "public expenditures" were lumped together and contrasted with "productive" private uses of capital.[20] The mass media reproduced this attitude: deficits that would have caused hysteria in a regime distrusted by business were viewed calmly in the Reagan-Bush years (although they were enough cause for concern to serve their function of constraining social outlays).

In fact, the destabilizing characteristics of more populist-oriented deficits are self-fulfilling effects of business and financial community preferences. Deficits arising from policies serving the wrong constituencies, or perceived as such by business as during the Carter years, quickly cause a loss of business and financial "confidence" and produce inflationary expectations and a flight from the dollar, which tends to bring such unsound policies to a halt. This is an important mechanism by which capital and its major institutions control politicians and economic policy.

Another reason for the growth of large deficits and their toleration by the Reagan and Bush teams and business community has been the short planning horizon of both.[21] Corporate managers are under pressure to produce results quickly, and the tax bonanzas that Reagan showered on business in 1981-82 did this handsomely. The negative effects of the associated cut-backs in public investment on infrastructure and human capital, and burgeoning deficits, come later. Here, as with the consumer spending boom, was a pretty case of "immediate gratification," an alleged characteristic of the culture of poverty, but demonstrably applicable to the affluent leadership of the corporate system.

The Reaganites brought the short planning horizons of corporations to national economic policy. Benjamin Friedman has pointed out that the "growth of our stock of government-owned capital (apart from military installations) has slowed even more dramatically than growth in our stock of business capital"; government capital "grew by 3.5 percent per annum during [1950-1979] but has slowed to just .9 percent since 1980."[22] Systematic cuts in funding for schools, job training, roads, bridges, water purification, and waste control will damage productivity, but both the productivity loss and associated costs appear with a time lag.

Louis XIV had the intelligence to recognize that his policies were creating serious problems for the future: *"après moi, le déluge" ("after me, the flood")*. The Reagan-Bush teams and their corporate constituency, despite their access to the best computers money can buy, are unaware (or perhaps do not care) that their actions merely postpone problems and threaten the welfare and even survival of future generations. It seems that the increased capability of computers has helped solve micro-problems alone; and with irrational and self-interested forces determining social direction, the solutions to macro-problems are as poorly understood and as little subject to rational planning as in less technologically advanced ages.

The Decline of the Employment Objective

Full employment as a national policy objective reached its zenith in the western capitalist states toward the end of World War II. It was widely believed that the Great Depression bore a heavy responsibility for the rise of German fascism and for the war itself. The not yet forgotten distress of the Depression and the relative strength of organized labor and the liberal-left also helped make the avoidance of mass unemployment an important postwar policy goal. Sir William Beveridge's 1944 *Full Employment in a Free Society* is a classic exposition of the costs of unemployment and the principles and mechanisms by which societies could maintain full employment, which Beveridge took for granted as the primary national economic policy objective. Indeed, most western governments developed policies and passed legislation oriented to this goal.

The trouble with a full employment policy, however, is that it commits the state to bolstering the power of labor. While it helps increase total demand, its fatal characteristic from the business view is that it keeps the reserve army of the unemployed low, thereby protecting wage levels and strengthening labor's bargaining power. Business will therefore fight such a policy, with an intensity proportional to the degree of pressure on profit margins. It will press the view that inflation is the prime threat, and that this makes full employment untenable. Thus, even though full employment was widely accepted as a policy goal immediately after World War II, the forces of capital in the United States were sufficiently strong to prevent any policy commitment to "full" employment— which the *New York Times* suggested "would in fact involve a completely planned economy." After a struggle, the language of the 1946 Employment Act committed the government only to "maximum levels of" production, purchasing power, and employment, and only by "all practicable means consistent with other essential considerations of national policy…" The watering down of the full employment goal in the United States began early.

The history of the period since 1946 has been one of gradual retreat from any commitment to full employment.[23] The proportion of unemployed workers defined as consistent with full employment has gradually risen in economics textbooks and policy analyses, from roughly 2-3 percent in the 1940s to 5-6 percent in the 1980s. The altered target has usually been rationalized in terms of a changed composition of the labor force, with many more workers—chiefly women and teenagers—having a "volatile" attachment to the workforce, which has allegedly elevated the "normal" level of unemployment. Thus any attempt by government to increase aggregate demand sufficiently to create jobs for all these marginal workers would generate inflation much faster than it would produce suitable jobs for them.

Conservative economists have even developed a concept of a "natural rate of unemployment,"* a metaphysical notion and throwback to an eighteenth century vision of a "natural order," but with a modern apologetic twist. The natural rate is defined as the minimum unemployment level consistent with price level stability, but, as it is based on a highly abstract model that is not directly testable, the natural rate can only be inferred from the price level itself. That is, if prices are going up, unemployment is below the "natural rate" and too low, whether the actual rate is 4, 8, or 10 percent. In this world of conservative metaphysics, anybody out of work is "voluntarily" unemployed. Unemployment is a matter of rational choice: some people prefer "leisure" over the real wage available at going (or still lower) wage rates; others choose to "search" for jobs by stocking up on more and more labor market information, instead of just taking any old job at whatever the market will offer![24]

Apart from the grossness of this kind of metaphysical legerdemain, the very concept of a natural rate of unemployment has a huge built-in bias. It takes as given all the other institutional factors that influence the price level-unemployment trade-off (market structures and independent pricing power, business investment policies at home and abroad, the distribution of income, the fiscal and monetary policy mix, etc.) and focuses solely on the tightness of the labor market as the controllable variable. Inflation is the main threat, the labor market (i.e., wage rates and unemployment levels) is the locus of the solution to the problem.

The erosion of the full employment objective is closely tied to the weakening of the power of labor and increasing competitive pressures on U.S. business. "Getting government off our backs" in the late 1970s and 1980s involved not only cutting the social wage directly, but cutting it indirectly as well by reducing government protections to labor formerly provided by the NLRB and OSHA, unemployment compensation, and macro-stabilization policies. Among its other achievements, Reaganomics reestablished the deliberate, substantial enlargement of the "reserve army of the unemployed" as a feasible means of regenerating business profitability. Before Reagan and

England's Margaret Thatcher, it was thought that postwar sensitivities and democratic politics precluded this. Our democratic leaders have proved that this is not the case.

Entitlements versus Subsidies

Neo-reactionary economic and social policy trends have been accompanied by appropriate semantic adjustments. The poor "take advantage of" (i.e., use) our allegedly generous social welfare system as we "coddle"* them. The word "coddle" is not used in reference to agribusiness or military contractors. From the Nixon years onward, "fat"* has regularly been found in social but not military budgets. In preparing the federal budget for Congress, military projections are regularly calculated on an inflation-adjusted basis; social budgets are presented in absolute dollar amounts. Aid to Families with Dependent Children (AFDC) program allotments fell in value by 30 percent during the 1970s, because the dollar payments remained the same on average while prices rose markedly; but this was stressed only in critical scholarly publications and the alternative media. It was not featured in the mass media's reporting of statements about the alleged generosity of the welfare system.

In the 1970s there was, in the business view, a "rising tide of entitlements."[25] This referred to legal claims on the state, such as the right to a pension at age 65 or unemployment compensation upon meeting certain technical eligibility requirements. "Entitlements"* being claims of weak clients, the word "entitlement" quickly acquired negative connotations of unwarranted grants or excessive obligations to some, which were burdensome to others and lacking social justification. Strong clients get "subsidies,"* incentives, or progress payments in connection with "security" or "defense" expenditures, or they benefit from leases and contracts to enhance efficiency and stimulate growth. Welfare budgets involve "handouts" and "doles"; government price supports or credit guarantees to agribusiness and other corporate entities are "subsidies," not doles or handouts.

A large fraction of the transfers from taxpayers to substantial citizens and business firms are so well hidden or presented in such a way that they are not even perceived as subsidies. Apart from tax breaks, which are an extremely important form of subsidy, subsidies may occur in the process of "privatization,"* in which public sector assets are disposed of at low prices and high sales commissions to powerful individuals and groups who acquired "access"* to government officials by supporting the selling party's last election campaign. Military contracts for unneeded weapons, negotiated under "golden handshake" conditions between contractors and friendly employees of the Pentagon (prospective future employees of the contractors), are subsidies hidden under formal contracts for services rendered.

Contracting for rights to coal, oil, minerals, and timber lands (see below under Looting the National Forests) is often carried out, especially in business friendly and "revolving door"* administrations like Reagan's, under conditions that make the contractual arrangements *de facto* subsidies. The Interior Department under James Watt rushed to lease federal coal lands to private interests in a period of depressed coal market conditions. A Federal commission looking into this leasing program found that it was "deficient in all its features," involved "serious errors of judgment," and that there was a "suspicion of wrongdoing" on the part of U.S. officials in at least one case where coal rights were sold for some $100 million under fair market value.[26] The Reagan era formula was to "Let a hundred Teapot Domes flourish."

The New Federalism and the Safety Net for the Deserving Poor

Among the semantic devices mobilized in the Reagan-Bush years to obscure the savaging of the weak is the concept of a "new federalism,"* which Nixon had already coined and described, in a wonderful parody of a then-current cliché, as "returning power to the people." The trick of Nixon's new federalism, used even more ruthlessly under Reagan and Bush, has been to turn expensive welfare programs back to state and local governments without providing commensurate resources, thereby assuring that they will be gutted in their more appropriate location "close to the people." Many of these programs had been undertaken by the federal government in the first place because the states and local authorities didn't have adequate resources or commitment to address the problems. State and local governments were also constrained by the force of interstate competition for business, which demanded low business taxes (hence low social budgets), a force even more potent in the 1980s, making the new federalism a cynical ploy.

Another claim of the Reagan era was that a "safety net" had been placed under the truly needy and "deserving poor."* As the Reaganites stripped protections from the poor based largely on their political weakness (as illustrated above in the case of the disabled), this was an exceptionally brazen use of doublespeak. The "undeserving poor"* are a truly growing class, based on the financial constraints built into Reaganomics, policies increasing unemployment and homelessness, and the insidious gradual reduction of eligibility of the really poor and powerless.

The Reagan Regulatory Counterrevolution

In 1981 the business community expected Ronald Reagan to weaken and reduce the costs of regulation. Carried out with enthusiasm and ideological fervor, the process revealed the administration's and corporate community's parochialism and truncated vision.

The EPA was gutted, and other agencies including OSHA, the Food and Drug Administration, Securities and Exchange Commission, and Federal Home Loan Bank Board (FHLBB) were seriously weakened in the interest of short-term gain. In pumping large resources into Reagan's campaigns in 1980 and 1984, the business community and the "market" simply *bought* the impairment of important sectors of the regulatory system, which were defunded and headed up by ideologues and hacks hostile to the regulatory mission, thereby demoralizing committed and quality bureaucrats and inducing them to leave public service.

The Savings and Loan Industry: Deregulation, Reregulation, and Bailout

The Reagan-Bush era savings and loan (S&L) crisis provides an important illustration of the nature of deregulation, the thoughtlessness of its design, and its consequences. The S&L crisis has not run its course, and some of its features also apply to the sagging banking and insurance industries. The partially deregulated financial sector is the probable locus of even more sensational future debacles.

The S&L industry was sponsored and protected by the government for many years to allow it to make mortgage loans that the banks did not care to provide. In exchange for legal confinement to mortgage lending and other restrictive regulations, the S&Ls received government deposit insurance and subsidized loans from the S&L central bank, the FHLBB. Their shares, essentially deposits, were eventually made payable on demand, while their assets were largely long-term mortgages. This imbalance in the maturities of their assets and liabilities made the S&Ls vulnerable to sharp increases in interest rates, which would drive up the costs of their liabilities but would not affect the revenue from their long-term (mortgage) assets. They were thus highly speculative ventures, dependent on continuing low interest rates. When interest rates rose in the late 1970s, the S&Ls were in trouble, and when rates skyrocketed in the Reagan-Volcker tight money crunch of 1981, they were in desperate trouble. Deregulation during this period allowed S&Ls to raise rates on their deposits, but they couldn't raise rates on their mortgage assets, and therefore suffered severe operating losses.

This "first crisis" of high interest rates caused numerous failures and left many of the remaining S&Ls badly damaged, with eroded capital. In the midst of this first phase, moreover, the Reagan administration, Congress, and several key states like California and Texas sanctioned further deregulation. Most critically, they allowed the weakened S&Ls to make more risky investments, such as the purchase of junk bonds, land investment, and construction loans. Meanwhile, they maintained government insurance on deposits— which was even raised from $40,000 to $100,000 coverage per account in 1980—and allowed the development of "brokered deposits" in which S&Ls could raise large sums by selling government-insured deposits through brokers, at a fee, to anybody. This set the stage for a second and larger crisis, as the already weakened S&Ls with low net worth had little to lose in "going for broke" with risky investments funded by government insured deposits. Heads I win, tails the government and taxpayer lose.

As the final ingredient in the Reagan era recipe for disaster, the early 1980s witnessed a substantial cutback in the FHLBB examiner force, in line with the general cutbacks in regulatory appropriations. This made it increasingly difficult to monitor and respond to the deteriorating quality of industry assets and the influx of crooks and self-dealing builders to take advantage of the new opportunities.

There was strong evidence from at least 1984 that a "second crisis" of fraud and excessive risk-taking was brewing. The insurance fund of the Federal Savings and Loan Insurance Corporation shriveled quickly, and the authorities had neither the money nor personnel to close down insolvent S&Ls. Knowledge of this regulatory paralysis induced further entry of crooks and additional fraud. The Reagan administration ignored this enlarging disaster up to the end of Reagan's term in office, because it did not want to spend money on this problem when it had so many commitments to the Salvadoran army, the CIA, SDI, Stealth Bombers, and other important programs. The press also remained quiet. Until Bush decided to bite the bullet upon entering office, the media hardly noticed the second crisis, once again recognizing a problem only after officials told them it was there. At no point has the media directed attention to the fact that the Reagan administration allowed the problem to fester for years to avoid a budget hit from the savings and loan industry.

Edwin Gray, chair of the FHLBB in 1984-86, fought a lonely battle to reimpose regulatory controls and increase the vigor of regulation as the second thrift crisis grew, but was frustrated by the industry, the Reagan administration, Congress, and the media. Reregulation, as is so common, came too late, and the bill to the taxpayer for bailing out the insured industry is large and still growing. The leaders of the establishment do not suggest that the beneficiaries of the Reagan era income counterrevolution pay for the Reagan era debacle; it is taken for granted that ordinary taxpayers will foot this bill. The Resolution Trust, established in 1989 to dispose of the assets of failed institutions, started slowly in the face of personnel and legal problems and soft real estate markets, and is not recouping large amounts from most sales and transfers.

The Bush early 1990s program of loosening restraints on the weakened banking industry, allowing it to move into new service areas, is an eerie throwback to the early 1980s deregulation of the S&Ls, demonstrating that experience does not produce wisdom and the rethinking of policy when it conflicts with ideology and the demands of the powerful. A larger debacle may be brewing in the banking sector.

Leveraged Ripoffs

The great merger movements in U.S. history have all been fueled to a very large extent by promoter-banker-manager self interest. Strategically placed individuals have long taken advantage of special financial market conditions, including investor ignorance, euphoria and speculative fervor, rising stock prices, and easy credit to "fleece the lambs" by selling securities at inflated prices and taking substantial fees and generous portions of the issued securities (or options) at favorable prices.[27]

This tendency of insiders and bankers to use "conjunctures of change" to feather their own nests was pointed out with clarity by Thorstein Veblen in *The Theory of Business Enterprise,* published in 1904. The interested parties and a significant body of professional economists, however, have always explained heightened merger activity as a response to the demands of technology and organizational and marketing evolution—that is, as part of the process of reallocating resources to enhance efficiency in the economy. This rationale was offered even for the hundreds of leveraged buyouts* (LBOs) of the middle and late 1980s, where the same managers usually remained in place after the acquisition, but with substantial ownership interest and a heavy debt load. We were asked to believe that these managers had been insufficiently motivated by mere salaries and stock options; they needed the promise of huge capital gains and the pressure of large interest charges to concentrate their minds!

Mergers were unleashed in the Reagan era by the eased legal environment, the huge tax bonanzas the administration gave to U.S. corporations, and the reluctance of business to build new capacity in the economic climate of 1981-83 and thereafter. The enlarged cash flows reaped by corporations went in good part into buying up other companies. These were "supply-side" mergers in the sense that they resulted mainly from the tax cuts and derived corporate surplus cash looking for a quick profit-making outlet, not from gains in efficiency.

A sizable financial apparatus developed to help and encourage business firms to "restructure."* Buying and selling companies involved new security issues and advisory and underwriting services (and fees). Bankers, brokers, institutional investors, and managers all moved more heavily into trading, in all facets of their businesses. In a now famous 1979 article in the *Harvard Business Review,* "Managing Our Way to Economic Decline," Robert Hayes and William Abernathy argued persuasively that under the regime of business school-trained managers and institutional investors interested in quarterly performance, the U.S. corporate system had lost its way—its managers had turned from "hands-on" attention to productivity, and from concern with long-run market share and efficiency, to trading, deal-making, and maneuvers aimed at short-run financial gain. Others have spoken of the U.S. business community as suffering from a "transactional disease," in which gains from transactions have come to predominate over gains from production and technical improvement.

The leveraged buyout blossomed in the 1980s. In its most common form, the management, in alliance with a group of bankers, bought up the company's outstanding stock with borrowed money. The managers and financial sponsors put up very little of their own money, but borrowed from banks and issued "high yield" (junk) bonds to institutional investors to raise the funds to acquire the stock. The bankers got large fees for arranging the transaction and placing the bonds, the institutional investors got high yields (although they were taking substantial risks), and the participating managers bought company stock at low prices (often with borrowed money) and positioned themselves for huge capital gains. The stockholders who were bought out got prices above the previous market levels, but they received less than they might have if the managers had solicited other offers.

Managers are supposedly hired by boards of directors to serve the stockholders interest, and this is their legal fiduciary obligation. In an LBO, however, the managers have an interest in acquiring the outstanding stock at the lowest possible price. In the huge RJR Nabisco deal of 1988, the initial management offer was $75 per share, whereas the final price after outsiders entered the bidding was $110 per share. According to the initial proposal by the management, CEO F. Ross Johnson and seven other top officials would have put up $20 million for an 8.5 percent share of the company which would have been worth $200 million upon completion of the deal, and, on certain moderate assumptions, over $2.6 billion within five years. That managers should be able to put themselves in this position of acute conflict of interest, carrying out what some business commentators have called "insider raids" on their own companies, without legal obstruction or media outcry is a testimonial to the power of the interests that have profited from these transactions.[28]

Many analysts and social critics have pointed to the large social costs of the Reagan era escalation of mergers and LBOs—the losses imposed on abandoned workers and communities; the diversion of investment funds and managerial talent to "transactions"; the further pressure to take a short view of business planning; and the potential damage from the large debts incurred, which reduced the maneuverability of managements, encroached on research and development outlays, and made the firms and the overall system more vulnerable to downturns in economic activity. Some part of the current difficulties of U.S. banks is a result of credit losses from LBOs. Furthermore, a significant portion of the gains from the LBO comes out of the pockets of the U.S. Treasury and taxpayers, as tax deductible interest payments are substituted for dividend payments to shareholders. This is a classic example of a private gain at a social cost. The importance of the tax factor in LBO gains poses the interesting possibility that LBOs might be used in continuous cycles, with the company "going public" after the tax gains are exhausted (many already have), then organizing a new LBO to create more tax gains in an endless loop.

An important rationale for the LBO has been that it stimulates the managers to greater efficiency, given their new stake in ownership and the pressure of large interest payments. These managers had previously issued themselves "golden parachutes,"* to assure their undying loyalty to the stockholders in case somebody tried to raid the company before they did—otherwise they might be tempted to resist an outside bid which would oust them from power and perks. We are clearly deep into the realms of hypocrisy and doublespeak. The argument that the LBOs will stimulate managers to greater efficiency implies that ordinary salaries and stock options are not enough, and that mainstream corporate America suffers from poor incentives and therefore inefficiency. This could of course be a mere rationalization for the management-banker ripoff in LBOs. Another possibility is that both statements are true.

The Looting of the National Forests

The privately owned forests—vast acreages held from giveaways and blatant corruption in the nineteenth century[29]—were widely subjected to a "cut-and-run" policy that eventually caused the timber companies to turn to the public domain.[30] A Timber Industry-Logger-Forest Service (TILFS) complex has firmly institutionalized the stripping of a unique public resource in its own interest, and has been busily clear-cutting and ripping off the last of the great Douglas fir and redwood forests in the United States, without any national debate. Like the military-industrial complex (MIC), the TILFS complex has mastered the art of mobilizing power to gain privileged access to the national forests and to get the relevant government agencies to run interference for it.

Like the Red Scares so useful to the MIC, the TILFS complex has played the game of "housing crisis" and timber shortage,[31] and, of course, the threat to jobs. Money to local congresspersons has helped to create a powerful congressional lobby, logrolling in the interest of looting the national forests.[32] A series of laws, beginning with the tax legislation of 1943, "turned the forest service into an adjunct of the timber industry."[33] The budget of the Forest Service as a whole, its secondary activities, and monies given to local communities were gradually tied to and made dependent on the volume of timber cut. Just as the MIC spreads contracts for a B-1 bomber or Star Wars widely, so the TILFS complex dispersed timber sales over many jurisdictions which "increased local and congressional support for additional logging."[34] This gave all parties a vested interest in rapid cutting. Effective mobilization of power in the timber industry interest was also brought about by TILFS complex attention to appointments to the Forest Service (and Bureau of Land Management), making sure that these bodies were dominated by friends of the ripoff, ardent believers in *using* the national forests, mainly for timber.[35]

In exact reversal of the government's treatment of poor people, where things are made deliberately unpleasant for them to receive "entitlements," the federal government has gone to extremes to make it easy for timber interests to decimate the national forests. It has built a road system, at taxpayer expense, that is eight times the length of the interstate highway system,[36] and it has set aside additional monies from the proceeds of public sales of timber to finance road construction by the timber companies in the national forests. It has written contracts with the timber companies with terms as long as 50 years for the sale of enormous tracts of still virgin and unroaded forests at generous prices,[37] and then, if timber prices fall, does not enforce the contracts[38]—exactly paralleling the "golden handshake" of MIC contracts. The subsidy component is obscured by Forest Service accounting, which writes off road construction expenses over as many as 2000 years, a technique that allowed the agency to hide $250 million in expenses in 1990.[39]

Even on the accounting basis used by the Forest Service, net losses are suffered in 98 of 120 national forests exploited for timber, with the 98 losers costing $256.8 million in 1990.[40] Robert Wolf, a former Congressional Reference Service and government consultant on timber sales, estimates that the tax loss on timber sales, 1980-1990 inclusive, was $3.2 billion, not counting either interest costs, the costs of environmental damage, or the foregone recreational and other benefits of intact forests.[41] The Wilderness Society has estimated prospective losses in the 1990s from below-cost commercial sales of national forest timber at around $2 billion. As Richard Rice expresses it, "Simply put, your tax dollars and mine are being used to subsidize environmental damage on the national forests."[42]

It is the theoretical function of government to offset the effects of market failure by taxes, subsidies, and by making public goods off limits to the market. The tragedy of the national forest story is that the capture of government agencies supposedly serving the public interest by market interests has undermined the proper government role and made the relevant government agencies into *servants of market failure*. This has rested on the crucial support of the national media, which has failed to make this perversion of function, and the highly important looting of the national forests, into important news stories regularly presented to the public.

Perhaps the most remarkable doublespeak feature of the rape of the national forests has been Reagan's, Watt's, Bush's and the timber companies' ability to wrap themselves in the flag while they leveled the country's patrimony and destroyed the material and aesthetic basis for their claims of U.S. greatness. From those "seas to shining seas" there are amber waves of grain, but a rapidly dwindling wilderness and ancient forests.

The doublespeak comes frequently in the rationalizations for unconscionable policies that require obfuscation. Under Nixon we had a proposed "National Forest Timber *Conservation* Act" [emphasis added], which would have applied "intensive management" techniques to the national forests; i.e., it would have increased the cut by 60 percent! Two years later the patriotic and conservation-minded Senator Mark Hatfield of Oregon introduced "The *American* Forestry Act of 1971" [emphasis added]. Jack Shepherd pointed out that the word "environment" appears more than a dozen times in this bill, which posed a deadly threat to the environment.[43] Nixon also came out strongly for clear cutting on the ground that this would avoid the damage to adjacent trees which would result from selective cutting, and would allow "new growth" in the national forests! Shepherd noted the analogy to Nixon's (and the United States') "saving" role in Indochina: "the national forests must be cut down in order to save them."[44]

After ripping up the magnificent old forests, and badly damaging the soil in the process, the timber barons and Forest Service regularly put up signs pointing to their reseeding efforts and the "new growth" prospects, *a la* Nixon's cutting down the forests to save them. One sign, shown in a photograph in Shepherd's *The Forest Killers*, sits overlooking a barren landscape, and reads: "Overmature Timber Harvested In Full Compliance With California Forest Practice Laws and Regulations. Helicopter Sowed 21 Million Seeds To Start A New Forest January 1965."[45]

The Commodification of Culture

While the former Soviet bloc receives accolades in the West for its steps toward a market economy, in the West itself the market extends daily into hitherto neglected areas and niches of opportunity. A December 1988 report in the *Wall Street Journal* noted the penetration of soda pop into the Saturday morning TV children's "junk food ghetto, glutted with commercials pitching candy, fast food hamburgers and sugary cereals to children." Seven-Up broke the soft-drink barrier in children's commercials, claiming that "kids are an underdeveloped market," children 12 and under accounting for only 15 percent of soft-drink consumption.

Every aspect of the culture is in process of commodification and linkage to the sale of goods. Advertisers have moved systematically into all places where people congregate and can be subjected to advertising materials, now called the "captive advertising market." There is a Health Club Television Network that beams programs and ads into health clubs, an Airport Channel, channels striking doctors' waiting rooms, and even a Checkout Channel testing the feasibility of TV directed to supermarket checkout lines.[46]

Sports and sports events have for a long time, but with steadily increasing intensity, been used by commercial interests as vehicles for marketing, and the force of the market has diminished the element of sport and play in sporting events, helped along by rampant chauvinism, so blatant in the 1984 Olympics and 1991 Superbowl. Players as well as managers and owners are becoming increasingly celebrity/businesspersons, and the sports page more and more belongs in the business section of the newspaper. Big name players make as much or more money from endorsements and commercial appearances as from contracts to play.

The games themselves are increasingly dominated by the demands of the market—the National Football League (NFL) is now considering moving to an 18- instead of a 16-week schedule to "better position the product," in the words of one NFL official. Pauses in the game are dictated as much by advertising needs as by those of the participants, and the advertisers' logos steadily increase their presence—extending to the names of the events, the ads shown in the stadiums and on players' attire, as well as in the increasingly frequent ads within the TV programs. In movies and other TV programs as well, brand name products are used, for a price, as program materials as well as in ads. Since 1982, "product placement" has become institutionalized in movies, with the price now averaging about $50,000 per item/incident. In magazines, also, the distinction between advertising and editorial material has been eroding under the force of competition for ads and advertisers' pressures for editorial "support" that will "add value" to the space they buy.[47] Beyond "advertorials," in which ads mimic editorial material, and editorial help in producing ads, the nature of the accompanying articles will obviously affect the value of advertisements. We now have "funded journalism," but more important than this is the overall approach to editorial materials in an environment of concern for helping to add value to advertising space.

The market has moved steadily into the schools, where the business community has long offered educational aids in the form of printed and video materials on their companies, products, industries, and the principles of free enterprise. More recently, companies have moved to "partnership" relationships with schools, with some 40 percent of all public schools now receiving assistance on this basis. The business community vigorously supports political parties and leaders who defund the schools, and bargains and fights for lower local taxes, but then gallantly offers small change to alleviate the troubling "crisis in the schools"!

A notable development of recent years has been Whittle Communications' offer of free equipment to schools in exchange for the right to offer students a news broadcast containing advertising. This camel's nose under the tent has been accepted by over 9,000 financially strapped schools, and the advertisement as part of the formal educational package has thus found a home. Whittle is planning a more direct entry into the school business, proposing a for-profit school network covering kindergarten through the 12th grade that would use its own materials, charging tuition, but also raising money by selling advertising to appear in the school's hallways, texts, and any broadcasting materials used in the program.[48] Whittle's plan fits well into the Bush educational proposals that envisage more "free choice" and private funding for model schools.

Museums and libraries have also been integrated more closely into the market. Debora Silverman has described how the New York Metropolitan Museum of Art's exhibits on China and pre-revolutionary France were linked to Bloomingdale's featured sales of items of the same genre.[49] Both the department store and art museum were being advised by the late Diana Vreeland, a long-time editor of *Vogue* magazine and consultant to Bloomingdales. The museum exhibits, which lacked historical or social context, seemed like museum versions of sales programs.

More generally, museums have increasingly felt the need to obtain corporate sponsorship for exhibits, and thus to adjust their overall orientation to attract this important source of funding. Corporate expenditures on the arts rose from $22 million in 1967 to close to a billion dollars in 1987. One curator noted that "Most corporate sponsors finance exhibitions based on centrist ideals and uncontroversial subject matter." The artist and radical critic of museums, Hans Haacke, states that "shows that could promote critical awareness, present products of consciousness dialectically and in relation to the social world, or question relations of power, have a slim chance of being approved...self-censorship is having a boom."[50]

The technological revolution in "informatics" has not only made it possible to use information more extensively and intensively within the business world and for social control, it has made information itself more marketable. The result has been a further commodification of information. Data bases in all kinds of fields have multiplied. This "for sale" information is collected and formatted in accordance with the needs of the parties best able to buy it. Public libraries are increasingly bypassed as repositories of information, and they have had to subscribe to some of the new private information services. The "free" library is thus on its way out, as libraries are compelled to impose charges for access to privately controlled information.

Another important development has been the tendency to reduce and privatize information collected by the government, much of which was traditionally subsidized as valuable to the public and fitting the concept of a "public good." For a public good, one person's use does not interfere with another person's use as well, so that imposing a price restricts use unnecessarily and the market "fails" when price is used as a rationing device. In the 1980s, government collected information was increasingly turned over to private users to sell on their own terms (even back to the government at a price). So in this "information age" information has been increasingly privatized and commodified, its public good quality ignored in the interest of serving "the market." This strengthens the position of those able to control and pay for such information (i.e., the business sector, especially its larger units), and weakens the position of scholars and the general public.[51]

While traditional, hard information is becoming less readily available to the public, advertising and PR have been growing at a steady clip. We may crudely generalize: hard data is being reserved for business and the elite; the information sector made increasingly available to the masses as public goods (with no direct charge) is *very* "soft," and of questionable, even negative, value.

Advertising* is the subsidized message provided by sellers of goods to facilitate sale. PR* is its institutional counterpart. These self-serving and inherently biased forms of communication are dominant in modern market economies and are geared to the demands of the owners/managers of firms that pay for them. They reinforce the values of acquisition, consumption and accumulation, and marginalize values of non-commercial interest (community, equality, ethical concerns, the sacredness of life and nature) although they may make occasional opportunistic use of these values for their own advantage. They have had a profound effect on broadcast media and the political process, as discussed earlier.

Epilogue: The End of History?

The unilateral withdrawal of the Soviet Union from the arms race and empire, and then its internal traumas, collapse of the Communist Party, and prospective integration of its remnants into the global market order (and threatened colonization by the West), have ushered in a new period of Western triumphalism. In the United States and Great Britain there was also a triumphal blip based on the great victory in the two-month long Gulf war of early 1991.

Triumphalism brings with it an acute loss of perspective. As the dominant forces celebrate and savor their victories, the political leadership and its intellectual and media epigoni suffer a further loss of already modest self-critical capabilities, history is rewritten with less constraint, and the seamy side of the victories and the growing problems the victors face (or rather, ignore) are given slight shrift.

In an earlier period of western domination, following World War II, there was an eerily similar phase of triumphalism in which it was pronounced that ideology was at an end[1] (except for the Soviet incubus), and that the Third World, with U.S. aid to market forces, would soon "take off into sustained growth" and become ever more like us.[2] This notion of the gradual homogenization of the globe was a bit inconsistent with the Grand Area conception of the Third World as a raw materials supplier and servant of the advanced industrial powers, and was in large measure an expression of ideology, playing a role similar to the more recent assumption and claims of U.S. devotion to democracy in the Third World. In actuality, although there have been pockets of rapid development and growth of per capita real incomes, inequalities within the Third World and between the Third World masses and the affluent West continue to grow. While the rich get richer in the West, ordinary citizens do not advance but suffer increased insecurity, and more than a billion people in the Third World live on the edge of catastrophe.[3] U.S. children "have more pocket money—$230 a year—than the half-billion poorest people alive."[4]

In an age of triumphalism, "ideology" ends because the prevailing ideology becomes obvious truth. "Even the communists" agree that the market is the only way to organize the economic and social order. Thus the word "reform"* comes to mean the liquidation of what used to be called "reform" in favor of the unimpeded operation of private markets and in accord with rules laid down by the IMF, implementing the truths of Adam Smith's "obvious and simple system of natural liberty." In short, blatant ideology ceases to be ideology.

The Cold War as Western Aggression

With the fall of the Soviet bloc and triumph of capitalism, we may be sure that the traditional view of the Cold War as western defense and containment of an aggressive and expansionist system will be even more firmly institutionalized. This will constitute acceptance of a special and mythical history, comparable, ironically, to the famed Stalinist construction of a Soviet history in accord with ongoing political demands.

The truth of the history of the Cold War must be traced back to the western invasion of Russia during and immediately after World War I to prevent a Bolshevik victory in a civil conflict. These were "active measures" that occurred even before the Communists had taken power. Western actions to isolate, weaken, and destroy the Soviet state were incessant from 1917 onward. A strenuous effort was made to turn Hitler toward the Soviet Union in the late 1930s and, following World War II, fascists were quickly rehabilitated in country after country to shore up the old order, boycotts and other forms of economic warfare were employed against the Soviet Union and its allies,[5] and a policy of armed encirclement and destabilization was put into place.[6] As stressed earlier, this was clearly recognized in U.S. official (but unpublicized) documents to be *offensive* activity,[7] while at the same time the public posture—transmitted without bothersome dissent by the ideological institutions—was that we were strictly on the defensive in crises of "containment."

Under the cover of the "Soviet threat,"* the United States and other western states fought against social revolution and independent development globally, but especially in the Third World. The incessant war against the Soviet Union was paralleled by a war against the Chinese revolution before and after 1949, against social revolution in Indochina from 1945 onward, against threatening social change in Iran in 1953, Guatemala in the years 1947-54, Brazil in the early 1960s, Chile in the early 1970s, Nicaragua after July 19, 1979, among many other cases. These were independent nationalist revolts against elite and foreign rule, but perceived as contrary to the interests of the United States and western corporate institutions, and therefore vilified, transformed into Moscow-led threats, and destabilized and attacked. In brief, the conventional view of the West as on the defensive against "aggression" in its interventionism in the Third World is straightforward mythology (captured in our dictionary definitions of Containment and Force).

The fall of communism, like the defeat of Allende in Chile and the successful undermining of the Nicaraguan revolution in the 1980s, is therefore in some substantial measure a victory of superior power and systematic use of coercion and violence. The Soviet Union, Cuba, Nicaragua, and Vietnam, throughout their years of control by elements deemed hostile to western interests, had to contend with *real* security threats, continuous economic warfare, and periodic active military attack. In the context of pre-conditions of economic backwardness, each of these countries developed command economies and less than democratic political systems that weakened their ability to cope with and meet their citizens' demands. It is possible that without systematic western attacks these states would still have faltered, but this will never be known.[8] It is clear, however, that western aggression put them under extreme stress and damaged their ability to succeed.

Who Will Contain Us as We Strive to Keep the Third World Masses in their Place?

The question of "who will contain us" is an oxymoron in the United States. By patriotic assumption, we have no interests that might conflict with legitimate interests of other peoples, and would not impose them by force if we did. But this perspective reflects the fact that citizens of every imperial power live in a closed and protective intellectual environment which bathes imperial policies in a benevolent light. In reality, from the vantage point of Third World majority interests and our role as Globocop enforcing the *status quo,* the United States badly needs to be contained.

With the retreat and dissolution of the Soviet Union, the problem has become even more serious because that country, whatever its very serious flaws and imperialism, did offer some aid and protection to Third World revolutions and deterrence to the United States. The problem is worsened by the antidotes recently developed against the dreaded Vietnam syndrome. The U.S. leadership has now found that a short war with few U.S. casualties brings a political bonanza to those leading the country into war. We are proud to beat up countries ranging from one-fortieth to one-thirty-six thousandth of our size (as measured by relative GNPs). The government has mastered the art of war-making propaganda, and the mass media have lost the capacity to challenge it by raising salient issues and forcing debate, so that matters like the number of enemy victims, the subsequent failure to pick up the pieces within the victim states, and matters of justice and law are kept out of public view.

As a result, the United States and its western allies should now have a freer hand in keeping the Third World masses in their place. Where traditional forms of subversion, the support of suitable "leaders,"* and IMF discipline won't suffice, *contra* armies and direct attacks on newly demonized Little Satans should be easier to deploy in the future.

Market, Growth, and Environment

With the triumph of the market and the accelerated advance of a global market order, who is going to protect the environment and ecological integrity of a seriously threatened planet earth? Although the fallen Communist regimes of Eastern Europe did very badly in environmental protection,[9] it surely does not follow that a free market world will do well. Brazil and Mexico are hardly models of environmental protection, and neither is the United States.

In principle, moreover, we would expect a market-based world to do very poorly in environmental protection. Environmental problems flow in large part from two factors that are integral to a capitalist market system: the drive for limitless growth and the desire to externalize costs of production (i.e., pass them on to the community at large) so as to minimize private expenses. A centralized authority is necessary to constrain growth. But such an authority runs counter to fundamental characteristics of a capitalist economy, where governments are kept weak and capital has dominant power over political choices and the formation of national and private goals. The growing hegemony of the market has been associated with the growth of individualism and consumerist goals, at the expense of concern for others and the community. It will be exceedingly difficult to alter such an ethos and deeply entrenched goals without a prior change in the structure of power and corporate domination that underlies goal formation.

Controlling externalities also requires a strong central power that can prevent their production and imposition on the community in the first place, or can effectively restrict and internalize the costs of those produced. But government in a market-based system has neither the knowledge nor power to prevent externalized costs, with minor exceptions. It controls new packaging materials and chemicals that enter and damage the environment only after the fact, as victims and complaints pile up and pressures to act become great. Furthermore, governments tend to be controlled or strongly influenced by business firms, limiting their ability to effectively regulate and control. As the market economy globalizes, controls over externalities weaken further as firms engage in "regulatory arbitrage,"* threaten governments with their ability to move if treated harshly, and exploit and abuse weak governments and countries. "Shakedown states" installed by western power (Brazil, Guatemala, Indonesia, Zaire) permit the rape of the environment, as well as the exploitation of a repressed labor force, with western connivance. Intensifying pressures on Third World governments and people based in part on their integration into the world market, with imposition of the "development model," heavy international borrowing, the shift to agro-exports and reduction of agricultural outputs for the home market, add to pressure on the environment as the land is stripped to provide the world market with logs, minerals, and cattle, and the local impoverished populace struggles to survive.[10]

Market-based governments tend to be parochial and self-serving. This has been dramatically evident in the Reagan-Bush years, during which the UN has been vilified,[11] UNESCO abandoned, the Law of the Sea Treaty dropped, and a narrow, national self-interested view has been displayed on issue after issue in the international sphere. The Reagan-Bush administrations have been premier *business* administrations, displaying the short planning horizons of the business world and reflecting their policy interests. The long-run protection of the environment is going to require constraints on growth as well as on externalities, but it is hard to imagine an administration evolving from the U.S. political economy that would minimally *cooperate*, let alone lead us into a new world *environmental* order.

The End of History?

We have arrived at another historical juncture where there is prophesied an "end of history." It is reminiscent of 1815, following the defeat of Napoleon and the crushing of the various rebellions of the post-French revolution era, when Prince Metternich and the rulers of the newly consolidated anti-liberal and anti-national regimes of elite rule felt comfortable that stability would prevail, and that the "police operations of the Holy Alliance"[12] would keep revolutionary movements from below in check.

Things didn't work out that way—history failed to stop. Great power rivalries, upheavals by the excluded and exploited majorities, and pressures for liberalization and more basic reforms could not be contained.

In the current version of end of history triumphalism, "police operations of the Holy Alliance" are downplayed but remain important. The role of these operations in undermining social democracy and socialism in the period from 1917 into 1992 has been greatly underrated, as described earlier. It is evident that the U.S. Globocop is rarin' to go in its role of keeping the

Third World safe for market occupancy and further penetration. Western Europe is readying its own counterrevolutionary force to enable it to compete with the United States in the role of global enforcer of freedom (i.e., open markets).

Francis Fukuyama and others who have pronounced the end of history claim that democracy, free choice, and the market have triumphed over the forces of political constraint and coercion. In their view, this is no victory of a holy alliance, rather it is the triumph of the free individual. This claim is given plausibility by the rush of the Soviet bloc states to join the market throng. But the "free individual" has not triumphed in the West itself, where democracies have become steadily more constrained, market-dominated, and largely nominal. Outside of the dominant western capitalist world, it is the transnational corporate system rather than the "free individual" that has been victorious, based in good part on the use of force. Many Third World revolutions have been aborted, badly damaged, or destroyed by externally instigated violence. Elsewhere, Third World peoples have been kept in such a terrible state of impoverishment and repression, helped along by joint venture arrangements between western and Third World elites, that needed revolutionary changes have not yet been able to materialize.

A number of analysts of the French revolution, most notably Alexis de Tocqueville, stressed that, contrary to the common view that the severe abuses of the French masses led to the revolution, in fact the French masses were far more prosperous and less repressed than those in Germany and Russia, and this relative prosperity was a necessary condition for successful revolution. The German and Russian peasants were too thoroughly crushed and oppressed to be able to revolt. A comparison of western Third World client states and the struggling, now rejected state socialist countries of the Soviet bloc, in terms of the material and social condition of the masses, shows that the latter look relatively quite well off.[13] If their peoples have risen to throw off their oppressors, this suggests that they had progressed to a point where a better and freer life seemed possible. And they had been repressed with less ferocity than those in revolt against U.S. clients in Latin America.

This suggests, finally, that not only has history not ended, but that the next phase of mass upheaval and the throwing off of the fetters of institutional oppression is also likely to come from the hundreds of millions of landless and marginalized people in the shantytowns and countrysides of the Free World. The "Cry of the People" in the Third World has not been heard in the West; but the explosive uprising, when it comes, may be beyond the repressive capabilities of Globocop and its public relations system. The unshackling of the "mere gooks" and "mere Arabs" is the future task of historical change, which brings its own surprises.

A Doublespeak Dictionary
for the 1990s

Which of the following is the...

a.) terrorist extremist
b.) moderate centrist
c.) defender of freedom
and democracy.

1.) A teenage Palestinian

2.) A Salvadoran President who has presided over the deaths of 75,000 of his people.

3.) An American President who kills more than 200,000 Iraqis for "jobs", or was it oil?, and spends $300 billion annually on his war machine.

M. WUERKER

A

Access.

What political investors buy when they give money to candidates and parties. Access is to be distinguished from buying influence or votes, which is dishonest graft.[1]*

Acheson, Dean.

An influential statesman noted for his advocacy of negotiations at some future date from a position of strength still to be attained.[2] (See *Containment, Diplomacy,* and *Negotiations.*)

Activist.

Someone pursuing change in an area best left alone; a pest.

Activist foreign policy.

Dropping bombs at the drop of a hat; pre-emptive Self-defense *(q.v.).*[*]

Adult market.

Porn.

Adventurism.

An enemy action or program, including assistance to an internationally recognized government defending itself against state-sponsored terrorism, which interferes with our plans.[3]

Adversary press.

One that fails to serve as an unquestioning flack and cheerleader for the government and corporate establishment. (See *Advocacy journalism* and *Responsible.*)

Advertising.

Expenditures to make indistinguishable goods distinguishable; value creation.

Advisers.

Members of our armed forces deployed in another country at the request of its legitimate government solely for training purposes and scrupulously avoiding combat activities.[4] (See *Subversion.*)

---

* Footnotes for the Dictionary begin on page 204. In the dictionary text, cross references are indicated by *q.v.,* the abbreviation for *quod vide* ("which see").

Advocacy journalism.

Reporting which does not merely transmit government and corporate press releases; journalism.[5]

Aggression.

Invasion of another country by someone other than ourselves without our approval; also, providing aid and comfort to the side that we oppose in a civil conflict;[6] also, resisting a U.S. attack.[7] (See *Aggression, Internal,* and *Aggression, Naked.*)

Aggression, Internal.

The taking up of arms by an indigenous population against a government that we support.[8]

THE EMPERORS' NEW WARS

DO YOU KNOW "NAKED AGGRESSION" WHEN YOU SEE IT?

a) Afghanistan   b) Panama   c) Kuwait

HE'S STARK RAVING MAD! WITHOUT A SHREAD OF RESPECT FOR INTERNATIONAL LAW!

Naked Aggression

Aggression, Naked.

An invasion and occupation of another country that threatens our interests. Morally, legally, and politically intolerable, this calls for immediate and complete ouster, reparations, and the teaching of a Lesson. (See *Aggression, Properly Attired,* and *Lesson.*)

Aggression, Properly Attired.

An invasion and occupation of another country by ourselves or an allied or client state, based on exceptional circumstances explained satisfactorily in official press releases.

Agitator.

The source of disaffection and riots among otherwise contented people.[9]

Aid, or AID.

Help in selling our goods abroad;[10] also, assistance in repressing, as in, "AID's task [in Vietnam] has been to assist the National Police in recruiting, training and organizing a force for the maintenance of law and order" (U.S. official Robert Nooter). Syn.—Secure, Protect. (See *Security*.)

Alleged.

Designation of an event or person whose reality the designator is not prepared to admit, as in "the alleged 'turkey shoot' of defeated Iraqi soldiers retreating from Kuwait," etc.

Alliance for Progress.

A program for the export of soft soap to Latin America.[11] In Spanish, "La Alianza Para El Progresso" (lit., "The Alliance Stops Progress"). (See *Bosch, Juan* and *Castro, Fidel*.)

Allies.

Me and my myrmidons.

Allowable cut.

The maximum volume of trees in the national forests that Congress will *allow* to be cut this year: the minimum volume that *will* be cut.

American roulette.

Stoking the nuclear arms race until the enemy either "says uncle" or we reach Armageddon on an accelerated basis. (See also, *Nuclear chicken*.)

Anarchy.

Protest against established authority. Also change, especially when rapid, unfamiliar, and not clearly beneficial to my interests.

Ancient forests.

Stands of overmature trees urgently in need of removal in order to "save" the forests. (See *Overmature* and *Save*.)

Another Hitler.

Last year's "moderate," now threatening our interests.

Anti-ballistic missile (ABM).

An expensive attack on the symptoms of a disease, which, after a brief lag, makes the disease more acute.[12]

Anti-communism.

The religion that inspired the crusades of the West from 1917 to 1988.

Antisemitism.

Formerly, bias and prejudice against Jews; now, open criticism of Israeli policy.

Apartheid.

An official system of separate and unequal facilities. (See *Ghetto*.)

Appeasement.

During the age of Hitler, the acceptance of Hitler's invasions and occupations of neighboring countries, despite his openly expansionist program, in a futile effort to satisfy him or divert his aggressions elsewhere; in the post-World War II era, the use of diplomacy rather than immediate resort to force.[13]

Apollo.

The American entrant into the celestial stock car race.

Armageddon.

A plausible scenario.

Armed minority.

The origin of a civil upheaval which we oppose. Military juntas are invariably armed and a minority, but they are never an Armed Minority.[14]

Armed pluralism.

A counterrevolutionary army organized and armed by us to overthrow a government that we oppose; as in, "Because the Sandinistas have prevented political pluralism in Nicaragua, what they are getting is armed pluralism against the regime" (Elliott Abrams).[15]

Arms agreement.

A settlement between Great Powers that regularizes the Arms Race *(q.v.)* by providing for the joint curtailment of weapon systems of proven ineffectiveness or in excess supply, while leaving the door open to new ones. The talks leading up to such agreements are usually designated by spices (salt, pepper, thyme) as they add zest to the pursuit of new weapons.[16]

Arms race.

The continuous competitive expansion of weapons systems, necessary to provide an incentive to the enemy to negotiate the next Arms Agreement *(q.v.)*. (See *Bargaining chips*.)

Arms sales.

Employment creation at home; providing for Self-defense and Peaceful Change abroad.[17] (See *Self-defense* and *Peaceful change*.)

Assassination.
Veto by selectively employed firepower.

Assets.
Things of value for the task at hand, like cash, inventories, machines, and assassins. (See *Disposal problem.*)

Assistance.
Providing aid and comfort to the side that we favor. (See *Aggression.*)

Atrocities.
Their deliberate and systematic killings of civilians, paramilitary personnel, and our armed forces.[18]

Attack, sneak.
A successful enemy foray, especially late at night, for which we are unprepared.[19] Syn.—underhanded, cowardly, dirty, dastardly, terroristic.

Attack, conventional.
Dropping bombs on villages from 20,000 feet.[20] Syn.—provoked, retaliatory, in measured response, successful.

Authoritarian.
Totalitarian but Free *(q.v.).*

Backlash.
　　The surfacing of some large, partially submerged lumps in the melting pot, upon a brief stirring of the ladle. They impart an unappetizing flavor to the entire dish.[21]

Bargaining chips.
　　New weapons systems that we will produce, not because weapons makers want to sell them, or to strengthen our capacity to fight, but rather to put us in a better position to bargain at some future date for the reduction of weapons systems.[22] (See *Arms agreement* and *Follow-on.*)

Bargaining from strength.
　　The rationale for allowing the Military-industrial complex to produce all the bargaining chips it wants.

Batista, Fulgencio.
　　Former manager of a formerly U.S.-owned vacation resort.[23]

Bay of Tonkin incident.
　　A fabricated attack on U.S. warships by the North Vietnamese on August 4, 1964, manufactured by the Johnson administration to obtain a blank check from Congress to move to a full-scale war with Vietnam. Assisted by a gullible media and supine Congress, the blank check was granted and a war of aggression was escalated.[24] (See *Escalation.*)

Bay of Tonkin principle.
　　That a military action against the Communist Enemy (for whatever reason) will raise a President's ranking in public opinion polls.[25] The effect is transitory, however, and increased doses are required for equivalent percentage effects in successive poll-raising efforts.[26]

Benign neglect.
　　Well-meaning and reluctant neglect; neglect for the good of the neglected; neglect resulting from the political needs of the Southern Strategy plus the economic demands of the Military-industrial complex. (See *Military-industrial complex* and *Southern Strategy.*)

Best and brightest.
　　The most arrogant, conventional, and well-placed in the Eastern Establishment. Engineers of the Vietnam War, their proudest moment was going to the brink of nuclear war with the Soviet Union in 1962,

bringing the world close to Armageddon, but with a "win" on the New Frontier.[27]

Best man.

The man best qualified to serve my political and ideological needs of the moment; as in, "I have chosen the best man available for this job" (George Bush, in nominating Clarence Thomas to be Justice of the Supreme Court).

Bipartisanship.

A tacit agreement between the two major parties to act as one on an important issue, to avoid serious debate, and to deny the public an option that large numbers might choose.[28]

Black.

Under; dirty; depressed; depressing. Also, the color of evil and the underworld; as in "It was a black day for Las Vegas when the Mafia moved in." (See *White.*)

Bleeding heart.

Lacking in fortitude in bearing with the suffering of others. (See *Stamina* and *Pragmatic.*)

Bloodbath.

What the forces of Evil would do to the forces of Freedom if we were to stop bathing them both.

Body bags.

U.S. military dead, on their way home from the battlefield; the only politically relevant costs of U.S. military operations abroad. (See *Mere gook rule.*)

Body-count.

The census of the Saved. (See *Save.*)

Boondoggle.

A small welfare expenditure. (See *Defense expenditures.*)

Bosch, Juan.

A Latin American statesman dedicated to the principles of the Alliance for Progress, whose threatened return to power provoked the U.S. military invasion of the Dominican Republic in 1965.[29]

Brain-drying.

A desiccation of the cortex resulting from long exposure to TV-tube radiation. Symptoms of this disorder are a glassy-eyed stare and a tendency to reach for a pearl-handled revolver in stress situations.[30]

Brain-washing.

(See *Indoctrination.*)

Braun, Werner von.

Formerly, Professor of Explosives, University of Heidelberg; subsequently a lecturer on Democracy and the Free World in the United States.[31]

Brilliant Pebbles.

Small homing rockets designed to intercept attacking missiles in their boost and midcourse phase; a spinoff of Star Wars, this has been featured as an economy-sized space weapon, after the extra-large model began to seem a mite expensive when the "enemy" opted out of the game. (See *GPALS* and *Star Wars.*)

Budget, Federal.

A compilation of the expenditures and receipts of the Defense Department; the finances of some lesser and more dispensable government operations are also thrown in. (See *Defense Department* and *Defense expenditures.*)

Bug.

A small electronic device for listening in on other people's conversations, widely used by the forces of Law and Order to "bring us all together" in the central files.

Bug out.

To abandon a course of action merely on rational considerations of costs and benefits.

Bully factor.

The discrepancy in size between ourselves and countries that we attack, invade and occupy. This is not a political deterrent in the United States as our actions against small countries are always police operations in a just cause. (See *Operation Just Cause.*)

Bunker.

An underground enemy military site hit by U.S. bombs. (See *Shelter.*)

Burden-sharing.

Mercenary funding; collective support for the new global Hessians.

Busing.

Conveying children to school on buses where the purpose or effect is racial integration or desegregation; a symbol of the policy of desegregation. Sometimes described by its detractors as a policy of "busing for arbitrary racial balance."[32]

Calculated risk.

An incalculable risk.

Captured documents.

Papers taken from enemy dead which reveal in detail his desperate straits and nefarious purposes. These documents turn up regularly in times of political stress, helping to allay public fears and hostility. They are ordinarily written in the style of Terry and the Pirates.[33]

Castillo-Armas, Carlos.

The first CIA-elected president of Guatemala.[34]

Castro, Fidel.

The father of the Alliance for Progress *(q.v.)*.[35]

Casualties.

Our casualties.

Celebratory liberal.

One who spends a third of his time lauding his country's achievements, another third denouncing its enemies, and the final third cautiously addressing its failings, in process of rectification.[36]

Censorship.

The sick leading the blind.

Change of course.

A change in policy based on a sudden new dedication to international law and democracy; immaculate conversion. This explains why, e.g., the United States was satisfied with nondemocracy in Nicaragua under the Somozas but on July 19, 1979 (Somoza out, Sandinistas in), suddenly became deeply concerned with elections and pluralism. Syn.—Seeing the Light.

Character.

In U.S. political life, adherence to traditional moral norms in behavior, or discretion where departing from such norms. Character is entirely unrelated to honesty, independence, thoughtfulness, or adherence to decent public values.

China.

From 1949 to 1971, a non-existent country with a billion inhabitants; subsequently a fledgling member of the Free World *(q.v.)*.

Christ, Jesus.

An irresponsible rabble-rouser of communistic tendency;[37] victim of an early witch-hunt.

Chutzpah factor.

Self-righteousness, arrogance, and a sense of superiority so great that gross double standards seem entirely reasonable and no self-interested action is beyond rationalization. This factor is positively correlated with size, power, and per capita income.

Christianity.

The principal religion of the United States. In one version, "Thou shalt love they neighbor as thyself" (Matthew, xix, 19). In modern form: "Now I would like to see them [the other 94 percent of the world's population] enjoy the blessings that we enjoy. But don't you help them exchange places with us because I don't want to be where they are" (President Lyndon B. Johnson).

City.

A sinking ship, long abandoned by the rats as a place of habitation. The males of the species still sneak in each morning for pieces of cheese.

Civilian irregular defense-group volunteer.

Mercenary *(q.v .)* [38]

Civilian Police Review Board.

A device sponsored by opponents of Law and Order to humiliate the police and encourage the Coddling of criminals. (See Coddling and Law and Order.)

Civilian rule.

In common parlance, government in which the main political offices are occupied by civilians, with corresponding powers to make decisions; in Latin America, civilian occupancy of high office, but with nominal power only, serving as a cover for continued army rule, or constrained in major decision areas by military veto power. [39]

Class warfare.

Raising taxes on the rich. [40] (See *Soaking the poor.*)

Classified information.

Information potentially damaging to official violators of the law, placed out of the reach of prying citizens and investigators in the alleged interest of the *national* security.

Cluster bomb.

(See *Guava.*)

Coddling.

Reliance on due process of law; also, the subordination of police efficiency to individual rights; also, stressing rehabilitation rather than punishment of offenders.

Cointelpro.

A massive, fifteen year-long (1956-1971) FBI program of surveillance, disruption, harassment, and terrorism of legal organizations perceived as threatening by FBI and other officials. Methods used included forgery, planting of fabricated evidence, thefts, false accusations, intimidation, agent provocateur acts of terror, and aid to and protection of terrorists attacking targeted individuals and groups.[41]

Collateral casualties.

In nuclear chicken analysis, civilians killed as a regrettable "spillover effect" of a nuclear attack on a military target; more generally, allegedly unintended casualties.

Commandos.

Assassination squads organized by ourselves or our friends; similar teams employed by enemy states are called terrorists.[42]

Commercial broadcasting.

A system which gives over to private businesses the exclusive use of the public airwaves, free of user charge or contractual obligations to the public, to sell audiences to advertisers.

Commitment.

Among the multitude of promises made and obligations incurred in the past, the one consistent with the line of action now planned. Sometimes a purely hypothetical obligation, self-imposed to lend moral sanction to actions decided upon today; in this case it is referred to as a "solemn commitment."[43] Syn.—Preference.

Communism.

The totalitarianism of the countries outside the Free World. (See *Junta* and *Free World.*)

Compassion.

Regretting what must be done to the unfortunate in the interest of reestablishing and maintaining self-reliance and the work ethic, and in order to avoid paying the people's tax money on their "whims," "new goodies," and "to help them."[44]

Compassion Fatigue.

The exhaustion of a previouly undetectable supply of compassion. (*See Guilt Fatigue* and *Panhandler Threat Fatigue.*)

Concentration camps.

Their detention centers. (See *Strategic hamlet.*)

Consensus.

General agreement about an issue by important people. If only unimportant people agree on a subject (e.g., opposing the attacks on Nicaragua in the 1980s), this reflects a disorder demanding medication.[45] (See *Vietnam syndrome* and *Isolationism.*)

Conservation.

A gnat on the back of the rhinoceros of Progress *(q.v.).*

Conservatism.

An ideology whose central tenet is that the Government Is Too Big, except for the police and military establishment.

Conserve.

Set aside for tomorrow's barbecue.

Consolidate.

To stand pat; as in "President Bush seems bent on consolidating past gains rather than breaking new ground in domestic policy."

Conspiracy.

The application of freedom of speech and organization to a point threatening to be effective.

Conspiracy theory.

A critique or explanation that I find offensive.

Constituency.

Formerly, the people who voted for a candidate in his or her own district; now, those who pay for a candidate's electoral campaign.[46]

Containment.

The exclusion of lesser powers from areas in which we intend to establish hegemony.[47] Syn.—Expansion, Attack.[48]

Contract nourishment.

Inflating the cost of a government contract by over-pricing changes in contract specifications.[49] This permits a contractor who has "bought in" to "get well later."

Controversial.

A position contrary to that taken by the government or other established authority;[50] also, a person taking such a position. Syn.—Dubious, Extreme, or Extremist.

Corruption drain.

The diversion of monetary aid to a client state, and bribes, into the pockets of its Leaders *(q.v.).* In a "shakedown state" like Indonesia, the rate of drain may run to 30 percent of the gross.[51]

Cost growth.[52]

(See *Cost overrun.)*

Cost overrun.

In military lingo, an excess of actual over contractual costs in the purchase of weapon systems; a frequent occurrence as a result of Golden Handshakes between the buyer and seller, plus the fact that contracts, once signed, can be "nourished." (See *Contract Nourishment.)*

Cost-benefit analysis.

A methodology for understating the worth of social projects and overstating the value of private investment, by giving private producers' claims full value, society's less definite, hard-to-measure costs and benefits, accruing mainly in the future, little or no value.

Counterinsurgency.

Counterrevolutionary military intervention; the international terrorism of the great powers.[53]

Counter-productive.
Tactics, weapons, and policies which eliminate one enemy in such a manner as to induce two others to take his place.[54] (See *Napalm.*)

Counterterrorism.
Approved terrorism. Syn.—Retaliation.

Credibility.
The public's willingness to swallow official lies. Credibility declines with the exposure of these lies, but recovers by virtue of the public's short memory and patriotic will-to-believe, and the mainstream media's regular presumption that official claims are true.

Credibility gap.
The excess of the flow of official lies over the public's swallowing capacity. When the flow is increasing steadily, the gap can be kept within bounds only by enlarging the public's credibility. This is the function of Public Information and a Responsible Press.[55] (See *Press, Public information* and *Responsible.*)

Crime in the streets.
The threat of blacks to white person, property and status.

Crisis of democracy.
The emergence of the majority from a state of political apathy, along with their threatening attempts to understand, organize, and participate in their own governance. Syn.—Excess of Democracy.

Crop denial.
A Vietnam War program for the destruction of the food supplies of peasants being saved from aggression,[56] thereby denying the aggressors sustenance. Any detrimental effects on the peasants whose crops were destroyed was collateral, inadvertent, and unintended. (See *Operation Ranch Hand* and *Save.*)

Culture of poverty.
Separate and unequal enclaves of people who have done themselves in by allowing their poverty to become self-fulfilling through lack of Moral Fiber *(q.v.)*, thereby making themselves Undeserving Poor. (See *Undeserving poor, Hard core,* and *Benign neglect.*)

Deals.

Diplomatic efforts and substantive negotiations to settle an issue, after it has already been decided to rely on a policy of force; as in, "we have no intention of making any deals with Saddam Hussein."[57]

Death squads.

Private sector subcontractors supplying the state with off-the-record political murder. One of the growth industries in Latin America during the years of enlarged U.S. Public Safety, Military Assistance, and International Military Education and Training programs.

Debate.

Eloquent speeches about the principles of keeping barn doors closed, given some time after the horse has taken his leave; as in, "Congressman Tom Foley said that we have debated the issue of war and peace, but it is now time to unite behind the President."

Decapitation.

In military lingo, killing leaders; in nuclear chicken analysis, the removal by deliberate nuclear targeting of the many heads that comprise the command and control structure of an enemy country, leaving it without effective leadership or authority.

Defense.

(See *Self-defense.*)

Defense Department.

A huge, blind machine seeking "defensible frontiers." These are now understood to extend at least as far as Mars.

Defense expenditures.

Outlays which, no matter how large, speculative, or mismanaged, are rendered sacred by their nobility of purpose. Since there can never be too much National Security *(q.v.)*, cavilling at a few billions is obviously out of the question. Such cavilling is reserved for the Boondoggle *(q.v.)*.

Defense intellectual.

A mercenary with a graduate school degree.

Defensive.

Our move.[58]

Defiant.

Stubborn, unyielding, or uncompromising; applied to a leader of an enemy state. (See *Resolute.*)

Deficit.

An excess of government expenditures over receipts, horrifying when liberal Democrats are in power, but only slightly troubling under right-wing Republican rule. Along with the urgency of Defense Expenditures *(q.v.)*, it provides the rationale for curbing outlays that serve the Special Interests *(q.v.)*.

Demagogue.

A foreign political or military figure who refuses to play ball with us. (See *Leader.*)

Democracy.

A system that allows the people to vote for their leaders from among a set cleared by the political investment community. In application to the Third World, it means rule by an elite that understands our interests and needs.[59]

Democracy, excess of.

A situation in which the forms of government by the people actually threaten to be infused with participatory substance. Syn.—Crisis of Democracy.

Democratic loyal opposition.

A domestic breed of rabbit, always hungry for green lettuce, that flees in terror when anyone shouts "Commie dupe!" (See *Loyal opposition.*)

Democratic resistance.

A guerrilla or mercenary force attacking a government that we oppose. As in the model case of Nicaragua in the 1980s, the force may be neither democratic nor a resistance, but a terrorist force organized to attack "soft targets"; nevertheless, it remains a Democratic Resistance, by rule of sponsorship.

Democrats.

(See *Democratic loyal opposition.*)

Demographics.

The age, sex, and income distribution of audiences, whose measurement provides a proper valuation of advertisements, hence of TV programs.[60]

Demonstration election.

(See *Election, Demonstration.*)

Desert Shield.

(See *Operation Desert Shield.*)

Desert Storm.

(See *Operation Desert Storm*).

Deserving poor.

A very tiny class. (See *Undeserving poor*).

Detente.

An agreement, as understood by us, that the enemy will withdraw behind his borders, leaving us free to bring stability everywhere on the globe, in exchange for our being nicer to him.[61] (See *Stability.*)

Deterrent.

Our attack capability. (See *Threat.*)

Development.

Putting to profitable use; exploitation.

Diplomacy.

Restating to the enemy the terms of our ultimatum. Syn.—Negotiations. (See *Negotiations.*)

Disposal problems.

The difficulty in getting rid of or silencing national security "assets" trained in assassination, bombing, torture, and committing general mayhem, following aborted or failed operations (e. g. , Cuban assets following the Bay of Pigs fiasco).[62] If they had been successful, the top-level assets would have become Leaders of some lucky state, as with Castillo-Armas in Guatemala in 1954. (See *Castillo-Armas* and *Leader.*)

Dissent.

The inalienable constitutional right of every American citizen to stab our boys in the back.[63]

Dissenter.

The sinister and aggressive modern Storm-Trooper,[64] fully armed with flower and picket sign.

Document retention strategies.

Strategies for the destruction of documents that might embarrass or incriminate government officials or their agents.[65] (See also, *Classified information.*)

Dole.

A government handout to insubstantial citizens; detrimental to efficiency. (See *Incentives* and *Subsidy.*)

Dominoes.
Countries which topple when they blow, but remain standing when we shove.

Double standard.
Criticizing our policy of Restraint *(q.v.)* without at the same time deploring their policy of Terrorism and Violence. (See *Terrorism* and *Violence.)*

Dove.
One who supports our aims in trying to democratize (e.g., Nicaragua 1981-90 or Guatemala 1950-54), but would prefer using only moderately illegal means;[66] also, one who favors the last escalation but is opposed to the next.[67]

Downwinder.
A person living in the path of winds blowing radioactive materials from a nearby nuclear generating, processing, or testing facility.[68]

Draft.
A system of forcible recruitment of military labor, which compels the underprivileged to serve their country at less than market wage rates. This offsets in some degree the overpayments to military suppliers of equipment and other services, thus permitting some rough justice to prevail overall. Sometimes referred to as Selective Service.

Drug runners.
Small-fry traffickers in substances deemed unhealthful in U.S. law and politics, not to be confused with domestic and international dealers in tobacco, alcohol, asbestos, pesticides, and other unhealthful substances produced by large companies with large ad budgets and PACs.

Dumbing down.
Removing intellectual substance from textbooks in order to placate the forces of Morality.

Eagle.
A savage and powerful bird of prey; selected as the official emblem of the United States in 1782.

Eco-extremists.
Those actively opposing development in the instant case. Syn.—Eco-freaks; Environmentalists.

Economic Recovery Act of 1981.
The Deficit-Maker, or Fat Cat Enhancement Act of 1981.

Education.
Our instructions on the merits of free enterprise and the horrors of communism. (See *Indoctrination.*)

Effete intellectual snob.
A book-reading know-it-all of doubtful sexual prowess who questions the truth revealed by our leader.[69] (See *Irresponsible* and *Vocal Minority.*)

Efficiency.
Anticipated cost reductions that explain and justify an acquisition of a company, and then, later, its divestment and sale. (See *Synergy* and *Value.*)

Eichmann, Adolph.
A notorious functionary, hanged for loyally carrying out the orders of those wielding power in his country.[70]

Election.
In the United States, a periodic opportunity for the public to choose among candidates cleared by the political investment community.

Election, Demonstration.
A circus held in a client state to assure the population of the home country that their intrusion is well-received. The results are guaranteed by an adequate supply of bullets provided in advance.

Fair Election

Election, Fair.

One in which, having stacked the deck conclusively in advance, we do not cheat in counting up our exact winnings. As in, "Within the limitations created by the exclusion from the ballot of certain popular candidates and the abuses that marked the earlier stages of the campaign [South Vietnam, 1967], most observers believe that on the whole the voting was fairly conducted" (*New York Times* Editorial, Sept. 4, 1967). Also, one in which our carefully selected observers see no one beaten up as they are escorted in limousines past carefully selected voting booths.

Election, Free.

A post-pacification election, in which the "hearts and minds" of the survivors are shown to have been won over by the force of pure reason.

Empowerment.

Formerly, giving people greater authority and resources; now, allowing people to deal with a problem previously dealt with by the government, without the burden of any federal assistance.[71] (See also, *Revenue sharing.*)

End of ideology.

The beginning of total adaptation to the existing power structure. (See *Expert.*)

Enemy.

A deluded foreign population that refuses to be Independent *(q.v.).*[72]

Enemy structure.

A thatched hut that we destroy.[73] (See *Vietcong.*)

Entitlements.

Claims to government aid by the Special Interests. (See *Special interests* and *Subsidy.*)

Environmental president.

One deeply concerned with the environment as a Vision Thing *(q.v.)* and insofar as it does not encroach on the budget or interfere with Development *(q.v.)*.

Environmental terrorists.

Extremists who hamper the efforts of loggers, miners, developers, and others trying to harvest the fruits of the commons.

Escalation.

Covering up mistakes by increasing their size and number. With a sufficient investment in mistakes, their correction involves undue loss of Face *(q.v.)*. We are then stuck on the Escalator *(q.v.)*.

Escalator.

A moving stairway leading to Kingdom Come.

Expert.

A technician paid to tell his employer what his employer wants to hear.[74] The Expert is sometimes permitted to offer Responsible Criticism. (See *Preferential method* and *Responsible.*)

Extremist.

An advocate of change sufficient to have an effect. Also, someone taking a position significantly different from my own; as in, "I deplore the actions of extremists on both sides—those who blow up schools and those who want to keep them open." (Eisenhower-Pfeiffer)

Face.

Something that we must save but the enemy must be prepared to lose. Sometimes the face to be saved is that of a leader, who would otherwise be obliged to admit having made serious errors of judgment. In this case, a diligent effort is made to transmute the face of the leader into that of the nation.[75] (See *Commitment.*)

Fair election.
> (See *Election, Fair.)*

Fair trade.
> Trade in which my own country's advantages are deemed natural, but those of other countries must be rectified by threats and unilateral retaliation. (See *Unfair trade.)*

Faith.
> My deeply held belief. (See *Fanaticism.)*

Fanaticism.
> His deeply held belief. (See *Faith.)*

Farsighted.
> Recognizing the political payoff, and possibility of bailout from domestic failures, in engineering a nice, winnable little war.[76]

Fat.
> The chronic condition of excessive resources of agencies and budgets concerned with health, education and welfare. (See *Lean.)*

Federal Communications Commission (FCC).
> A government agency regulating broadcasting, nominally responsible for protecting the public interest; in reality, serving to create the illusion of government protection, while managing the steady encroachment of advertising and erosion of public interest programming.[77] (See *Commercial broadcasting* and *Public broadcasting.)*

Feminism.

Another 'ism' (like anarchism, communism, etc.); a source of Politi-cally Correct ideas offensive to believers in the Really Correct; a destroyer of the male hegemonic *status quo* at home and work. (See *Politically correct* and *Really correct.*)

Feminist.

An aggressive, uppity member of the weaker sex, compensating for personal inadequacies by disturbing the peace.

Firepower.

The first and last recourse of U.S. diplomacy.[78] (See *Acheson, Dean,* and *Negotiations.*)

Fledgling democracy.

A regime which has our imprimatur and goes through the motions of a democratic electoral process; democratic *substance* is not relevant to the designation.

Flexibility.

My own compromises with principle, made reluctantly in recognition of the demands of political survival. (See *Opportunism.*)

Flexible freeze.

A Bush era budgetary concept according to which social expenditures are frozen in nominal terms (and therefore decline in real value with inflation), while military outlays are allowed an inflation premium, which preserves their real value.

Follow-on.

A militarily pointless successor to an existing weapons system, nec-essary to maintain the level of jobs and keep weapons suppliers in business, to provide a Bargaining Chip *(q.v.),* and to preserve the balance of power between the military services. (See also, *Modernization.*)

Force.

The principal language of the stronger; by a process of transference, said to be the only language *they* understand. (See *Firepower.*)

Forced integration.

Integration.[79]

Foreign aid.

Welfare payments made to Third World leaders to help them bail out their sinking economies, fund the level of repression needed for their survival, and to arrange for their possible retirements on the Riviera. (See *Leader.*)

Founding Fathers.

The moral equivalents of the Nicaraguan contras (Ronald Reagan).

Free.

Non-communist. Syn.—Good.

Free Enterprise.

The use of privately or publicly-owned property for private profit.[80]

Free fire zone.

An area in which, by military proclamation, "there are no friendly forces or populace and in which targets may be attacked on the initiative of U.S./Free World commanders."[81] By definition any individual incinerated or shot in such territory is a Vietcong (*q.v.*). American policy during the Indochina wars may be summed up as: the gradual transformation of larger and larger parts of that region into free fire zones.

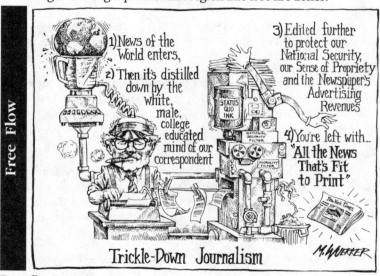

Trickle-Down Journalism

Free flow.

A condition in which media and other communications messages are privately owned and controlled; also, the right of the powerful in the communications industries to pursue their material interests without constraint. Free flow is not impeded by media monopoly, large-scale government propaganda operations, or systematic reductions in government disclosure of information. (See *Government control.*)

Free World.

The group of countries that maintain a door open to private foreign investment.[82]

Freedom.

(See *Free* and *Free World*.)

Freedom, Abuse of.

The use of Freedom. (See *Dissent*.)

Freedom fighter.

Fighter against freedom; mercenary. Also, an airplane (F-4, Phantom jet) built by the United States for its own use and for that of Free World forces in South Vietnam, South Korea, Taiwan, Brazil, etc.

Freedom House.

A small fabricator of credibility; a wholly-owned subsidiary of the White House.

Führer principle.

That our leader, undoubtedly in possession of secret information unavailable to the rest of us, knows best the true National Interest, and should be followed loyally and unreservedly by all patriotic citizens. (See *National interest* and *Responsible*.)

Further studies.

A way to avoid action and expenditures. The major Reagan-Bush program for dealing with the threat of acid rain and the greenhouse effect.

Gap.

A frightening but mythical deficiency relative to some foreign power in a weapons system—dreadnought, bomber, missile, anti-missile-missile, megatonage, etc. Although sometimes attributed to faulty intelligence, gaps are more often a result of manipulated intelligence. They play an important role in generating business for the Military-Industrial Complex. Gaps regularly disappear shortly after the contracts to fill them are signed.[83] (See *Military-industrial complex* and *National security*.)

Genocide.

The end product of arrogance, dehumanization, and superior force. (See *Gook.*)

Getting the message.

Accepting our terms in view of our ability and willingness to kill mere gooks (or mere Arabs) without limit. (See *Mere gook rule.*)

Ghetto.

An urban preserve maintained for the lower forms of human life. In some countries the ghetto is officially organized; in the United States it is a product of free choice.

Global Protection Against Limited Strikes (GPALS).

A scaled-back version of Star Wars, whose primary mission is to protect that program from major budget strikes. It combines space and ground missile defense plans, the former comprising a thousand Brilliant Pebbles *(q.v.).* It shares with Star Wars "the old program's bias toward space weapons, its collision course with the Anti-Ballistic Missile (ABM) treaty, and its strategic incoherence."[84] (See *Star Wars.*)

Goals.

Nominal objectives fabricated on a day-to-day basis to meet a changing market demand.

God.

Another one of our founding fathers.[85]

God that failed.

Communism; also, social reform.

God that succeeded.

Mammon; also, the market.

God's Will.

My preferred course of action, or that of my country's leaders.

Golden parachute.

Large severance payments fixed by managements to induce themselves not to forget that they are working in the stockholders' interest, in the event of a merger offer that threatens to end their power and prerogatives.

Goldwater's Law.

That poverty increases in proportion to expenditures made to alleviate it. This law is revived by politicians and the Experts during each period in which the dominant elite is eager to scale back the social wage.[86]

Gook.

A small, stubborn, yellow aborigine of Southeast Asia; lacking modern technology this inferior breed was slaughtered mercilessly,[87] but escaped extinction because the U.S. public was impatient and got tired of killing without chalking up a win.

Government control.

Government interference that conflicts with the interests of private media corporations, including limits on advertising and protection of national media independence and sovereignty. It does *not* include government aid to private media firms, or governmental programs of disinformation and aggressive media management, or government cutbacks on information, secrecy and cover-ups, which are all compatible with Free Flow *(q.v.)*.

Graham, Billy.

Salesman, public relations manager, and trustee for Jesus and Billy Graham Enterprises, Inc.

Grantsman.

Government troughsman.

Grantsmanship.

The art of earnestly desiring to do what the available money wants done. (See *Expert.*)

Great Man.

A man of large impact on the world, usually measured by the number of corpses left in his wake.[88]

Great Power.

A state with a large Gross National Product and arms establishment, which is thus able to maintain a large retinue of clients. For each Great Power, the clients are referred to as Independent States, freely entering into an alliance with the Great Power. (See *Independent.*)

Growth.

The philosopher's stone of modern economics; unfortunately it neglects both garbage and the second law of thermodynamics.[89]

Guilt fatigue.

Exhaustion at having to walk past hungry and sick people needing help that one is not prepared to give. Their "God bless you's" as one walks past add insult to injury. (See *Compassion fatigue* and *Panhandler threat fatigue*.)

Guava.

A pineapple dropped in great numbers on villages throughout Indochina during the Vietnam War;[90] part of the imperial American program of Food for Freedom. Syn.—Area Denial Bomb, Cluster Bomb.

Hard-boiled.

Possessing great fortitude in bearing with the sufferings of others. Syn.—Tough. (See *Bleeding heart* and *Tough.*)

Hard core.

Not readily amenable to social management; untouchable.

Historical lies.

Lies, partial lies, or truths that conflict with well-established official lies; as in, "The rancor over *JFK* arises from the realization that historical lies are nearly impossible to correct once movies and television have given them credibility" (Brent Staples).

Homelessness.

The free choice and preference of millions of citizens in the Reagan-Bush era, demonstrating a renewed U.S. devotion to the great outdoors (see Mark Twain, *Roughing It*).

Honoraria.

Cash payments to politicians for their kindness in making a brief appearance at a gathering of a group with an axe to grind.

Hoover's Law.

That the Communist Menace varies inversely with the number of communists, the threat approaching infinity as the number approaches zero. It was to counter this threat that the FBI subsidized the *Daily Worker* and caused FBI personnel to account for an ever-increasing fraction of CP members.[91]

Hope.

The "soft money" of political visionaries. The hard money is jobs, contracts, subsidies and tax benefits.

Horton, Willie.

George Bush's opponent in the presidential election of 1988. (See *Quotas.*)

Hostages.

Prisoners taken by our enemies. (See *Prisoners.*)

Hostile forum.

An international institution or agency that decides against us.[92] The very same institution or agency becomes a respected international authority when it rules in our favor.

Humanitarian aid.

In international law, assistance designed strictly for alleviating human suffering and provided without discrimination among the civilians in an area of conflict; in U.S. practice in Nicaragua, any non-military aid given exclusively to the mainly military personnel on the side we favor.[93]

Hypocrisy.

A bridge of rhetoric that spans the gap between ideals and actions.[94]

Idealistic.

With scruple. (See *Pragmatic.*)

Ideologue.

One who adheres to principle without regard to political cost; also, someone who disputes my action on the basis of principle.

Ideology.

(See *End of ideology.*)

Imperialism.

Direct or indirect subjugation of other states, resulting from a search for defensible frontiers and a desire to preserve the Freedom and Independence of the states being subjugated.[95] (See *Free* and *Independent.*)

Voo-Doo Economics 101
The "Invisible Hand" wields the "Carrot and Stick"...

The Rich need the incentive of more "Carrots" to stimulate the economy...

While the poor need the "Stick" of reduced benefits and the threat of homelessness to overcome their laziness and keep their noses to the grindstone.

Incentives

Incentives.

Energy releasing devices which call for Golden Parachutes and a large stake in ownership for managers, low taxes for investors, and the threat of unemployment for workers.

Incidents.

Nuclear accidents releasing fissionable materials into the environment. Syn.—Events, Transient Events, Reactor Excursions.

Incursion.

An invasion of another country by us or one of our allies or clients, provoked and for just cause. (See *Aggression.*)

Independent.

Allied with us. (See *Puppets* and *Satellite.*)

Individualism.

A belief in the value and sanctity of each member of my in-group. In the limiting case, the in-group consists of me.

Indoctrination.

Their propaganda on the merits of planning and horrors of capitalism. (See *Education.*)

Industrial policy.

In the United States, supporting the Military-industrial complex.

Inequality.

The I-word. Ordinarily not discussed because inequality is part of the Natural Order *(q.v.)*. Its naturalness and beneficence are very much on the minds of owners of, and advertisers in, the mass media, along with PAC-managers and other funders of elections.

Infiltration.

Their movement of troops into contested fighting areas.[96] (See *Assistance* and *Reinforcements.)*

Infotainment.

Entertainers exploring the seamy side of personalities.

Instability.

(See *Unstable.)*

Intellectual.

Possessor of a graduate school degree; formerly, holder of a college degree.

Intensive management.

In Forest Service lingo, increasing the Allowable Cut *(q.v.).*

Internal aggression.

(See *Aggression, Internal.)*

Internationalism.

Support for our imperial ventures. (See *Isolationism.)*

Interrogation.

Torture.[97]

Intervention.

Their unilateral intrusion into the affairs of other countries.[98] (See *Assistance, Save,* and *Subversion.)*

Inventory shrinkage.

Theft.

Iran-contra hearings.

A congressional inquiry into the crimes of patriots, conducted by friends of the patriots and the Democratic Loyal Opposition *(q.v.).*

Iraqis, killed by Saddam Hussein.

A large set of slaughtered people, attended to with zeal and indignation by a patriotic media, well-schooled in identifying worthy victims.

Iraqis, killed by us.

A non-existent set, disappeared by rule of patriotic media self-censorship.

Irresponsible.

Concerned with the substance rather than the form; also, questioning the motives and honesty of those wielding power.[59] (See *Responsible.*)

Isolationism.

Internal opposition to a country's unprovoked assault on another country. Syn.—Neo-Isolationism. (See *Internationalism.*)

Jobs.

The basis and justification for any enormity.[100]

Judeo-christian ethic.

A creed for all seasons; or, anything goes.

Junta.

During the 1950s through 1970s, the principal form of government of the Free World. Because of desperate economic conditions in the 1980s, many juntas retired temporarily to the barracks in favor of Civilian Rule *(q.v.)*. They remain available for service in case of renewed Subversion *(q.v.)*.[101]

Kahn, Herman.

Leading intellectual of the crackpot realist school;[102] author of its classic text, *Gamesmanship and Annihilation: Toward a Theory of Rational Genocide.*

Kill.

What the enemy does in military operations and terrorist activity. (See *Neutralize* and *Termination with extreme prejudice.*)

Ky, Marshal Nguyen Cao.

A North Vietnamese playboy and former collaborator under the French colonial regime;[103] the only head of state following World War II to proclaim Adolf Hitler as his hero.[104] Specially selected by the United States to represent the Free World in South Vietnam, Marshal Ky had great support in that country; unfortunately, none of it was indigenous.[105]

Land reform.

Generally, redistributing the land of inactive and absentee landlords to those working the soil; in South Vietnam, taking land formerly redistributed to the peasantry and giving it back to the landlords.[106]

Law.

The form. (See *Law enforcement.*)

Law enforcement.

The reality.[107] (See *Law.*)

Law and Order.

Order. Also, internal pacification.

Leader.

A foreign political or military figure, not necessarily popular with his own people, who guides his country into alignment with us.[108] (See *Demagogue.*)

Lean.

The chronic state of our preparations for Armageddon. (See *Defense expenditures* and *Fat.)*

Legislation.

The golden handshake at the end of the political rainbow.[109]

Lesson.

Don't cross us.

Leverage.

That which we seek in aiding amenable tyrants, but which we find unaccountably without effect on their actual behavior.[110]

Leveraged buyouts (LBOs).

Internal raids on companies by their own managers, with the help of bankers and institutional investors.

Liberal.

A responsible critic and reformer. (See *Responsible.)*

Limited accidental damage.

Total destruction of a target theoretically off-limits; as in, "Pentagon spokesmen said the Bach Mai hospital and Gia Lau airport apparently suffered 'some limited accidental damage' during the intensive U.S. bombing."

Limousine liberal set.

Traitors to the limousine owning class.[111]

Linkage.

Trade-offs and bargaining exchanges essential to diplomacy and highly regarded when extracting concessions from enemy states, but treated as immoral when suggested for use in dealing with allies and client states.[112]

Little brown brothers.

A native people about to be attacked, slaughtered, and civilized.

Load-shedding.

Cutting back the budgetary claims of the Special Interests *(q.v.)*, thereby releasing resources to serve the National Interest *(q.v.)*.

O.K. **BUB!** YOU GOT AWAY WITH THAT IRAN/CONTRA SCAM, BUT REMEMBER WHO YOU'RE **MESSING** WITH!!...

AND WE'LL LET THAT SEXUAL HARASSMENT GO (IT IS ONLY THE SUPREME COURT)... BUT DON'T **PUSH ME!**

O.K., GATES CAN SLIDE BY TOO - WOULDN'T WANT TO MAKE A STINK OVER ARMS FOR HOSTAGES, DRUG MONEY, B.C.C.I., ET ALL, NOW WOULD WE?

BUT *HEY* REMEMBER IT'S A **TWO PARTY** SYSTEM - CHECKS AND BALANCES, RIGHT? *ISN'T IT?*

M. WUERKER

Loyal Opposition

Loyal opposition.

In recent U.S. political history, a second party that is more "loyal" than "opposition," thereby establishing a two-sectored party of property. (See *Bipartisanship* and *Democratic loyal opposition.*)

Loyalist.

Siding with the oligarchy, police, and us.

Loyalty.

The subordination of morality to the demands of the organization.

Lucrative targets.

Large concentrations of enemy soldiers, supplies, or habitations, making the payoff from a bombing raid a rich one.[113]

Lynch mob.

Critics of malfeasance by the powerful, as in "This is a kind of lynch mob atmosphere" (Ronald Reagan, referring to press commentary on Attorney-General Edwin Meese's financial dealings with the Wedtech Corporation and an Iraqi pipeline project).[114]

MAD.
 Mutual Assured Destruction; a nuclear strategy whose acronym tells all.

Magic bullet.
 One that wends its way through several bodies, smashing bones on the way, but ends up in pristine condition, conveniently located for police attribution to the gun of choice.

March, patriotic.
 An expression of faith in one's leaders and solidarity with the forces of Law and Order *(q.v.).*

March, protest.
 An incitement to riot.

Market.
 A western totem, according to which life is best and perhaps exclusively organized around the private search for gain.

Market intelligence.
 Inside information on government contract terms and negotiations; a valuable asset for which there is a strong market demand and supply, greatly enlarged and realized during market-friendly administrations.[115] (See *Operation Ill-Wind.*)

Marxist-Leninist.
 Designation of a government about to be destabilized, "Marxist" indicating its dogmatic left tendency, "Leninist" pointing to a Moscow link. The designation has no necessary connection to the actual beliefs or linkages of the government in question, but is conjured up for symbolic value, to justify making it a target of attack.[116]

Mercenarization.
 The process of pacifying and controlling a foreign population by means of a sufficiently large investment in the purchase and supply of a mercenary army. This is often described as "getting the [Asians, Vietnamese, Guatemalans, etc.] to fight their own battles."

Mercenary.
 A soldier fighting for pay. Mercenaries may be external or internal,[117] and they may be contracted for on an individual basis[118] or as a group by a broker (who collects a commission).[119]

Mere gook rule.

That deaths and injuries to lesser breeds who stand in our way may be ignored in law and policy-making; technically, the marginal cost of a dead gook (Arab, etc.) is zero. The rule is based on the fact that gooks do not value life and feel pain like we do; besides which, they stand in our way.

Micro-management.

Legislative interference with presidential authority, as in "The irrational conduct of Iraq has convinced me that this is not the time to begin to micro-manage the SDI programs" (Senator Alphonse D'Amato, "explaining his flipflop on an SDI amendment").[120]

Military contracting.

A system of government buying and private selling of weapons through a Revolving Door in which gains are private, losses are nationalized. (See *Revolving door.*)

MILITARY CODEPENDENCY · COMPLEX

I KNOW, I KNOW... HE'S ROUGH ON MY ECONOMIC COMPETITIVENESS, ABUSIVE OF MY ENVIRONMENT... AND THIS NATIONAL SECURITY THING IS A JOKE, BUT I CAN'T IMAGINE LIFE WITHOUT HIM

Military-Industrial Complex

Military-industrial complex.

The Pentagon and its Hundred Neediest Cases.

Military Keynesianism.

Using military spending as the fiscal underpinning of economic stability. This benefits the Military-industrial complex, and avoids the damaging effects of increased social outlays on the National Interest *(q.v.).*

Military pressure.

An instrument serviceable for pushing the Sandinistas toward democracy and the Vietnamese toward compromise on Cambodia, but entirely perverse in effect if employed on South Africa or Israel,[121] and "the ultimate arrogance of power" if used to influence the Greek police state in the late 1960s.[122]

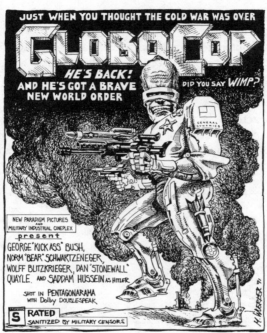

Military solution.

Our last resort, after we have exhausted Diplomacy *(q.v.)*, Negotiations *(q.v.)* and a Search for Peace *(q.v.)*. (See also, *Force.*)

Missing person gratuity.

A pay-off to a vocal relative of the victim of an official U.S. murder.[123]

Moderate.

In domestic politics, a spokesperson and representative of the National Interest *(q.v.)*, or of the consensus—of sponsors of PACs *(q.v.)*. In reference to the Third World, a Leader *(q.v.)*.

Modernization.

The replacement of old but still serviceable weapons systems with new ones, the obsolescence of the former following from the availability of the latter, and the need to keep production lines rolling.[124]

Money.

Something that does the job for the National Defense, but which is "not the answer" to educational and social problems; money is quietly appropriated for the former, it is futilely "thrown at" the latter.

Morality.

Adherence to conventional standards of dress, hair style, comportment; respect for hard work, money, the flag, and established institutions; and hostility to protest based on the stubborn pursuit of ethical values.

Moral fiber.

A willingness to get screwed continuously without impairment of work efficiency.

Multiversity.

A brainpower refinery and service station.

Mutual respect.

A phrase employed by politicians to convey the impression of tolerance and compromise, frequently placed in the same speeches which refer to Bums, Rotten Apples, and the overriding need for Law and Order *(q.v.)*.[125]

My fellow Americans.

The opening words of a political speech, meaning, "Ignorant children, for whom my contempt is about to be shown by a stream of contradictory banalities."

Naked aggression.

(See *Aggression, Naked.*)

Napalm.

A murderous fire bomb which, when dropped on villages, has the remarkable property of creating two enemies where one existed before.[126]

Nation-building.

Nation-busting.[127] (See *Save.*)

National Endowment for Democracy (NED).

A U.S. government sponsored and funded international PAC, designed to turn the politicians of the entire globe into PAC-men.[128] (See *PAC, Pac-men, Democratic loyal opposition.*)

National interest.

The demands and needs of the corporate community.

National security.

Perceived interests abroad, large or small.[129] A National Security "threat" is subject to Hoover's Law *(q.v.)* : the smaller the apparent threat the greater the real one.

Nationalism.

Kickapoo war juice. Large quantities are essential to provide the stamina needed for protracted conflict. (See *Stamina.)*

Natural order.

A privately-owned market system, as spelled out by Adam Smith in *The Wealth of Nations*(1776) and reaffirmed by Milton Friedman, George Gilder, and Michael Novak in the late twentieth century.

Natural rate of unemployment.

The rate of unemployment preferred by the propertied classes. As inflation is their bugaboo, not unemployment, the "natural" rate of unemployment is the level consistent with no inflation. Although historically there has been considerable inflation, in the new economics of the rich the "natural" rate of inflation is zero.

Need.

A good or service offered for sale, as advertised on national television.

Negotiations.

The process of accepting the surrender of the ill-gotten gains of the enemy.[130] Negotiations in its archaic meaning referred to the process of arriving at a settlement by mutual concessions. This is now recognized to be appeasement. Syn.—Victory.

Neo-isolationist.

One opposed to my policy of Responsibly Winding Down and Withdrawal without Bugging Out or Failing to Honor Our Commitments thus assuring that this will be the Last War. (See *Commitment.)*

Neutralize.

Kill *(q.v.).*

New federalism.

Giving state and local governments the responsibility for allocating reduced sums for weak clients. Syn.—Empowerment, Returning Power to the People. (See *Empowerment* and *Revenue sharing.)*

New World Order Exam

1.) As a matter of Principle, the U.S. will go to war to defend the lives and rights of which of the following?

a.) Kuwaitis

b.) Kurds

2.) What's so new about the New World Order?

New World Order.

The Old World Order stripped of any major obstructions to our helping our Little Brown Brothers *(q.v.)* enter the Free World *(q.v.)* and become Independent. (See *Independent.*)

News anchors.

Cheer leaders for the national establishment.

Nixon Doctrine.

Reducing our acknowledged commitments and manpower inputs in neo-colonial wars, while stabilizing or enlarging our real obligations, capital outlays, and wars by proxy.

Nuclear chicken.

Roulette played on a global scale with megatons and mega-deaths. Nuclear chicken games and strategic thinking are useful in getting us adjusted to the unthinkable. (See *Thinking the unthinkable.*)

Nuclear power plants.

White elephants built on the ground. (See *Star Wars*)

Obscenity.
Sex without a Moral Lesson.

Off.
Kill.

Off-loading.
Transferring a covert and illegal program of state terrorism to deeper cover and under the nominal authority of quasi-private operatives.[131]

Offensive.
Their move.[132] (See *Defensive.*)

Operation Budget Shield.
A "demonstration war," providing a controlled display of weapons, a solid win against a small victim, and a lot of exhilarating fun and games, serving to rally support for a threatened military budget.

Operation Chaos.
An illegal CIA project for monitoring domestic dissident groups during the 1960s, carried out under the pretext that foreign influence was being exerted on legal protest groups.[133] (See *Cointelpro.*)

Operation Clean-Up.
A Somoza campaign to quell a Nicaraguan insurrection in 1978, in which it was "a crime to be a male between the ages of 12 and 30."[134]

Operation Condor.
A collective program involving six National Security States of Latin America, begun in 1976, sponsored by the United States and managed by Chile, designed to monitor and murder political refugees from other states. Hundreds were tortured and killed under this cooperative venture in state terrorism.[135]

Operation Desert Shield.
The label for the first phase of the U.S. attack on Iraq, designed to convey the false impression that the U.S. move of forces into the area was for defensive purposes only.

Operation Desert Storm.
The label for the open war against Iraq, designed to suggest that impersonal forces rather than human agencies were leveling that Third World country.

Operation Ill-Wind.

Code name for a Reagan era investigation of military contractor purchases of inside information on military contracts from consultants, many former Pentagon officials. The sky-rocketing of such abuses was rooted in an enormous growth in contract volume, a sharp increase in conflict-of-interest appointments, and an "emasculated civil service."[136] Other proposed code names: Operation Built-In; Operation We Asked For It; Operation Inevitable.

Operation Just Cause.

In general, a U.S. external action designed to remove an undeserving person or government who is out of step with our needs and objectives; specifically, the code name applied to the U.S. invasion of Panama in December 1989.

Operation Mongoose.

A major terrorist program carried out against Cuba under the Kennedy Administration in 1962-1963, which included numerous sabotage raids, contamination of food supplies, bombings, boycotts by intimidation, and assassination attempts against Fidel Castro.[137] Part of a larger on-and-off effort that was one of the two largest state-sponsored programs of international terrorism in the Western Hemisphere over the past 40 years (the other was the Reagan-Bush attacks on Nicaragua during the 1980s).

Operation Paper Clip.

A covert program under which hundreds of Nazis that could serve U.S. scientific and intelligence programs were illegally brought to the United States and protected from prosecution for war crimes.[138]

Operation Phoenix.

A major U.S. program for the murder of civilians possibly linked to or supporting the enemy in Vietnam, 1967-1971. Headed by William Colby, it resulted in the deaths of between 25-40,000 people.[139] Colby was subsequently elevated to head the CIA.

Operation Provide Comfort II.

The name given a strike force of "allied" soldiers in Turkey ready to enter Iraq if Saddam Hussein attacked the Kurds. This program existed at the same time as the one starving the Iraqi population as a means of weakening Saddam Hussein, the latter without any known code name, but perhaps the missing Operation Provide Comfort I.[140]

Operation Ranch Hand.

A program for the spraying of dioxin-based chemicals on the crops of South Vietnamese peasants being saved from aggression, in order to deny food to any aggressors in the neighborhood. (See *Crop denial* and *Save.*)

Operation Rat-Killer.

A U.S. military campaign of 1951-1952, designed to wipe out North Korean guerrillas;[141] the terminology reveals an early version of the Mere Gook Rule *(q.v.)*.

ANOTHER DAY OF BLISTERING INTERROGATION ON THE HILL

Operation Truth.

The code name for "a huge psychological operation of the kind the military conducts to influence a population in denied or enemy territory," but carried out by the State Department to convince U.S. voters that the contras were Freedom Fighters and Nicaragua a totalitarian dungeon.

Opportunism.

My opponent's repudiation of principle in the interest of political advancement. (See *Flexibility.*)

Orwell, George.

A British optimist.

Over-kill.

The investment in nuclear weapons and delivery systems in excess of that necessary to kill all of our enemies once only. The principal surplus of the United States, evolved from the New Deal concept of an Ever-Normal Granary.

Overmature trees.

In timber company and Forest Service lingo, trees which may live in splendor for another 500 years, but which would make damned fine boards today.

Overzealous.

Engaging in illegal acts on my behalf; as in, "overzealous people in campaigns can do things that are wrong" (Nixon on Watergate, Press Conference of Aug. 29, 1972).

PACs.

Political Action Committees. The guiding light in U.S. politics, revealing to politicians what the important people with effective demand want in the way of political services.

PAC-men.

Politicians highly sensitized to the call of the PACs and the demands of the National Interest *(q.v.).*[142]

Pacification.

Returning a restive population to its traditional state of apathy by killing on the requisite scale; subjugation.[143]

Panhandler threat fatigue.

Exhaustion at coercive requests for money from down-and-outers, who provide a convenient basis for overcoming Guilt Fatigue *(q.v.).*

Parties.

Businesses serving investors in Legislation *(q.v.).*[144]

Party system.

An arrangement in which two or more parties compete to convince the vested interests that they are more likely to fool the public this time.

Patriotism.

Judging disputes on the basis of place of residence.

Paveway III.

A laser-guided bomb, clean, smart, and cozy, sent by the forces of freedom to hone in on bunkers while carefully avoiding shelters. (See *Bunker, Shelter,* and *Scud.*)

Peace.

In the years 1945-1975, a communist slogan designed to induce us to Lower Our Guard; subsequently, what the U.S. government strives for in all its foreign dealings and ventures, along with Stability *(q.v.)*. (See also, *Peace process.)*

Peace dividend.

A threatened diversion of resources from the military budget to civilian use, terminated with extreme prejudice by means of Operation Budget Shield *(q.v.)*.

Peace-making.

Job destroying.

Peace process.

Whatever the U.S. government happens to be doing or supporting in an area of conflict at the moment. It need not result in a termination of conflict or ongoing pacification operations in the short or long term.

Peace with honor.

Victory *(q.v.)*.

Peaceful change.

Repression punctuated by Free Elections *(q.v.)*; as in "It is true El Salvador's path has been a hard one. Peaceful change has not always been easy or quick" (Reagan, speech to the longshoremen, July 18, 1983).

Peacekeeper missile.

A new nuclear missile developed by us, which will contribute to peace because it adds to our strength and we are peacekeepers.

Peaceniks.

Extremists who demonstrate in the streets, stand in front of tanks, and practice other forms of civil disobedience that disrupt our military celebrations. (See *People power.*)

People power.

The forces of democracy in other countries who demonstrate in the streets, stand in front of tanks, and practice other forms of civil disobedience that disrupt their military celebrations. (See *Peaceniks.*)

Perfectly clear.

Somewhat murkier now than previously.

Persian Gulf war.

The greatest show on earth, with a cast of thousands, shown on TV screens in living color, and funded by tax revenues and foreign donations.

Pesticides.

The cocaine of the farm sector; "they promise paradise and deliver addiction" (Paul Ehrlich).[145]

Piggyback exploitation.

The dependence of an exploiting imperial power on a ruthless exploitative local elite to extract a surplus sufficient to meet the demands of both.

Plausible deniability.

An arrangement whereby high officials who are responsible for decisions that violate the law and involve the commission of serious crimes are hidden behind their hit men as they deny knowledge of the acts they have ordered and sanctioned.[146] This system works best when we have a Responsible Press.

Pledge.

A solemn political promise, whose common use is dependent on reciprocity of abuse, plus the public's short memory.

Police.

The Fifth Estate, and the only one outside of the law. Its function, as stated by Chicago Mayor Richard B. Daley, is "to preserve disorder" (Press conference, Sept. 9, 1968).

Police brutality.

    A myth built on a mountain of cracked skulls.

Police State.

    A society pacified or in process of Pacification *(q.v.)*.

Political fund raising.

    Fighting money with money.[147]

Politically correct.

    The challenge of dissidents and minorities to traditionally biased usages and curricula, as perceived by the vested interests in existing usage and curricula and those seeking a basis for attacking the current challengers. (See *Really correct.*)

Politicize.

    To raise issues viewed as closed or off-the-agenda by established authority.

Politics.

    The art of winning investors, and then voters.

Pollution.

    The poisonous exudations of industrial societies, which increase in proportion to their corpulence. They reduce the real but not the nominal Gross National Product.

Pollution rights.

The rights of polluters to sell any unused permission to pollute, thereby assuring that society will not be permanently deprived of their foregone pollution. The main form of "rights" enlarged in the Reagan-Bush era.

Poor.

Lacking in get-up-and-go.

Power.

Justice.

Practical.

Without scruple. (See *Idealistic.*)

Pragmatic.

Recognizing that if I don't do this thing which is nasty (but profitable) somebody else will; or that if I do something decent (but costly) its effect will be insignificant. This is sometimes referred to as the "Principle of the Impotent Microcosm." Syn.—Practical. (See *Idealistic*).

Prayers for peace.

Campaigns organized by political leaders to direct citizens' demands for peace to appeals to Heaven rather than elected officials in Washington, D.C.

Pre-dawn vertical insertion.

The 1983 Grenada invasion (as described in a military briefing to the press).

Preferential method.

The rigorous selection of those facts and authorities that support the hypothesis to be proved. The scientific method employed by the Expert *(q.v.)*.[148]

Prejudice.

Your moral judgment. (See *Value.*)

Presidential war.

One initiated by the chief executive at his sole discretion for any reason satisfactory to himself, including pique, proving non-wimpery, a desire to use up large and aging military inventories, or for political advantage. Satisfactory nominal reasons are developed by trial and error and through polling public opinion.

Press.

A written medium serving as a conduit of Public Information *(q.v.)*.

Press conference.

A carefully tooled precision machine for the manufacture of Public Information *(q.v.)*. The product is dumped on the market without further processing by a Responsible Press. (See *Responsible.*)

Pretext.

Their nominal reason for a course of action undertaken for other and ignoble purposes. Syn.—Excuse. (See *Provocation.*)

Prevent wars.

Enlarge the arms budget.[149] (See *Security, Price of,* and *Peace process.*)

Prisoners.

Hostages taken by us or our allies. (See *Hostages.*)

Privatization.

Disposing of public sector assets at low prices and high sales commissions to powerful groups and individuals who generously supported the ruling party's last election campaign. It provides short-run cash windfalls to the government, while weakening its power and its cash flows in the years to come. In the Third World, a means of making valuable assets available to First World creditors and investors at fire sale prices in a situation of virtual state bankruptcy.

Progress.

Displacement; also, movement toward Reform. (See *Reform* and *Urban Renewal.*)

Pro-life

Pro-life.
Strongly supportive of the rights of the fetus; often associated with a below average concern for post-fetal life.[150]

Propaganda.
Their lies. (See *Public information.*)

Protective reaction.
An attack on enemy supply lines, bases, anti-aircraft or radar stations, infrastructure, or free-standing people, based on the obligation of our government to Protect Our Boys and the Citizens of Waukegan, Ill.[151] (See *Reinforced protective reaction.*)

Protest.
A public appeal to one's fellow citizens and government to alter a line of policy deemed in error. This irresponsible action has no effect whatsoever on the elected representatives of the petitioners, but it consistently misleads the enemy into believing that policy will change. If they were not so misled, the enemy would enter into Negotiations *(q.v.).*[152]

Protest March.
(See *March, Protest.*)

Provider.
The nickname of an airplane that dispersed chemicals to destroy the crops of South Vietnamese peasants. It "provided" the peasants with protection against aggression—they would have no food to be used by the Vietcong aggressors—as well as a further testimonial of U.S. solicitude for their welfare.[153] (See *Aggression* and *Operation Ranch Hand.*)

Provocation.
The last straw in a series of unprovoked enemy actions, that causes us finally and after much soul searching to make a defensive response. Syn.—Reason. (See *Pretext, Defensive,* and *Protective reaction.*)

Public broadcasting.
A small and underfunded broadcasting service designed to reduce the pressures on commercial broadcasters to provide programs that will not sell, without encroaching on their market for advertising. Because of the threat of programs not policed by advertisers, public broadcasting itself has been pushed into the commercial market.

Public diplomacy.
The Reagan era name given to a large-scale government propaganda operation, which included massive disinformation and intimidation of

the media, designed to manage public opinion. A part of this program was called Operation Truth *(q.v.)*.[154]

Public information.

Our lies.[155] (See *Propaganda*.)

Public relations.

The substitution of words for performance.[156]

Public service.

In broadcasting, originally, the provision of programming and airtime for public affairs, education, children's programs, and cultural and other programming for minority groups and audiences; subsequently, when all airtime could be sold to advertisers, providing anything people can be induced to listen to or watch.[157]

Puppets.

(See *Satellites*.)

Push-button.

A mechanism which permits us to achieve results without knowledge of the processes involved. (See *War, Push-button*.)

Qualification for public office.

Record of financial support and personal loyalty to the leader and his party.

Quiet diplomacy.

A negotiating effort to oust a Properly Attired Aggressor from its illegally-held possession, carried out gently over many years, with due consideration of its "security needs,"[158] and without either complete removal or required reparations for damage, looting, or murder. Syn.— Constructive Engagement. (See *Aggression, Properly Attired*.)

Quotas.

George Bush's prospective opposition in the election of 1992. (See *Horton, Willie,* and *Southern Strategy*.)

Radical nationalists.

Groups, parties, and governments in the Third World that are not on the U.S. payroll, are unwilling to take orders, and propose an independent line of development. Radical nationalism generates instability. (See *Unstable.*)[59]

Rand Corporation.

A tank, owned by the U.S. Air Force, stocked with Defense Intellectuals *(q.v.).*

Ratings.

The operative measure of a program's merits.

Reaganomics.

The economics of "immediate gratification," corporate version; a program of Robin Hood in reverse.

Reality.

A nightmare, unbelievable during waking hours.

Really correct.

The *status quo* in politicized language and curricula; also, whatever line the government and establishment want to take on an issue. (See *Politically correct.*)

Reciprocity.

Your wallet in exchange for the removal of my foot from your face. (See *Negotiations.*)

Reform.

Sloughing off government outlays helping the distressed and eliminating devices protecting individuals and firms from competition and the state from foreign domination; unleashing market forces in accord with IMF criteria. Formerly, the term meant the opposite, and increasing inequality and malnutrition were seen as signs of deterioration calling for intervention (i.e., "reform"). It is now recognized that these effects are transitory costs of progress, and that benefits will trickle down to the masses in the long run.[160]

Regulation, Old.

A cartel arrangement carried out under government auspices, nominally to serve the public interest, but in reality mainly allowing the cartel members to restrain competition.

Regulation, New.

Governmental efforts through agency rules and enforcement to protect the public from the negative effects of corporate activity on product quality, worker safety, and the environment. Because of its threat to corporate welfare, it is under steady attack for excesses and threats to jobs and competitiveness, and is the main target of business-sponsored political campaigns to "get the government off our backs."

Regulatory arbitrage.

Choosing the site for an economic activity on the basis of the weakness of its regulatory controls.[161]

Reinforced protective reaction.

Protecting Our Boys and the citizens of Waukegan, Ill. by bombing an enemy with a force in excess of 100 aircraft.[162] (See *Protective reaction.*)

Reinforcements.

Our troops moved into contested fighting areas. (See *Infiltration.*)

Reinterpretation.

My abrogation of an agreement. (See *Violation.*)

Rejectionism.

Refusing whatever terms we or our allies and clients propose, however brazenly unjust they may be, and even if they are obviously put forward for public relations purposes only.[163] Rejectionism by us or our allies and clients is an oxymoron.

Reregulation.

Trying to put Humpty-Dumpty back together again, after having watched him fall off the wall without lifting a finger.

Resolute.

Stubborn, unyielding, uncompromising, merciless; a term applicable to our own and allied leaders. (See *Defiant* and *Ruthless.*)

Responsible.

Pertaining to the form but not the substance, as in "Responsible Criticism." Also, starting from the premise that those wielding power seek admirable ends on the basis of superior knowledge.[164]

Restraint.

Killing fewer people than is within our technical capability.[165]

Restructuring.

Closing down, or drastically reducing employment; also, rearranging in accordance with managerial and banker interest; the private seizure of corporate opportunities, plus the zapping of labor.

Revenue enhancement.

Increasing taxes.[166]

Revenue sharing.

Revenue bleeding.[167]

Revolution without borders.

The threat of the mouse to home and tradition, as seen by the cat.[168]

Revolving door.

A door connecting the private sector to government purchasing and regulatory agencies, through which officials move back and forth, gaining know-how in the private sector and then putting their expertise to the service of the public in the government sector. (See *Operation Ill-Wind* and *Market intelligence*.)

Rightful leaders.[169]

Leaders *(q.v.)*.

Riot.

A deplorable outburst of violence by the inhabitants of the cracks in the floor of society. They are ordinarily invisible.

Rotten apples.
Individuals lacking faith in their leader and that spirit of "mutual respect and mutual forbearance that is the essence of a civilized society."[170] If people possessing such faith and spirit beat up or eliminate Rotten Apples, the Apples have only themselves to blame.

Ruthless.
Merciless and brutal; a term used to describe rulers of enemy states. (See *Resolute* and *Tough.*)

Safeguard.
The follow-on to the Sentinel ABM, first proposed for protection of selected cities, but with the residents strongly objecting to the plan, quickly shifted to protection of Minuteman silos against a quickly refurbished Soviet first strike threat.

Safety net.
A porous mesh made from the guts of the deceased welfare state, through which will fall the Undeserving Poor *(q.v.)*.

Safety of our nationals.
The initial rationale for an invasion designed to preserve a friendly military junta, pending the putting together of a better rationale at our leisure.[171]

Sale.
Business consummation. The Moses and all the prophets of industrial statesmanship.

Sanctions.
Punitive measures short of military attack, imposed to pressure violators of human rights and international law to cease their abuses. Sanctions are never imposed on *us*, and they are neither severe nor strictly enforced when imposed on our friends, but they are vigorously applied to enemy states. In the Gulf war of 1991 they served to provide a softening up phase prior to a full scale attack on an enemy state.

Sanctuary.
An enemy haven or source of supplies that has not yet been attacked;

hence the explanation of military failure[172] and the target for the next Escalation *(q.v.)*

Satellite.

Aligned with them. Syn.—Puppet. (See *Independent.)*

Save.

Destroy. As in, "It became necessary to destroy the town in order to save it."[173] An application of a fundamental adage "better dead than Red," which the United States applies to Third World countries to help them understand where their true interest lies. Syn.—Help.

Scud.

A dumb, evil-doing bomb dropped indiscriminately on innocent people by Another Hitler. (See *Another Hitler, Paveway III,* and *Smart Bombs.)*

Search and destroy.

A mission involving the occupation of a hamlet, the killing of all males attempting to flee, impounding the others for Interrogation *(q.v.)*, and destroying all animals, food, and houses "to deprive enemy forces of sustenance and shelter"; the principal activity of U.S. ground forces in South Vietnam from 1965-1971.

GEORGE SHULTZ HUNTS FOR PEACE IN CENTRAL AMERICA —NEWSITEM

CONTRA AID

MILITARY AID TO HONDURAS

MILITARY AID TO EL SALVADOR

M. WUERKER

Search for peace.
Public relations ploys that will allow us to continue to pursue war.

Security.
Control by force or the threat of force; as in "political identification of the people with the government [Saigon] has not proceeded as fast as the security situation has..." (William Colby, head of the Phoenix Program in Vietnam). Syn.—Insecurity. (See also, *Phoenix Program* and *National security*.)

Security forces.
Armed forces under government command whose function is to provide the populace with Security *(q.v.)*.

Security, price of.
Whatever the arms establishment goes after.

Self-appointed.
Someone who has undertaken a public service effort which I find offensive; as in, "Ralph Nader, the self-appointed consumer advocate," etc.

Self-defense.
Our, and our closest allies', right to attack anybody at discretion for any reason satisfactory to ourselves.[174] Enemy states responding to direct attacks from outside their borders are not engaging in self-defense, they are showing their inherent aggressiveness and the threat of a Revolution Without Borders *(q.v.)*.

Self-determination.
The right of a people to select a government acceptable to us.[175]

Self-hating.
Lacking in chauvinistic fervor; failing to revel in patriotic gore.

Sentinel.
An early anti-ballistic missile program whose justification for deployment was the threat of Chinese missiles that did not yet exist and the use of which would admittedly have been suicidal. But the MIC was hard-pressed for a rationale to get the taxpayer to fund this weapon. (See *Safeguard.*)

Service.
The prime motive of my quest for office.

Shake-down state.
One whose Leaders insist on an extra payoff for their special services to the dominant members of the Free World. (See *Corruption drain, Free World,* and *Leader.*)

Shelter.
An underground facility that houses civilians seeking protection from bombing attacks, unless we hit it with a bomb, at which point it becomes a Bunker *(q.v.).*

Sincerity.
The last refuge of an apologist for a scoundrel.[176]

Skunk hunting.
A three-plane battle tactic involving a lure, the dropping flares, and the killing of trapped skunks.[177]

Smart bombs.
Bombs intelligent enough to fall only on military targets and to avoid civilians and civilian structures.

Soaking the poor.
Improving incentives, getting government off our backs, and rectifying past improprieties in the tax structure. (See *Class warfare, Incentives,* and *Reaganomics.*)

Sortie.
A destructive and killing mission by an aircraft that carries numerous bombs which explode and propel at high speed metal fragments and materials that tear and burn human flesh.

Southern Strategy.

Encouraging white opposition to black demands for equality in the hope of capitalizing politically on the effects of racial polarization; part of the Republican Party's plan for "bringing us all together."

Soviet Threat.

A large and formidable beast of prey, the size of whose claws and fangs varied with the demands of the Military-Industrial Complex for Modernization. Unfortunately for the MIC and Modernization, this creature expired suddenly in 1988. (See *MIC* and *Modernization*.)

Space shuttle.

A long lead-time device for digging up and filling holes in outer space.

Special interests.

Workers, women, students, farmers, the aged and infirm, the unemployed, and blacks and other minorities; the general population; unimportant people.

Sport.

Competition between professionals carried out on a business-like basis.

Sports page.

Part 2 of the business section of the newspaper.

Spots.

An acne suffered by commercial broadcasting that increased in severity and unsightliness the greater its prosperity.

Stability.

Political and economic conditions that satisfy our interests.[178]

Stamina.

The capacity to inflict and absorb injury without permitting the intervention of either narrow self-interest or sentimental humanity.

Star Wars.

A white elephant to be built in the sky. (See *GPALS*.)

Step toward democracy.

In reference to a client state, any verbal assurance no matter how vague and remote, and any formal act, no matter how empty of substance.

Strategic hamlet.

A specially constructed Vietnam war settlement under military surveillance and control, housing an uprooted enemy population.[179] These settlements helped win hearts and minds by protecting the women and children from attack and subversion by their husbands, fathers and sons.[180] Syn.—Agrovilles, Peace Camps, Relocation Centers, etc. (See *Concentration camps.*)

Strict construction.

Loosening constitutional restraints on the rights of police; also, a return to constitutional interpretation of *circa* 1898.[181]

Subsidy.

A compensation payment to substantial citizens to offset price instability or market weakness or to call forth an otherwise unavailable output, in the interest of equity or National Security. (See *Dole.*)

Subversion.

Any organizational or protest activity from below that threatens privilege.[182]

Super-aggression.

Leveling a Third World country following a provocation, real or contrived, that provides a superpower with an excuse to destroy a threatening rival, reestablish control over an important disputed territory, and teach Third World countries a lesson in proper behavior. (See *Lesson.*)

Synergy.

The mystical force that lowers costs when two dissimilar companies are combined; sometimes expressed by the equation 2 + 2 = 5.

Take out.

Kill.

Taking advantage of.

Using. (See *Vocal minority.*)

Tax abatements.

Tax concessions which sometimes cause businesses to build and invest in place X instead of Y.

Tax avoidance.

Dodging taxes within the law. (See *Tax evasion.*)

Tax bubble.

A tax structure fixed under Reaganomics *(q.v.)* whereby those with taxable incomes of $200,000 a year or more had a lower marginal tax rate (28 percent) than those with somewhat smaller incomes (33 percent), the latter group suffering the "bubble" between lower rates on either side.

Tax efficiency.

Minimizing tax payments by any legal route; as in, "There's an estimated $1 trillion out there among people seeking [sic: i.e., able to pay for] tax efficiency. And there are four good reasons for coming to us—zero taxes, secrecy, security, and service" (George Moore, Chairman, Gibralter Trust Bank, Ltd.)

Tax evasion.

Dodging taxes in violation of the law. (See *Tax avoidance.*)

Tax loophole.

Legislated means of tax avoidance, often arranged and even written by the beneficiaries.

Tax reform.

Reducing taxes on business firms and the wealthy to improve their incentives to save, invest and work. These reductions can be offset by reductions in welfare expenditures and benefits to the impoverished and working poor to improve *their* incentives to work.[183] (See *Incentives, Reaganomics* and *Reform.*)

Taxes.

Obsolete term. (See *Revenue enhancement.*)

Technical violations.

Illegal acts carried out by the forces of Law and Order; as in, "with regard to the matter of handling campaign funds, we have a new law here in which technical violations have occurred and are occurring, apparently, on both sides" (Nixon). Because they are only "technical," such violations are subject only to token prosecutions, dropped as soon as this can be done without undue publicity.

Television.

The real U.S. school system.

Termination with extreme prejudice.

Murder by the forces of Law and Order.

THE POT CALLING THE KETTLE BLACK

TERRORIST!

Terrorism

Terrorism.

Killing civilians retail.

Thinktank.

A tank stocked with intellectuals on the take.

Thinking the unthinkable.

Establishing the moral basis for doing the unthinkable.

Thousand points of light.

What is projected upon the opposite wall when a light is shined in the ears of the U.S. electorate, well-ventilated by television *(q.v.)*.

Threat.

Their attack capability.[184] (See *Deterrent.*)

Tough.

Brutal, inhumane, and murderous; a term used in reference to our own or allied leaders.[185] Syn.—Firm, Resolute. (See *Ruthless.*)

Tragic error.

Any action by ourselves that kills large numbers of innocent people and which cannot be kept under the rug or blamed on enemy provocations. The usage follows from the postulate of our benevolence along with the rule that invidious words (terrorist, murderer) cannot be applied to us.

Trees.

Leading polluters; also, timber.

Trouble-maker.

Someone interfering with the Containment and Pacification efforts of the world's policeman.[186] (See *Containment* and *Pacification.*)

Trujillo, Raphael.

    A brutal, gangster-dictator of the Dominican Republic, sponsored by the U.S. Marines, and recognized and aided by the United States for three decades; anti-communist.[187]

Truth.

    Emissions from the mouths of the powerful.

Turnout.

    The statistical proof of the public's devotion to the military junta and security forces in U.S.-sponsored elections; the index of successful intimidation in those sponsored by the enemy.

Unauthorized conveyance.

    Stealing, when done by important people.[188]

Undeserving poor.

    People with very low incomes who are not also blind, deaf, dumb, and without the use of two or more limbs. Syn.—Poor.

Unfair trade.

    Arrangements in which the special advantages of our trading rivals are used as we do our own.

Unilateral disarmament.

    Increasing our stock of overkill at a diminishing rate, or at a rate lower than our overkill production capacity, as in, "over recent years we've followed a policy of kind of unilaterally disarming and the idea that maybe others would follow suit" (Reagan in 1985).[189]

United Nations (UN).

    An odd organization which vacillates between demagoguery and irresponsibility (voting against us), and showing promise of providing the basis for the establishment of global peace and order (voting with us).

United States.

    The big PX;[190] also, Globocop.

Unprocessed news.
Unsupported rumors.[191]

Unstable.
Not satisfactory to our interests. Following the Communist takeover of China in 1949 that country was unstable; Nicaragua failing to do our bidding in 1909 was declared unstable, and marines were sent in to provide Stability *(q.v.)*.[192]

Upscale
High on, or climbing up, the income ladder; worthy of commercial attention and political solicitude.

Urban renewal.
Negro removal.[193]

V

Value.
My moral judgment; also, price. (See *Prejudice.)*

Value free.
Unbiased, except that the choice of problem and parameters within which it can be solved may be shaped by the demands of money and power.[194] (See *Expert.)*

Victory.
Annihilation. (See *Save.)*

Vietcong.
A Vietnamese peasant, especially one that we have killed.[195] (See *Enemy structure.)*

Vietnamization.
The pacification of South Vietnam by means of a sufficiently large investment in an internal mercenary army. For domestic purposes this was referred to as "getting the Vietnamese to fight their own battles." Vietnamization was a special case of Mercenarization *(q.v.).*

Vietnam syndrome.

An ailment of the body politic in which a majority of ordinary citizens, partly in response to memories of a costly war of aggression built on official lies, are opposed to an Activist Foreign Policy *(q.v.)*. (See also *Consensus* and *Vietnam war.*)

Vietnam War.

A lengthy U.S. war against self-determination fought 10,000 miles from the U.S. shoreline as part of a policy of Containment *(q.v.)*. (See *Containment* and *Aggression, Internal.*)

Violation.

Their abrogation of an agreement. (See *Reinterpretation.*)

Violence.

Force employed ineffectually, on a small scale, and without official sanction (e.g., actions by John Brown versus General William T. Sherman; Weather Underground versus Richard Nixon).

Vision thing.

A hope and a prayer for improvement in an area we cannot afford to spend money on now.

Visit.

Bombing raid.

Vocal minority.

People "taking advantage of" our free institutions to sow the seeds of doubt in the minds of their fellow citizens and giving aid and comfort to the enemy. (See *Taking advantage of.)*

War.

When initiated by us, peace-keeping or "violence processing. "[196]

War, just.

The war in which my country is presently engaged. (See *Patriotism.)*

War, limited.

A localized military venture where combat experience can be gained, new weapons tested, surplus military inventories disposed of, and freedom and independence defended, all simultaneously, at a Calculated Risk *(q.v.).*

War of national liberation.

A civil upheaval provoked by gross injustice and misgovernment.[197] When inconvenient to a great power, intervention on behalf of the rejected government is carried out on the ground that aid given the rebels by outsiders makes this a case of Aggression *(q.v.).* If this won't wash, the populace is guilty of Internal Aggression. (See *Aggression, Internal.)*

War, preventive.

An attack on another country initiated now to avoid the difficulties of getting under way later. It is based on the principle that "a bird in the hand is worth two in the bush." For purposes of Public Information, however, the relevant principle is said to be "the need to undertake a war now in order to prevent a larger one in the future."[198]

War, push-button.

A clean war in which damage is inflicted from a distance, on the basis of moral principles, without any unpleasantness disturbing the eyes, ears, nostrils, or hearts of the pushers of buttons. Highly conducive to stamina in doing what must be done to save face, etc.

War on drugs.

Replaced the ill-conceived war on poverty by substituting Third World police tactics and suspension of civil rights for Bleeding Heart social programs in an effort to keep a lid on the inner cities. (See *Ghetto.*)

War, the last.

This war, which I am trying hard to package and sell to a reluctant public.

Waste.

Kill.

Welfare.

Payments made to shiftless and lubricious nonworkers which encourage them to continue their immoral behavior at the expense of the taxpayer.

Welfare expenditure.

(See *Boondoggle* and *Dole.*)

White.

Above; clean; decent; cheerful. The color of joy and the heavenly hosts. Thus, in speaking of a kindly act we say "That was white of you."

White Paper

White paper.

A collection of truths, half-truths, and fabrications, compiled after the fact to justify a mistaken decision in process of enlargement.

Widow-makers.

The nickname adopted by a battalion of the 101st U.S. Air Cavalry Division, in celebration of their efficiency in decimating the aboriginal male population of Vietnam.[199]

Window of vulnerability.

The Carter-Reagan era "gap" in nuclear weaponry, which supposedly made possible a relatively costless Soviet first strike, calling for rapid U.S. rearmament. This gap ignored U.S. nuclear-armed submarines and bombers, and exaggerated Soviet technical prowess, along with assorted other fabrications and worst-case assumptions. The window closed in 1983 when the President's Commission on Strategic Forces announced that our retaliatory forces "guaranteed deterrence."[200] By that time, the contracts based on the threat of the "window" were signed.

Wounded bear theory.

That the Soviet leadership, unable to perform at home, would be inclined to recoup their political fortunes by foreign adventures. There is no corresponding theory applicable to the U.S. leadership; see, however, *Presidential war* and *Wounded eagle.*

Wounded eagle.

A large bird of prey which, injured and in decline, moves to a diet of baby rabbits.

Zap.

To shoot down in cold blood, especially a Gook *(q.v.).*

Zippo squads.

U.S. soldiers assigned the duty of burning down the homes of South Vietnamese peasants. This now-conventional term is derived from the name of a common cigarette lighter used in this saving enterprise.

Notes

Preface

1. See Joe McGinnis, *The Selling of the President, 1968,* New York: Trident Press, 1969; and Mark Hertsgaard, *On Bended Knee: The Press and the Reagan Presidency,* New York: Farrar Straus Giroux, 1988.
2. See Erik Barnouw, *The Sponsor,* New York: Oxford University Press, 1978; Hertsgaard, *op. cit.*; Robert Westbrook, "Politics as Consumption," Richard Fox and Jackson Lears, *The Culture of Consumption: Critical Essays on American History, 1880-1980,* New York: Pantheon, 1983; essays by Gerald Benjamin, Erik Barnouw, Thomas Patterson and David Everson, in Gerald Benjamin, ed., *The Communications Revolution in Politics,* New York: Academy of Political Science, 1982.
3. Letter to W.T. Barry, August 4, 1822, *Letters and Other Writings of James Madison,* New York: R. Worthington, 1844, vol. 3, p. 276.
4. Senator Arthur Vandenberg's oft-quoted phrase on what the natural leaders were obliged to do in 1947 to manufacture mass consent for an aggressive foreign policy. Cited in Eric Goldman, *The Crucial Decade,* New York: Vintage Books, 1960, p. 59.
5. *A Collection of Essays,* New York: Harcourt Brace Jovanovich, 1946, p. 167.
6. George Orwell, *1984,* New York: Signet Books, 1949, p. 163.
7. "Reagan, the actor, has absolutely no moral sense about truth or falsity. Truth, to him, is what he happens to be saying at the time. Even when he is repeating some hoary old lie about welfare cheats which has been exposed in the press a hundred times, he still looks as though he is telling the truth and I'm sure he thinks he is telling the truth." Alexander Cockburn, *Corruptions of Empire,* London: Verso, 1987, p. 346.
8. Shultz is quoted in Philip Taubman, "Shultz Criticizes Nicaragua Delay," *New York Times,* Feb. 6, 1984; also, *Security and Development Assistance,* Hearings before the Senate Foreign Relations Committee, 98th Cong., 2nd Sess., Feb. 22, 1984, p. 83.
9. On March 10, 1982, two weeks before the election, a Salvadoran death squad circulated a death list of 35 Salvadoran and foreign journalists, another notable contribution to intimidation of the press corps. See Edward S. Herman and Frank Brodhead, *Demonstration Elections: U.S.-Staged Elections in the Dominican Republic, Vietnam, and El Salvador,* Boston: South End Press, 1984, pp. 120-121.
10. The mainstream media also did not report the journalist death list noted in the preceding footnote. The morgue story was spelled out in detail by a journalist in the documentary *In the Name of Democracy.*
11. See Edward S. Herman and Noam Chomsky, *Manufacturing Consent: The Political Economy of the Mass Media,* New York: Pantheon, 1988, pp. 129, 132-33.
12. At the conclusion of election day, March 28, 1982, Dan Rather exulted: "A triumph! A million people to the polls." The same Rather had nothing to say about the large turnout in the Nicaraguan election on November 4, 1984.
13. See Herman and Chomsky, *Manufacturing Consent,* pp. 129-137; Jack Spence, "The U.S. Media Covering (Over) Nicaragua," in Thomas Walker, ed., *Reagan Versus the Sandinistas,* Boulder, Col.: Westview Press, 1987.

14. "Clear Choices in Salvador, Murky Plans in Nicaragua," *New York Times*, March 12, 1984.
15. Herman and Chomsky, *Manufacturing Consent*, pp. 107-110.
16. The *New York Times* even stated editorially on March 1, 1973, that "useful purpose" should enter into the calculus of news reporting. In connection with the Israeli shooting down of a civilian airliner in February 1973, the paper stated that "No useful purpose is served by an acrimonious debate over the assignment of blame for the downing of a Libyan airliner in the Sinai peninsula last week." As there was no question of who was to blame, this was a euphemism for not reporting very much, including condemnation or material details regarding the circumstances or victims. On the biased treatment of plane shootdowns, see further pp. 30-32 below.
17. See the quotations from the *New York Times* editorials on the U.S. shooting down of an Iranian airliner in 1988 and the Soviet Union shooting down a Korean airliner on p. 31.
18. See *Manufacturing Consent*, pp. 175-86.
19. Forty-six of the 48 top positions in the FDN's military hierarchy were held by former members of Somoza's National Guard as of April 1985. Despite this, Langhorne Motley, Assistant Secretary of State for Inter-American Affairs, told Congress in January 1985 that contra leaders "are without exception men who opposed Somoza." See Peter Kornbluh, *Nicaragua: The Price of Intervention*, Washington: Institute for Policy Studies, 1987, pp. 38-39.
20. The Reagan administration had exceedingly warm relations with the military government of Argentina before its overthrow in 1983, as well as with the governments of Pakistan, Saudi Arabia, Morocco, and Indonesia, among many others.
21. See *Manufacturing Consent*, pp. 71-86; Americas Watch, *Guatemala Revised: How the Reagan Administration Finds "Improvements" in Human Rights in Guatemala*, New York: Americas Watch, 1985.
22. See Edward S. Herman, "The United States Versus Human Rights in the Third World," *Harvard Human Rights Journal*, Spring 1991, pp. 98-103.
23. In discussing the Reagan policy toward Nicaragua, Tom Wicker, the liberal columnist for the *New York Times*, stated that "the United States has no historic or God-given right to bring democracy to other nations..." implying that the Reagan administration was actually aiming at that objective ("That Dog Won't Hunt," Aug. 6, 1987).
24. Andrew Rosenthal, "Bush Not Pressing Kuwait on Reform: President Is Said to Feel He Cannot Force Democracy," *New York Times*, April 3, 1991.
25. Rightwing critics who assail the mainstream press most furiously, like Michael Ledeen and Reed Irvine (Accuracy in Media), have a steady presence in the letters and Op. Ed. columns of the *New York Times* and *Wall Street Journal* that exceeds that of any liberal or leftwing media critic in the country.

1. The Unfree Flow of Information

1. See Ward Churchill and Jim Vander Wall, *Agents of Repression: The FBI's Secret Wars Against the Black Panther Party and the American Indian Movement*, Boston: South End Press, 1988; Carlos Muñoz, *Youth, Identity, Power: The Chicano Movement*, New York and London: Verso, 1989.
2. See Frank Donner, *Protectors of Privelege: Red Squads and Police Repression in Urban America*, Berkeley: University of California Press, 1990; Frank Donner, *The Age of Surveillance*, New York: Vintage, 1981; David Kairys, "Freedom of Speech," in Kairys, ed., *The Politics of Law*, New York: Pantheon, 1982.

3. In 1964, for the first time, the Supreme Court "made explicit the principle that seditious libel—criticism of the government—cannot be made a crime in America and spoke in this connection of 'the central meaning of the First Amendment.' " Jamie Kalven, citing a Brennan opinion, in Harry Kalven, *A Worthy Tradition: Freedom of Speech in America,* New York: Harper & Row, 1988, p. 66. The decision in *Times v. Sullivan* states in part that "Although the Sedition Act was never tested in this Court, the attack upon its validity has carried the day in the court of history." 376 U.S. 254, at 276 (1964). See further Kalven, *A Worthy Tradition,* p. 66.

4. Kairys, p. 148.

5. *Ibid.,* p. 149.

6. *Ibid.,* p. 152. The postmaster was upheld in 1917 for refusing to deliver a newspaper that expressed negative opinions about the conduct of the war (*ibid.,* p. 153). For a more extended discussion of the postal authorities as an obstruction to free speech, Jon Bekken, "'These Great and Dangerous Powers': Postal Censorship of the Press," *Journal of Communication Inquiry,* Winter 1991, pp. 55-71.

7. Kairys, p. 152.

8. Nicaragua in the 1980s was held to a much higher standard than this by the U.S. establishment and press, although Nicaragua was under serious military attack from without, whereas there was no threat of invasion of the United States in World War I. I have never seen this comparison made in the U.S. press. The point is discussed at length in John Spicer Nichols, "The Media," in Thomas Walker, ed., *Nicaragua: The First Five Years,* New York: Praeger, 1985.

9. Kairys notes that in the McCarthy era, "the judiciary essentially collapsed," *op. cit.,* p. 164. For the events of the period and clearing of the ground, see David Caute, *The Great Fear: The Anti-Communist Purge Under Truman and Eisenhower,* New York: Simon and Schuster, 1978.

10. See Ross Gelbspan, *Break-ins, Death Threats and the FBI: The Covert War Against the Central America Movement,* Boston: South End Press, 1991. Also, "Special Issue on Domestic Surveillance," *CovertAction Information Bulletin,* No. 31, Winter 1989.

11. These included efforts to damage the Mississippi Freedom Democratic Party in 1964, to destroy civil rights groups and discourage civil rights activists, to discredit and even destroy Martin Luther King, Jr., and to undermine black student organizations. These activities included the large-scale use of forged documents, as well as continuous illegal break-ins and thefts of membership lists, intimidation, agent provocateur acts, and encouragement of gang warfare, among other illegal techniques. See Noam Chomsky, "Introduction," in Nelson Blackstock, *Cointelpro: The FBI's Secret War On Political Freedom,* New York: Vintage, 1975, pp. 7-19; Donner, *Age of Surveillance,* pp. 177-204.

12. Quoted in Blackstock, *Cointelpro,* p. 18.

13. Donna Demac, *Liberty Denied,* New Brunswick: Rutgers University Press, 1990, p. 78.

14. "In America the majority raises formidable barriers around the liberty of opinion; within these barriers an author may write what he pleases, but woe to him if he goes beyond them. Not that he is in danger of an auto-da-fe, but he is exposed to continued obloquy and persecution." *Democracy in America,* New York: Vintage Books, 1954, Vol. I, p. 274 (originally published in 1835 and 1840).

15. See esp., Erik Barnouw, *The Sponsor,* New York: Oxford University Press, 1978; also, Ben Bagdikian, *Media Monopoly,* Boston: Beacon, 1987.

16. Recent decades have witnessed the growth of corporate-funded flak machines, like Accuracy in Media, the Media Institute, and the Center for Media and Pub-

lic Affairs, designed to put steady pressure on the media to toe a line acceptable to the corporate community. See Herman and Chomsky, *Manufacturing Consent*, pp. 26-28.

17. A model of how this works is spelled out in chapter 1 of *ibid*.

18. See *ibid.*, chapter 7. It is a commonplace of apologetics for the mainstream media that such criticism implies that reporters are dishonest. This, like the issue of sincerity discussed in the Preface, is a red herring. Frames imposed by the powerful may be internalized by reporters; they may recognize what stories and facts will be accepted upstairs, and accommodate to this, sometimes trying to evade these constraints as best they can. Some, it is true, are dishonest. See, for example, the discussion of James LeMoyne's and other *New York Times* reporters' treatment of arms flows from Nicaragua to El Salvador in Noam Chomsky, *Necessary Illusions*, Boston: South End Press, 1989, Appendix IV, "The Craft of 'Historical Engineering'". See also the analysis of LeMoyne's and the *New York Times'* extreme gullibility and resultant support of a government propaganda line in Edward S. Herman, "LeMoyne and the Times on the Murder of Herbert Anaya: Disinformation as News Fit to Print," *CovertAction Information Bulletin*, No. 31, Winter 1989, pp. 65-69.

19. See Barnouw, *Sponsor,* pp. 140-47; Steve Rhodes, "Public Service, Private Ideologies," *EXTRA!,* July-August 1991, pp. 14-15.

20. The increased competition from cable has caused the networks to pursue large advertisers more aggressively, entering into special joint-selling promotions, and engaging in deals which give advertisers greater control over programming. See Joanne Lipman, "Advertiser-Produced TV Shows Return," *Wall Street Journal,* Aug. 15, 1988; Lipman, "Brand-Name Products Are Popping Up in TV Shows," *Wall Street Journal,* Feb. 19, 1991; Kevin Goldman, "CBS May Give Prizes to Lure More Viewers," *Wall Street Journal,* May 15, 1991; Lipman, "ABC to Relax Longstanding Guidelines for Ad Content," *ibid.,* Sept. 5, 1991.

21. *Grave New World,* New York: Oxford University Press, 1985, p. 111.

22. Speaking of photos of injured Iraqis, Irvine said, "But that is very effective propaganda simply because it is true. And if you insist that you're going to show that, you're going to undermine the enthusiasm of people in this country for the war." Transcript of the NPR program "All Things Considered," Feb. 12, 1991.

23. For a discussion of Braestrup's study, see Herman and Chomsky, *Manufacturing Consent*, pp. 211-228 and Appendix 3.

24. Bill Keller, "Soviet Official Says Press Harms Army," *New York Times,* Jan. 21, 1988, p. A3.

25. On her dominant role and uncritical treatment in the mainstream media, see Edward S. Herman and Frank Brodhead, *The Rise and Fall of the Bulgarian Connection*, New York: Sheridan Square Publications, 1986, chapter 7.

26. Some six months after publication by Fairness and Accuracy in Reporting of a devastating analysis of McNeil-Lehrer's extreme pro-official bias and marginalization of dissidents, Noam Chomsky made his first appearance ever on the show, along with a few others like Erwin Knoll of *The Progressive.* The small spurt that followed this publication receded quickly in the wake of the Gulf crisis and war.

27. See Robert Murray, *Red Scare, A Study in National Hysteria 1919-1920,* Minneapolis: University of Minnesota Press, 1955, pp. 142-65.

28. For proof of this statement, see: on the terrorist threat, Edward S. Herman and Gerry O'Sullivan, *The "Terrorism" Industry: The Experts and Institutions That Shape Our View of Terror,* New York: Pantheon, 1990, chapters 1-3, 7-8, and Noam Chomsky, *Pirates & Emperors: International Terrorism in the Real World,* New York: Claremont Research and Publications, 1986. On Kadaffi, see Chomsky's *Pirates & Emperors,* chapter 3 and William Perdue, *Terrorism and*

the State: A Critique of Domination Through Fear, New York: Praeger, 1989, chapter 6. On the KGB plot to kill the Pope, Herman and Brodhead, *Rise and Fall of the Bulgarian Connection.* On the KAL 007 shootdown, see the text below, pp. 30-32.

29. On the differential attention to shootdowns, see Edward S. Herman, "Gatekeeper Versus Propaganda Models," in Peter Golding, Graham Murdock and Philip Schlesinger, eds., *Communicating Politics,* Leicester: University of Leicester Press, 1987, pp. 184-94, and the text below, pp. 30-32.

30. For a discussion of these alternative frames, see Edward S. Herman, "U.S. Mass Media Coverage of the U.S. Withdrawal From UNESCO," in William Preston, Jr., Edward S. Herman and Herbert Schiller, *Hope & Folly: The United States and UNESCO, 1945-1985,* Minneapolis: University of Minnesota Press, 1989, pp. 228-239.

31. See *ibid.,* pp. 233-34; Alcira Argumedo, "The New World Information Order and International Power," *Journal of International Affairs,* Fall-Winter 1981, pp. 17-88; David Felix, "Economic Development: Takeoffs Into Unsustained Growth," *Social Research,* Summer, 1969, pp. 267-93.

32. On this consistent bias, see Herman, "U.S. Mass Media Coverage," pp. 229-39.

33. *Ibid.*

34. *Liberty Denied,* p. 96.

35. On the importance of Reagan's myth construction in his public utterances, see Paul D. Erickson, *Reagan Speaks: The Making of an American Myth,* New York: New York University Press, 1985. On the centrality of lying, see Chomsky, *Necessary Illusions.*

36. Demac, *Liberty Denied,* pp. 139-42.

37. Richard Curry, "Paranoia—Reagan Style: Encounters With the USIA," in Curry, ed., *Freedom at Risk: Secrecy, Censorship, and Repression in the 1980s,* Philadelphia: Temple University Press, 1988, pp. 178-91.

38. Quoted in Demac, *Liberty Denied,* p. 97.

39. Quoted in John Lloyd, "The Ferret," *The New Statesman,* Jan. 30, 1987.

40. Committee to Protect Journalists, "Journalists Killed or Disappeared Since 1976," report of December 1986.

2. The Weapons Culture

1. "They [key U.S. leaders] dismissed, both publicly and privately, Soviet military power and the threat of war, thinking, to quote John Foster Dulles, that 'economically the nation is still weak...the Soviet military establishment is completely outmatched.'" Joyce and Gabriel Kolko, *The Limits of Power,* New York: Harper & Row, 1972, pp. 336-7. George Kennan wrote that "In no way did the Soviet Union appear, at that moment, as a military threat to this country. The Soviet Union was utterly exhausted by the exertions and sacrifices of the recent war." "Containment: Then and Now," *Los Angeles Times,* Dec. 29, 1985.

2. See Noam Chomsky, *Turning the Tide,* Boston: South End Press, 1985, pp. 196-98; John Loftus, *The Belarus Secret,* New York: Penguin Books, 1983, chapter 5.

3. Richard Halloran, "Pentagon Draws Up First Strategy for Fighting a Long Nuclear War," *New York Times,* May 30, 1982.

4. Was the United States shaping countries in "our image" when it put the Shah of Iran in power in 1953? helped install Pinochet as dictator of Chile in 1973? displaced Lumumba with Mobutu in Zaire in 1961? placed Diem, Ky and Thieu in office in South Vietnam? helped bring into power and supported for decades the Somozas in Nicaragua and Trujillo in the Dominican Republic?

5. Kolko and Kolko, *Limits of Power,* pp. 408-10.

6. A typical article in their vein, by Stephen Kinzer, is entitled "Nicaragua's Edge in the Arms Race," *New York Times,* Nov. 27, 1985, which stresses the sad disabilities of the Nicaraguan contras in the face of new Sandinista helicopters, "which are considered extraordinarily potent against guerrilla forces..." Kinzer also notes that "Their adversaries...have expressed fears that a strengthened air force, particularly with new jet fighters, could be used against nearby countries."

7. As Saul Landau stresses, the United States regularly transforms any nationalist development in the Third World into a global threat, "a universal formula that could be applied against revolutions everywhere." Castro's policies from 1959 quickly "became an area of national security 'crisis,' " and with Vietnam there was the urgent need to avoid the basic fact: that it was, "from its outset, a war to stop a communist led independence movement that had taken power in the summer of 1945 on the heels of the Japanese defeat before the French could reassert colonial domination." *The Dangerous Doctrine: National Security and U.S. Foreign Policy,* Boulder: Westview Press, 1988, pp. 66, 72, 94-95.

8. An excellent book by Ralph Lapp is entitled *The Weapons Culture,* New York: Penguin, 1969.

9. Good accounts are given in Richard Kaufman, *The War Profiteers,* Indianapolis: Bobbs-Merrill, 1970, and Gordon Adams, *The Politics of Defense Contracting: The Iron Triangle,* New York: Council on Economic Priorities, 1981.

10. Peter Prugh, "The War Business, Mendel Rivers' Defense of Armed Forces Helps His Hometown Prosper," *Wall Street Journal,* June 17, 1969.

11. Orwell, *1984,* p. 29.

12. For a history of these emendations, see Holzman's letter to the *New York Times,* Oct. 25, 1989, under the heading "How C.I.A. Concocts Soviet Defense Numbers;" Michael Wines, "CIA Accused of Overestimating Soviet Economy," *ibid.,* July 23, 1990, p. A6.

13. As Tom Gervasi pointed out, the Scowcroft Commission of 1983 "had begun its report by recognizing that our missiles at sea deterred all such strikes. With this reminder, it closed the 'window of vulnerability' our land-based missiles faced." However, in order to rationalize building the MX, it quickly opened up a new window based on the hypothetical threats of larger Soviet missiles and a larger number of warheads. *The Myth of Soviet Military Supremacy,* New York: Harper & Row, 1986, p. 140.

14. See Center for Defense Information, "U.S.-Soviet Military Facts," *The Defense Monitor,* vol. 13, no. 4, 1984.

15. Gervasi, *Myth,* pp. 44-127.

16. *Ibid.,* pp. 112-127. It is worth noting that the *New York Times* never reviewed Gervasi's book, although it was referred to on its jacket by former CIA director William Colby as "a remarkably painstaking analysis of the greatest intelligence gap of all: the exaggeration of Soviet power," and although it was a major work on an issue of urgent importance.

17. On the ways in which the MIC lobby used the foolish Soviet ABM emplacements to justify another massive spurt in the nuclear arms race, see Lapp, *Weapons Culture,* pp. 33-36, 150-175, 209-226; Seymour Hersh, "The Great ABM Pork Barrel," *War/Peace Report,* Jan. 1968.

18. The quotes are from the Pentagon's "Fiscal Year 1984-1988 Defense Guidance," taken from Halloran, "Pentagon Draws Up First Strategy."

19. I. F. Stone, "Nixon and the Arms Race: The Bomber Boondoggle," *New York Review of Books,* Jan. 2, 1969.

20. Lapp, *Weapons Culture,* pp. 153-54.

21. *Ibid.,* pp. 37-60.

22. Quoted in *ibid.,* p. 151.

23. *Ibid.*, p. 3.
24. Quoted in *ibid.*, pp. 3-4.
25. William Broad, "A New Course for 'Star Wars,' From Full to Limited Defense," Jan. 31, 1991, p. A18.
26. "Cauldron in Central America: What Keeps the Fire Burning?" *New York Times,* Dec. 7, 1980 (a colloquy with reporters, Kirkpatrick and others).
27. The Nixon administration felt compelled to sign the Paris agreements in 1973 and then proceeded to ignore them because a political basis for U.S. and client state control in the South still did not exist.
28. Douglas Pike, *Vietcong,* Cambridge: MIT Press, 1966, pp. 91-92, 101.
29. *New York Times,* Feb. 26, 1965.
30. *Road to Oblivion,* New York: Simon and Schuster, 1970, p. 230.
31. This was eventually acknowledged in an editorial in the *New York Times* entitled "The Lie That Was Not Shot Down" (Jan. 18, 1988). The editorial failed to explain why the *Times* had succumbed to the lie and exploited it very aggressively, and in addition, why the paper had never uncovered the truth, but instead waited for somebody else (Representative Lee Hamilton) to use the Freedom of Information Act to do so.
32. In its editorial of August 4, 1988, the paper wrote: "From what is now known of the report [on the incident], the incident still must be seen not as a crime but as a blunder, and a tragedy... The shootdown still seems the type of mishap almost impossible to avoid in the context."
33. "The *Vincennes* Incident," *Proceedings* (U.S. Naval Institute), September 1989, pp. 87-92.
34. George Wilson, "Fellow Officer Faults USS Vincennes Skipper," *Washington Post,* Sept. 1, 1989, p. A4.

3. The Search for Defensible Frontiers...

1. Tacitus, "The History," in *The Complete Works of Tacitus,* New York: Random House, 1942, p. 646.
2. See Michael Salman's review of Karnow: "In Our Orientalist Imagination: Historiography and the Culture of Colonialism in the United States," *Radical History Review,* Spring 1991, pp. 221-32.
3. See John Weeks and Phil Gunson, *Panama: Made in the USA,* London: Latin America Bureau, 1991; James Ferguson, *Grenada: Revolution in Reverse,* London: Latin America Bureau, 1990.
4. See especially, Miles Wolpin, *Military Aid and Counterrevolution in the Third World,* Boston: Lexington, 1972, and Jan Black, *United States Penetration of Brazil,* Philadelphia: University of Pennsylvania Press, 1977.
5. Black, *United States Penetration of Brazil,* pp. 64-77.
6. See Philip Agee, *Inside the Company: CIA Diary,* New York: Bantam, 1975, pp. 112-216; Edward S. Herman, *The Real Terror Network,* Boston: South End Press, 1982, pp. 132-37.
7. Mike Clary, "U.S. says it paid Noriega to spy in Panama, not to make drug deals," *Philadelphia Inquirer,* May 31, 1991.
8. Indignation is usually expressed in the U.S. media by quoting—"objectively"—government officials and establishment experts who express the indignation, along with appropriate photos, editorials, and placement and headings that show the importance of the news that the Soviets or Cubans are doing something dubious.
9. *Alleged Assassination Plots Involving Foreign Leaders,* Interim Report of the Select Committee to Study Governmental Operations with Respect to Intelligence

Activities, U.S. Senate, Rep. No. 94-465, 94th Cong., 1st Sess., Nov. 20, 1975, pp. 71ff.

10. Warren Hinckle and William Turner, *The Fish is Red*, New York: Harper and Row, 1981, p. 293; "Former Pentagon Researcher Says CIA Tampered With Cuba's Weather," *WIN*, Aug. 4, 1977, p. 16.

11. See the reference to Marshal Ky in the *Doublespeak Dictionary*.

12. Chomsky and Herman, *Washington Connection*, pp. 61-66.

13. Malcolm Browne, *The New Face of War*, Indianapolis: Bobbs-Merrill, 1965, p. 211.

14. The classic illustration of the avoidance of such considerations was Henry Kamm's 1981 report on how capitalist nations in Southeast Asia were thriving, while the Indochinese communist powers were "sadly" lagging. In the course of his account, Kamm never mentioned any possible relevance of boycotts or ten million tons of bombs dropped on the latter set of countries. Kamm, "In Mosaic of Southeast Asia, Capitalist Lands Are Thriving" (Nov. 8, 1981), discussed in Herman, *Real Terror Network*, pp. 167-70.

15. See Chomsky and Herman, *Washington Connection*, pp. 210-15 and works cited there.

16. According to Leifer, "By contrast [with conditions under Sukarno], the past quarter of a century has been distinguished by stability and economic development. These achievements have been attributed to the political sobriety and managerial skills of Indonesia's second and incumbent president, Suharto." ("Uncertainty in Indonesia: The Politics of Succession," *World Policy Journal*, Winter 1990-91, p. 139.) Leifer doesn't mention that Sukarno was subject to serious destabilization efforts by the army and United States. In keeping with the liberalism of the *World Policy Journal*, Leifer does mention that "It needs to be stressed, however, that his [Suharto's] political dominance has been maintained by authoritarian practices and at the expense of human rights. Furthermore, the benefits of economic development have been very unevenly distributed." These two sentences exhaust Leifer's coverage of these matters that demand "stress."

17. See Juan DeOnis: "Rightist Terror Stirs Argentina," Aug. 29, 1976; "Argentina's Terror: Army Is Ahead," Jan. 2, 1977; and "Argentine Leadership Leans Toward Democracy," June 26, 1977; and Edward Schumacher, "Populist Figure [Robert Viola] For Argentines," Oct. 6, 1980.

18. Quoted in Noam Chomsky, *Deterring Democracy*, London: Verso, 1991, p. 41.

19. *The Economist* (London), Aug. 15, 1987.

20. See the comparison between the *New York Times'* treatment of Cuba and El Salvador, "Headlines and Omissions," in *Lies of Our Times*, May 1990, p. 11. In a frenetic article "Qaddafi Plays Quietly, But He's Still in the Game," Clifford Krauss speaks of Kadaffi's "current strategy of aggressive subversion," and quotes a Defense Department official that "If there's trouble...you'll find his people." (*New York Times*, March 17, 1991.)

21. For an account of selectivity in treatment as between El Salvador and Nicaragua, see Edward S. Herman. "Labor Abuses in El Salvador and Nicaragua: A Study of New York Times Coverage," A Special Report on Human Rights and The Media, *EXTRA!*, Summer 1989, pp. 24-26.

22. The basic sources here are Amnesty International's *"Disappearances": A Workbook*, London: AI, 1980; AI, *Testimony on Secret Detention Centers in Argentina*, London: AI, 1980. See also Herman, *Real Terror Network*, pp. 110-19 for a summary, table, and further citations.

23. Editorial of May 26, 1976.

24. On the differential treatment by the *New York Times* and other mainstream media of "worthy and unworthy" victims, see Herman and Chomsky, *Manufac-*

turing Consent, chapter 2. For a specific recent illustration of how the *Times* re-fuses to present evidence linking client state leaders to state-linked murders (here, Cristiani to the murder of the six Jesuits and their two employees in November 1989), see Edward S. Herman, "Responsibility at the Top: East and West," *Lies of Our Times,* Nov. 1990, pp. 5-6.

25. See Herman and Chomsky, *Manufacturing Consent,* pp. 49-53, 100-103.
26. Michael McClintock, *The American Connection: Volume One, State Terror and Popular Resistance in El Salvador,* London: Zed Books, 1985, pp. 229-302. See also the citations in note 22.
27. Herman and Brodhead, *Demonstration Elections,* pp. 9-16, 119-26.
28. This was extremely important in the Dominican Republic after the U.S. invasion of 1965, where Juan Balaguer, the U.S.-supported candidate was able to argue, with cogency, that only he could do business with the United States. It was widely believed that a Bosch victory would even precipitate a coup, as well as prolong the occupation. See *ibid.,* pp. 36-42.
29. The Guatemalan elections were not literally organized by the United States, but they were welcomed by U.S. officials as providing a means for legitimizing a client state leadership they supported, and the Reagan administration sent an official observer team to give the election the U.S. imprimatur. See Herman and Chomsky, *Manufacturing Consent,* Appendix 1.
30. See *ibid.,* chapter 3; Herman and Brodhead, *Demonstration Elections,* chapter 7.
31. Stephen Kinzer, "Christian Democrat Takes Big Lead in Guatemala," *New York Times,* Nov. 5, 1985.
32. Many such instances are described in *Manufacturing Consent* and *Demonstration Elections.* An important case in point is the finding by the media that the rebels were trying hard to disrupt the 1982 election, in keeping with the government's stress on this point, but without evidential support. See *Demonstration Elections,* pp. 164-67.
33. "The Electoral Process in Nicaragua: Domestic and International Influences," Report of the Latin American Studies Association Delegation to Observe the Nicaraguan General Election of November 4, 1984, p. 4.
34. Lord Chitnis, "Observing El Salvador: The 1984 Elections," *Third World Quarterly,* Oct. 1984.
35. David Binder, "Nicaragua: Victory for U.S. Fair Play," *New York Times,* March 1, 1990, p. A26.
36. Edward S. Herman, "The Times on the Nicaraguan Election," *Lies of Our Times,* April 1990, p.10.
37. According to Edward Tufte, "the main propositions...of the politicians' theory of the impact of economic conditions on election outcomes [is that]: 1. Economic movements in the months immediately preceding an election can tip the balance and decide the outcome of an election; 2. The electorate rewards incumbents for prosperity and punishes them for recession." *Political Control of the Economy,* Princeton: Princeton University Press, 1978, p. 9.
38. See 11 CFR sec. 110.4, which codifies U.S. law and prohibits foreign nationals from directly or indirectly contributing to U.S. elections. Foreign nationals "shall not direct, dictate, or directly or indirectly participate in the decision-making process of any person [including organizations]...with regard to such person's Federal or non-federal election-related activities..." [subsection (a)(3)].
39. A *New York Times* article of March 1, 1990 was entitled "Turnover in Nicaragua: Goliath and the 14 Davids." Another was entitled "The Sandinista Machine vs. Avid Opponents" (Mark Uhlig, Feb. 6, 1990). For a comparison of *Times* headlines on an election in Chile and the one in Nicaragua, see "Bias in Language

and Tone: Chilean and Nicaraguan Elections," *Lies of Our Times,* April 1990, p. 11.

40. For an excellent account, see Chomsky, *Necessary Illusions,* Appendix IV, "Demolishing the Accords."

41. Robert Pear, "Shultz's 'No' to Arafat; Personal Disgust for Terrorism is at Root of Secretary's Decision to Rebuff the PLO," *New York Times,* Nov. 28, 1988, p. 1.

42. See Israel Shahak, "Letter from Jerusalem," *Lies of Our Times,* May 1991, pp. 14-15.

43. See Edward Tivnan, *The Lobby,* New York: Touchstone, 1987.

44. Excellent analyses can be found in Noam Chomsky, *The Fateful Triangle,* Boston: South End Press, 1983; Simha Flappan, *The Birth of Israel,* New York: Pantheon, 1987; David Hirst, *The Gun and the Olive Branch,* London: Faber and Faber, 1977.

4. Repelling Naked Aggression...

1. See Part 6, pp. 85-93, and citations therein.

2. See Herman and Chomsky, *Manufacturing Consent,* pp. 285-86.

3. "There's a third thread that deserves note: cooperation between Moscow and Washington. Both sides have supported Iraq." "Stirrings of Peace," editorial, July 31, 1988.

4. Bruce Ingersoll, "GAO is Critical of Export Credits Extended to Iraq," *Wall Street Journal,* Nov. 21, 1990, p. A16.

5. This sabotaging of international law was carried out by U.S. Ambassador to the United Nations Daniel Patrick Moynihan, who described with pride his effort to assure that "the United Nations prove utterly ineffective in whatever measures it undertook" to cope with Indonesian aggression, a task which "I carried...forward with no inconsiderable success." (Daniel Moynihan, *A Dangerous Place,* New York: Little Brown, 1978, p. 247.) On the failure of the reviews of Moynihan's recent book on international law to mention this episode and its significance, see Noam Chomsky, *Deterring Democracy,* pp. 199-200.

6. Philip Shabecoff, "Murder Verdict Eased in Vietnam," *New York Times,* March 31, 1970, p. 4.

7. Gary Grass, "Panama: Laundering Casualty figures," *Lies of Our Times,* Dec. 1990, p. 9.

8. Stefan Schindler, "Deconstructing Eisenhower," *Lies of Our Times,* Feb. 1991, pp. 14-15; Jon Halliday and Bruce Cumings, *Korea: The Unknown War,* New York: Pantheon, 1988, pp. 71-82; I.F. Stone, *The Hidden History of the Korean War,* New York: Monthly Review Press, 1952, Part I.

9. See Chomsky, *Deterring Democracy,* chapter 5, or his article "Nefarious Aggression," *Z Magazine,* Oct. 1990.

10. Murray Waas, "Who Lost Kuwait?," *Village Voice,* Jan. 21, 1991.

11. See Al Kamen, "Amid Disinformation and Confusion, Wartime Truth is Hard to Come By," *Washington Post,* Jan. 19, 1991, p. A23. Kamen explains that disinformation comes from Iraq and is not feasible in the United States.

12. See Part 1, note 24 and accompanying text.

13. In the lead for doublespeak deception, and one never caught in the mainstream media, was the navy's initial reporting of a 90 percent "success" rate for Tomahawk missiles, success being defined as the Tomahawk's actually emerging from the launcher (the rate at which they hit their targets being admittedly unknown). See Eric Arnett, "Awestruck press does Tomahawk PR," *Bulletin of Atomic Scientists,* April 1991.

14. Information on the "turkey shoot" and the number and disposition of Iraqi bod-

ies after that phase of the "killing sands" was carefully avoided, along with any discussion of the use of fuel air explosives.

15. This was pointed out in the May-June 1991 issue of *EXTRA!*

16. The bombing of nuclear reactors is in conflict with a number of protocols of international law, notably the 1977 Geneva Protocols I and II, Articles 35 (3), 51 (e), 55 (a), and 56. See Francis Boyle *et al.*, *In re: More Than 50,000 Nuclear Weapons: Analyses of the Illegality of Nuclear Weapons Under International Law,* Northampton, MA: Alethia Press, 1991, pp. 89-91.

17. Michael Kinsley, "Dead Iraqis," *New Republic,* March 18, 1991. See also, Paul Abrahams and Victor Mallet, "U.S. tries out fuel air bombs on Iraqis," *Financial Times,* Feb. 16-17, 1991.

18. See especially Lisa Peattie, "Normalizing the unthinkable," *Bulletin of Atomic Scientists,* March 1984.

19. This was a phrase used by GIs in Vietnam during the Vietnam war to describe their home country.

20. *Third World Resurgence,* (Penang, Malaysia), February 1991.

21. For a good summary of press treatment of the UN when it does not serve U.S. interests, see Noam Chomsky's "The Media and International Opinion," *Necessary Illusions,* pp. 218-222.

22. See Noam Chomsky, "Letter From Lexington" [on the "Peace Process"], *Lies of Our Times,* May 1991, pp. 12-13.

23. Phyllis Bennis, "Bush's tool and victim: the U.N. in the New World Order," *CovertAction Information Bulletin,* Summer 1991; "Security Council Votes: Some Incentives," *The NECEF Report* [Near East Cultural and Education Foundation of Canada], April 1991, p. 2.

5. The Crisis of Democracy at Home

1. The best statement of the constraining force of advertising is Barnouw, *The Sponsor.*

2. For evidence, see Thomas Ferguson and Joel Rogers, *Right Turn,* New York: Hill and Wang, 1986, chapter 1.

3. Watt "remains the most sought-after GOP fund-raiser except for President Reagan and Vice President Bush." Dale Russakoff, "Watt brings candidates big money, big problems," *Philadelphia Inquirer,* April 14, 1982 (a *Washington Post Service* report).

4. It was the plaint of Professor Samuel Huntington in the "crisis of democracy" years of the early 1970s, that in the good old days, "Truman had been able to govern the country with the cooperation of a relatively small number of Wall Street lawyers and bankers," in Michael Crozier *et al.*, *Crisis of Democracy,* p. 97.

5. For an excellent recent account of the 1960s from the viewpoint of a sympathetic participant, Hans Koning, *Nineteen Sixty-Eight,* New York: W. W. Norton, 1987.

6. Herman and Chomsky, *Manufacturing Consent,* chapter 3.

7. Murray, *Red Scare,* Minneapolis: University of Minnesota Press, 1955, pp. 121-65.

8. *Ibid.,* p. 146. See also, Murray B. Levin, *Political Hysteria in America,* New York: Basic Books, 1981, p. 131.

9. See Caute, *The Great Fear,* p. 349 and *passim;* Charles J. V. Murphy, "McCarthy and the Businessmen," *Fortune,* April 1954, p. 180.

10. Kenneth O'Reilly, "Liberal Values, the Cold War, and American Intellectuals:

The Trauma of the Alger Hiss Case, 1950-1978," in Athan Theoharis, ed., *Beyond the Hiss Case,* Philadelphia: Temple University Press, 1982.

11. See Part 1 above.

12. That the development model put in place by National Security State generals created a revolution which did not previously exist is stated explicitly in a 1977 Brazilian statement by the International Movement of Catholic Intellectuals and Professionals, "Voice From Northeastern Brazil to III Conference of Bishops," Mexico, Nov. 1977, reprinted in *LADOC,* May-June 1978, p. 15.

13. A good statement of the character of this instruction is in Wolpin, *Military Aid and Counterrevolution in the Third World*; see also , Black, *United States Penetration of Brazil,* chapters 8-13.

14. George Miller, "White House Sleaze Is Back," *New York Times,* Op Ed, June 8, 1991.

15. Speech in Cleveland, June 26, 1934, quoted in Corwin Edwards, "Preserving Competition versus Regulating Monopoly," *American Economic Review,* March 1940, p. 167.

16. Donner, *Age of Surveillance,* p. 184. Another official, William C. Sullivan, told the Church Committee that: "Never once did I hear anybody, including myself, raise the question: 'Is this course of action legal, is it ethical or moral.' " *Ibid.,* p. 183.

17. Iran-Contra plaintiffs who merely lied under oath generally escaped jail. However, "Iran-contra figure Thomas G. Clines, convicted in September of filing false income-tax returns, was sentenced yesterday to 16 months in prison, the stiffest imprisonment imposed on any of the eight defendants convicted in the scandal." "Ex-CIA official gets 16 months for Iran-contra conviction," *Philadelphia Inquirer,* Dec. 14, 1990 (reproduced from the *Washington Post).* A longer prison sentence was given to an underling in the Department of Housing and Urban Affairs. "'Robin HUD,' a former real estate agent who said she stole from the government to give to the poor, was sentenced today to serve almost four years in prison and pay $600,000 in restitution." Jason DeParle, "'Robin HUD' Given a Stiff Sentence," *New York Times,* June 23, 1990, p. 6.

18. For a good news account, Fred Kaplan, "Judge's surprise sentence for North," *Philadelphia Inquirer,* July 9, 1989 [reprinted from *Boston Globe*]. See also letters in the *New York Times,* July 16, 1989, under the heading "North's Sentence Teaches Wrong Lessons."

19. By the Bush years, the United States had more people in jail and the highest incarceration rate in the world. "U.S. Leads World in Imprisonment," *New York Times* (Associated Press), Jan. 7, 1991, p. A14. For a survey, with comparisons to other countries and an analysis of U.S. political imprisonments, see "Attica: 1971-1991, A Commemorative Issue," ed. by Robert Weiss, *Social Justice,* Fall 1991.

20. A leftwing radical, Laura Whitehorn, received a 20 year sentence in 1990 for pleading guilty to bombing the Capitol, although no one was injured. One of her co-defendants, Linda Evans, "was ordered to serve five years for her role in the bombing conspiracy after completing a 35-year term she is already serving for illegally buying guns." "Radical Gets 20-Year Term in 1983 Bombing of U.S. Capitol," *New York Times* (Associated Press), Dec. 8, 1990, p. 14.

21. For many other quotes, see David Schmitz, "'A Fine Young Revolution'..." in *Radical History Review,* Sept. 1985.

22. See above, Part 3, p. 39.

6. The Struggle for Incentives...

1. Sometimes deregulation also means removing unreasonable impediments to competition. In the ongoing market ideology, it is assumed that this is *all* the word implies.
2. See Part 1, especially the discussion of the use of "free flow," pp. 15-18.
3. "The Ends and the Means," Feb. 22, 1981.
4. William Greider, "The Education of David Stockman," *Atlantic Monthly*, Dec. 1981, pp. 50, 52.
5. For a good account of the long history of anti-welfare ideology in Great Britain, see Peter Golding and Sue Middleton, *Images of Welfare: Press and Public Attitudes to Poverty*, Oxford, England: M. Robertson, 1982.
6. Ellen Hume, "Argument of 'Losing Ground' is That Aid Cripples Poor; Manna for Conservatives," *Wall Street Journal*, Sept. 17, 1985.
7. Benjamin Friedman, *Day of Reckoning*, New York: Random House, 1988, chapter X.
8. Greider also pointed out that on election day the media were already announcing that a tax increase was in the offing, but expressed no surprise, contrition, or anger, although they had uncritically swallowed Reagan's line that everything was fine and that no new taxes would be needed. "Educating Ronnie," *Rolling Stone*, Jan. 31, 1985, p. 23.
9. Greider, "Education of David Stockman," p. 51.
10. Karen Davis, "Reagan Administration Health Policy," *Journal of Public Health Policy*, Dec. 1981, p. 321.
11. Michael Katz, *In The Shadow of the Poor House*, New York: Basic Books, 1986, p. 286.
12. According to a Congressional Budget Office Study; see R. A. Zaldivar, "Study: poor earn less, but pay more in taxes," *Phildelphia Inquirer*, Feb. 17, 1990.
13. This according to calculations of Citizens for Tax Justice, cited in David Hess, "U.S. tax burden has shifted to lower incomes, study says," *Philadelphia Inquirer*, March 9, 1990.
14. This is well displayed in the Moynihan focus on the breakdown of the black family as the centerpiece of analysis and policy, leading readily to a policy of benign neglect (leaving it to the black families to take on minimum responsibilities). George Will rehashes the Moynihan model with clockwork regularity. See his "Not Recognizing the Newness of Urban Family Breakdown Will Worsen Things," *Philadelphia Inquirer*, Sept. 26, 1991. For a cogent critical analysis of this line of thought, see Carl Ginsburg, "Race and Media: The Enduring Life of the Moynihan Report," Institute for Media Analysis, Monograph Series No. 3, 1989.
15. This factor is stressed in Samuel Bowles, David Gordon and Thomas Weisskopf, "Right-Wing Economics Backfired," *Challenge*, Jan.-Feb. 1991, pp. 8-9.
16. *Day of Reckoning*, p. 174.
17. Bowles, Gordon and Weisskopf, "Right-Wing Economics Backfired," p. 5.
18. Friedman, *Day of Reckoning*, p. 198.
19. In the *New York Times*, May 13, 1978, quoted in Richard DuBoff, "The U.S. Budget Deficit: Love It Or Leave It," *Monthly Review*, Dec. 1989.
20. In his Business Council remarks, in 1988, Wriston said that "The familiar refrain that every family must balance its budget, so why shouldn't the government, has a nice ring to it, but no family I know of expenses its home...All in all, capital expenditures added up to 13.2 percent of federal outlays, a not inconsiderable amount of expense, and if funded in a capital budget, would produce near balance in the operating budget." Quoted in Robert Heilbroner and Peter Bernstein, *Debt and Deficit*, New York: W. W. Norton, 1989, p. 65. Ironically, Wriston is using this double standard to defend Reaganite budgets, which represent spendthrift and irresponsible use of government resources as no other

government in modern times. A second irony: Heilbroner and Bernstein use this quote in support of their position that the deficit is overrated as if it is a principled business analysis, without anywhere noting Wriston's completely opportunistic use of the argument.

21. For a further discussion of this point, see below, pp. 99-101.
22. *Day of Reckoning,* p. 205.
23. See Richard DuBoff, "Full Employment: The History of a Receding Target," *Politics and Society,* 1977, pp. 1-25.
24. See Gardner Ackley, *Macroeconomics: Theory and Policy,* New York: Macmillan, 1978, pp. 469-77; DuBoff, "Full Employment," pp. 18-22.
25. Leonard Silk and David Vogel, *Ethics and Profits: The Crisis of Confidence in American Business,* New York: Simon and Schuster, 1976.
26. Philip Shabecoff, "Report Finds Interior Department Mismanaged Coal Lease Program," *New York Times,* Feb. 9, 1984, p. 1.
27. This history is discussed in Richard DuBoff and Edward S. Herman, "The Promotional-Financial Dynamic of Merger Movements: A Historical Perspective," *Journal of Economic Issues,* March 1989.
28. See Louis Lowenstein, "Management Buyouts," *Columbia Law Review,* May 1985; Laura Saunders, "How the Government Subsidized Leveraged Buyouts," *Forbes,* Nov. 28, 1988, pp. 192-96.
29. For a summary, see Jonathan Lash, Katherine Gillman and David Sheridan, *A Season of Spoils,* New York: Pantheon, 1984, pp. 224-231.
30. According to one estimate by an official of the Department of Interior, "80 percent of the private forest lands have been cut, and have not been put back into timber production." Quoted in Jack Shepherd, *The Forest Killers,* New York: Weybright and Talley, 1976, p. 38. For further documentation, Shepherd, pp. 34-47.
31. *Ibid.,* p. 69.
32. *Ibid.,* pp. 70-81.
33. *Ibid.,* p. 93.
34. Richard Rice, *The Uncounted Costs of Logging,* vol. 5 of a series on the national forests, Washington: The Wilderness Society, 1989, pp. 4-5.
35. One commentator, philosopher Thomas Birch, noted in 1971 that "The mentality that governs Forest Service management decisions is characterized by a near and complete failure in morality, a failure predicated on the fallacious conviction that everything that is there is for our use, and, therefore, must be utilized for our purposes and cannot simply be left alone." Quoted in Shepherd, p. 94.
36. Rice, "Uncounted Costs," p. 11.
37. "On the Tongass National Forest in Southeast Alaska, for example, the Forest Service entered into a number of 50-year contracts with timber purchasers that featured guaranteed supplies of timber at highly subsidized rates." *Ibid.,* pp. 4-5.
38. See Shepherd, *Forest Killers,* pp. 105-6.
39. Richard Rice, "Below Cost Timber Sales on the National Forests," Speech dated May 21, 1991.
40. Richard Rice, "Memorandum on below-cost timber sales," May 2, 1991, p. 2.
41. Robert Wolf, "Promises to Keep," *The Environmental Forum,* July-Aug., 1990, p. 10.
42. Rice, "Below Cost Timber Sales," p. 1.
43. Shepherd, *Forest Killers,* pp. 82-86.
44. *Ibid.,* p. 89.
45. It is often pointed out that the damage to the soil in the heavy logging of the overmature trees frequently makes the reseeding ineffectual. See Shepherd, *Forest Killers,* pp. 109, 133, 152, 358-60.

46. Patrick M. Reilly, "Media Firms Target Captive Audiences, Taking a Page Out of Whittle's Book," *Wall Street Journal*, Feb. 28, 1990.

47. Joanne Lipman, "Hurt by Ad Downturn, More Magazines Use Favorable Articles to Woo Sponsors," *Wall Street Journal*, July 30, 1991; Lipman, "Brand-Name Products Are Popping Up in TV Shows," *Wall Street Journal*, Feb. 19, 1991.

48. Michael Vitez, "Education, Inc.," *Philadelphia Inquirer*, July 21, 1991; Gary Putka, "Whittle Develops Plan to Operate Schools for Profit," *Wall Street Journal*, May 15, 1991.

49. *Selling Culture: Bloomingdale's, Diana Vreeland, and the New Aristocracy of Taste in Reagan's America*, New York: Pantheon, 1986.

50. These quotes are taken from Herbert Schiller's *Culture, Inc.: The Corporate Takeover of Public Expression*, New York: Oxford, 1989.

51. These matters are discussed with clarity and power in *ibid*.

Epilogue: The End of History?

1. See Daniel Bell, *The End of Ideology*, New York: Free Press, 1960. For commentary and critique, see Stuart Hall, "The Rediscovery of 'Ideology,' " in Michael Gurevitch *et al.*, eds., *Culture, Society and the Media*, London: Methuen, 1982.

2. The classic statement is Walt W. Rostow, *The Stages of Economic Growth*, New York: Cambridge University Press, 1960.

3. The World Bank's *World Development Report 1990* states that "more than one billion people in the developing world are living in poverty," defined as those "struggling to survive on less than $370 a year." (p. 1.)

4. Lester Brown, *State of the World, 1991*, New York: W. W. Norton, 1991, p. 153.

5. Gunnar Adler-Karlsson, *Western Economic Warfare, 1947-1967*, Stockholm: Almvist & Wiksell, 1968.

6. See above, Part 2, pp. 19-21.

7. *Ibid.*

8. Journalist Paul Berman has repeatedly asserted that the Sandinistas failed because of straightforward mismanagement, but he has never indicated how he isolates management failure from the effects of systematic attacks by a superpower whose design was to divert attention and resources from constructive activity to defense.

9. These regimes did badly in part because they were following the western tradition of equating progress with GNP growth.

10. See Naomi Roht-Arriaza, "The Politics of Environmental Destruction," *Report on Guatemala*, pp. 4-5, 11-12.

11. Except when serviceable to western aims, as during the Persian Gulf war. See the *Doublespeak Dictionary* definition of United Nations.

12. E. J. Hobsbawm, *The Age of Revolution: Europe 1789-1848*, London: Weidenfeld and Nicolson, 1962, p. 104.

13. See Noam Chomsky, *Deterring Democracy*, London: Verso, 1991, pp. 215-48.

Notes to *Doublespeak Dictionary*

1. "Everybody knew that lobbyists gave money to buy access and, whether indirectly or overtly, to gain some influence over legislation. So the more money lawmakers took, the more most of them professed to dislike it. Coelho's ethical code was common among lawmakers. Doing official favors for donors was permitted. The unforgivable sin was to make the connection explicit." Brooks Jackson, *Honest Graft,* New York: Knopf, 1988, p. 104.

   "Aspin told a newspaper in his district that the defense contractors know they must contribute 'if they want to talk to the chairman.' Not surprisingly, after Aspin ascended to the chairmanship [of the House Armed Services Committee], the campaign contributions he received from the PACs of defense contractors in the first ten *months* were nearly 50 percent above the total for the previous six *years.*" Philip Stern, *The Best Congress Money Can Buy,* New York: Putnam, 1988, p. 64.

2. "We are ready to negotiate, but not at the expense of rousing false hopes which would be dashed by new failures...The only way to deal with the Soviet Union, we have found from hard experience, is to create situations of strength." (Speeches of Dean Acheson reprinted in the State Department *Bulletin,* March 20 and March 27, 1950.)

3. In an article "Soviet Union: How to Make a Comeback After Your Empire Folds," in the *Washington Post Weekly,* Sept. 17, 1990, Michael Dobbs wrote that the Soviet Union is "exhausted by foreign adventures." He quotes an unnamed Soviet analyst as saying that "There is now a consensus against foreign military adventures abroad." Dobbs referred to "forays into developing countries, such as Afghanistan and Nicaragua" as illustrations of this adventurism. Reagan also spoke of the Soviet's "helping the Sandinista regime in Nicaragua subvert its neighbors" as bad business, suggesting that "the Soviets must give up these military adventures" if the world "is to know true peace." Statement of Aug. 29, 1987, quoted in Chomsky, *Culture of Terrorism,* p. 184.

4. "Throughout 1961 and 1962, as the Kennedy team debated whether or not to send U.S. troops to Cuba, they also had begun to send over thousands of military 'advisers' into Southeast Asia. The use of the word 'adviser,' however, misled Congress, the press, and the public. The men who advised were Green Berets, elite shock troops, specially trained for counterinsurgency warfare." Landau, *Dangerous Doctrine,* p. 88.

5. "Editors would also cloak themselves in the mantles of 'balance' and 'objectivity,' complaining that they could not be expected to engage in 'advocacy journalism' by examining official statements and policies too closely, when all they might be expected to advocate by so doing was the public interest." Gervasi, *Myth of Soviet Military Supremacy,* p. 120.

6. According to the estimate of Anthony Eden, in the fighting which preceded the Geneva Accords of 1954, "The Americans had put in nine times more supplies of materials than the Chinese..." (*Full Circle,* Boston: Houghton Mifflin, 1960, pp. 126-7.) President Eisenhower stated that not only was there "no incontrovertible evidence of overt Red Chinese participation in the Indochinese conflict," but that the leader of the forces we were fighting also would have won a crushing victory in a free election (*Mandate for Change,* Garden City, NY: Doubleday, 1963, pp. 340, 372). Nonetheless, in 1953 the United States tried to organize a coalition to fight an alleged Chinese "aggression" in Vietnam. See Eden, *Full Circle,* pp. 100 *ff;* Victor Bator, *Vietnam: A Diplomatic Tragedy,* Garden City, NY: Doubleday, 1965, *passim.*

In 1962 the United States had over 10,000 troops in South Vietnam, and "one-third to one-half of all combat missions, whether in Vietnamese or unmarked planes, have been flown by U.S. pilots." ("The New Metal Birds," *Newsweek,* Oct. 29, 1962.) In the latter part of 1962, according to Robert Scigliano, U.S. officials in Saigon estimated that "about one-half of the South Vietnamese support the National Liberation Front..." *South Vietnam: Nation under Stress,* Boston: Houghton Mifflin, 1963, p. 145.

In June 1966, Senator Mike Mansfield stated that at the time of the escalation of the war to North Vietnam in February 1965 there were about 400 North Vietnamese troops in South Vietnam. This figure was subsequently confirmed by the Defense Department as "essentially correct." In early February 1965 there were over 23,000 U.S. troops in South Vietnam. *Washington Daily News,* June 23, 1966; *Birmingham News,* February 9, 1965.

7. Senator Dave Durenberger, chair of the Senate Select Committee on Intelligence, speaking to the National Press Club in March 1985, supported a U.S.-sponsored invasion of Nicaragua, if other nations could be brought into a collective "response to Sandinista aggression." Durenberger did not support the charge of aggression, but by implication it was Nicaragua's not following orders and having the audacity to defend itself against Globocop. Quoted in Noam Chomsky, *Turning the Tide,* Boston: South End Press, 1983, p. 171.

8. Adlai Stevenson used this term in a UN speech in 1964 as he explained the basis for U.S. intervention in Vietnam. The United States was then furiously resisting all efforts to settle the conflict there peacefully, as its leaders understood that its political position in Vietnam was weak; hence the need to make the indigenous population an aggressor against itself. See Chomsky, *Turning the Tide,* p. 89.

9. "J. Edgar Hoover told the Commission [on Civil Disorders] that 'outside agitators' had played a role in this summer's Negro riots." Roy Reed, "Riot 'Agitators' Cited By Hoover," *New York Times,* Aug. 3, 1967. Ronald Reagan used the term to explain the basis of the Intifada in the Israeli-occupied territories. Susan Rafsky, "Outside Agitators Foment Palestinian Riots, Reagan Suggests," *New York Times,* Feb. 25, 1988.

10. See Teresa Hayter and Catherine Watson, *Aid: Rhetoric and Reality,* London: Pluto Press, 1985; Frances Moore Lappe and Joseph Collins, *World Hunger: Twelve Myths,* New York: Grove Press, 1986, chapter 10; William Borden, *The Pacific Alliance: United States Foreign Economic Policy and Japanese Trade Recovery, 1947-1955,* Madison: University of Wisconsin Press, 1984; Tom Barry and Deb Preusch, *The Soft War,* New York: Grove Press, 1988; Chomsky, *Necessary Illusions,* p. 363, n. 21.

11. "The inability to score a success even in the public relations aspect of the Alliance was especially noteworthy because with the ignorance which had marked the U.S. economic policy determinations, this was alone the field where a measure of success might have been expected. As Senator Case...has noted when asked whether he thought the Johnson Administration had lost ground in its appeal to the great mass of Latin American people... 'I don't think the Kennedy Administration achieved very much. I think its heart was in the right place but I don't think we got very far, frankly. It was more a public relations matter.' Yet, even the public relations effort failed." Simon G. Hanson, "The Alliance for Progress: The Fourth Year," *Inter-American Economic Affairs,* Autumn, 1966, p. 8.

"Many Latin-American governments have used the Alliance as a bargaining lever to obtain increases in United States aid precisely so as to avoid changing their domestic situation." Chilean President Frei, in *Foreign Affairs,* April 1967.

12. "The decision to deploy a 'light' antiballistic missile defense system costing $5 billion seems hard to justify in terms of anything except political expediency... There is little doubt that the present system is the prelude to a heavy system, if

only because once any system is deployed it is almost impossible to resist the politically potent argument to 'improve' it. Thus we pursue the impossible goal of perfect security in response to not very acute threats, while the acute ones—worldwide hunger, poverty and discontent, racial injustice, and a poisoned environment—remain overshadowed, largely ignored, and wholly unmet. It is hard to resist the conclusion that the decision to deploy an ABM system, which is a clear victory for the military-industrial complex, is not a victory for democracy." Robert Gomer, "The ABM Decision," *Bulletin of the Atomic Scientists,* November 1967, p. 29.

13. This follows from the fact that the United States has had predominant military power but a relatively weak political position in the Third World. Appeasement as giving ground merely on the basis of political weakness fits well the demands of a country with great power to exercise force. See *Acheson, Dean,* and *Force.* See also, Chomsky, *Turning the Tide,* "The Rule of Law and the Rule of Force," pp. 89-95.

14. "I believe it must be a policy of the United States to support free peoples who are resisting attempted subjugation by armed minorities or outside pressures." President Harry Truman, March 1947, in seeking support for the armed minority government of former collaborators in Greece. See *Junta* and note 101.

15. Statement made by Abrams in support of Contra aid, June 20, 1986, USIA Foreign Policy Briefing Transcript, p. 15.

16. See Richard Levine, "A Grain of Salt: U.S.-Soviet Arms Pact May Be More a Symbol Than Effective Rein," *Wall Street Journal,* May 26, 1972; Richard Burt, "Limited Ceiling: Treaties That Slow Up The Arms Race Usually Speed It Up," *New York Times,* Dec. 24, 1978.

17. "These sales are employing American labor and they are providing profits to American business. I think we should be encouraged and congratulated on making these arrangements." (Robert McNamara, quoted in *New York Times,* July 31, 1967.) Back in July 1967, the United States was also allegedly selling arms as "a contribution to peace and stability" ("U.S. Selling Arms To Sustain Peace, State Dept. Says," *York Gazette and Daily,* July 21, 1967), just as it was doing in 1981 (Judith Miller, "Buckley, Outlining Reagan Policy, Calls Arms Sales Abroad 'Vital' Tool," *New York Times,* May 22, 1981). And then again in the immediate aftermath of the Gulf War in the spring of 1991, "To a cynic listening to Defense Secretary Cheney last week, the new world order might have sounded surprisingly like the old one. Mr. Cheney, returning from a 10-day trip to Europe and the Middle East, announced arms sales worth $2.1 billion." "Same Old Arms Sales," *New York Times,* June 9, 1991, p. F2.

18. "In the OCO offices in Saigon, I was offered a freshly typed list of Viet Cong acts of terror committed during the previous week... As I looked down the list I noticed that it included an attack on a U.S. army post! 'Is that terrorism?' I wondered, pointing. The official studied the item. 'No. It doesn't belong there,' he admitted, poring over the type-sheet with mystified air, like on awakening from a dream. 'We'll have to correct that,' he added briskly. It was clear that he had offered me those figures in *good faith,* having seen nothing wrong with them; to him an attack on a U.S. army unit, even in wartime, was dastardly." Mary McCarthy, *Vietnam,* New York: Harcourt, Brace, 1967, p. 55.

19. Speaking of the Vietcong attack at Pleiku, in early February 1965, Secretary McNamara stated that "The fact is that the attack was carried out in the dead of night; it was a sneak attack." *New York Times,* Feb. 8, 1965.

20. "Dixie Station had a reason. It was simple. A pilot going into combat for the first time is a bit like a swimmer about to dive into an icy lake. He likes to get his big toe wet and then wade around a little before leaping off the high board into the numbing depths. So it was fortunate that young pilots could get their first taste

of combat under the direction of a forward air controller over a flat country in bright sunshine where nobody was shooting back with high-powered ack-ack. He learns how it feels to drop bombs on human beings and watch huts go up in a boil of orange flame when his aluminum napalm tanks tumble into them. He gets hardened to pressing the firing button and cutting people down like little cloth dummies, as they sprint frantically under him. He gets his sword bloodied for the rougher things to come." Frank Harvey, *Air War-Vietnam,* New York: Bantam, 1967, p. 2. Harvey also refers to hitting "'warm-up' targets in the Mekong Delta" from Dixie Station, p. 13.

21. "'These are good people,' Father Foley [St. Rita's Church, Chicago Lawn] said stubbornly. 'Policemen and schoolteachers and working men. Put yourself in their place. You've given 20 years to building up your property—you're in a nice neighborhood now, you have a little house worth fifteen or twenty thousand dollars maybe. Some colored moves into your block, and your property drops down two, three thousand dollars... Now you know how they live— pretty soon their friends move in and there are six or seven families living in the house.'" Gene Marine, "I've got nothing against the Colored, understand," *Ramparts,* Nov. 1966, p. 15.

22. William Beecher stated that the "defense establishment [was] conceived by its planners to...maintain a credible bargaining position in further efforts to limit strategic nuclear arms..." "Military Budget: A Look Behind the Figures," *New York Times,* Feb. 4, 1973. The *New York Times* has supported this notion editorially time and again: "True, the bill reduced spending on Star Wars from $4.8 billion to $4 billion. But that's still a tidy sum, large enough to maintain bargaining leverage with Moscow in the strategic arms reduction talks." "All Politics, No Defense," Aug. 7, 1988. Later in the same year, assailing Dukakis, the editorialists wrote: "The Democrat still talks about scrapping the two new land-based missiles, MX and Midgetman, and hints vaguely at an alternative. There's nothing here to show that Mr. Dukakis appreciates the value of a bargaining chip." "The Soviet Challenge, Unanswered," Oct. 23, 1988.

23. Just prior to the Cuban revolution, U.S. interests owned over 90 per cent of telephone and electric facilities, 50 per cent of public service railways, 40 per cent of raw sugar production, most of the cattle ranches and major tourist facilities, and together with the British, virtually the entire oil business. U.S. Dept. of Commerce, *Investment in Cuba,* 1956, p. 10.

24. James Stockdale, a pilot on the aircraft carrier U.S.S. Ticonderoga, flew above the two U.S. cruisers allegedly being attacked by North Vietnamese gunboats on August 4, 1964, and saw nothing. James and Sybil Stockdale, "I Saw Us Invent the Pretext for Our Vietnam War," *Washington Post,* Oct. 7, 1984, p. D1. See also, Landau, *The Dangerous Doctrine,* pp. 90, 97.

25. The Harris poll, taken shortly after the Bay of Tonkin incident, indicated that "The Vietnam action has brought President Johnson up from 45 per cent of the vote in the South to an even 50-50." *Philadelphia Inquirer,* Aug. 14, 1964.

26. An earlier version of this principle was stated by Thorstein Veblen in 1917: "It is quite a safe generalization that when hostilities have once been got fairly under way by the interested statesmen, the patriotic sentiment of the nation may confidently be counted on to back the enterprise irrespective of the merits of the quarrel... A corollary following from this general theorem may be worth noting in the same connection. Any politician who succeeds in embroiling his country in a war, however nefarious, becomes a popular hero and is reputed a wise and righteous statesman, at least for the time being." *An Inquiry into the Nature of Peace and the Terms of Its Perpetuation,* New York: B.W. Huebsch, 1917, p. 22.

27. As Chomsky points out, this crisis in which the best and brightest accepted "a high probability of global destruction to establish the principle that the US

alone has the right to keep nuclear weapons on the border of an enemy...surely must be one of the low points of human history. It is a fact of some significance for the future that it is generally regarded here as a glorious moment, 'one of the finest examples of diplomatic prudence, and perhaps the finest hour of John F. Kennedy's Presidency,' in the words of the same respected scholar [Graham Allison]." *Turning the Tide,* pp. 172-73.

28. "Bipartisanship eliminated meaningful congressional debate about the premises and day-to-day exercise of foreign policy... Congress still could obstruct, delay, and cause problems, but it could not truly participate in the crucial decisions of global power. However, the top officials in the national security bureaucracy were able to control discussion and debate on key foreign policy questions through control of information. The obsessive need for secrecy allowed the president, or those acting in his name, to invoke national security not only in times of national difficulties but whenever it became convenient." Landau, *The Dangerous Doctrine,* p. 48.

29. "The 1964 Mann, or Mann-Johnson, policy in the Dominican Republic implicitly sought to prevent the restoration of the constitutional Bosch government. After recognizing the post-Bosch regime, the Johnson administration in February 1964 appointed a new ambassador, W. Tapley Bennett, Jr., who proceeded to establish the closest personal and political ties with the new rulers. The United States poured more money into the country after Bosch's overthrow—about $100,000,000 in direct and guaranteed loans—than had ever been made available to any Dominican regime before." Theodore Draper, "The Dominican Crisis," *Commentary,* Dec. 1965, p. 36.

"What the record reveals, in fact, is that from the outset of the upheaval [in April 1965] there was a concentrated U.S. Government effort, if not actually a formal decision, to checkmate the rebel movement by whatever means and whatever cost." Philip Geyelin, *Wall Street Journal,* June 25, 1965.

30. A major finding of the Gerbner-Gross-Morgan-Signorielli studies of the impact of TV violence on the TV audience is that heavy viewers tend to be insecure and tend to favor the use of force to solve social and international problems. George Gerbner, Larry Gross, Michael Morgan and Nancy Signorielli, "Charting the Mainstream: Television's Contributions to Political Orientations," *Journal of Communication,* Spring 1982, pp. 100-127.

31. The information in Von Braun's security evaluation of February 26, 1948, says that "he was a member of the [Nazi] Party from 1 May 1937 and was also a Major in the SS, which appears to have been an honorary commission. The extent of his Party participation cannot be determined in this Theater. Like the majority of members, he may have been a mere opportunist. Subject has been in the United States more than two years..." Quoted in *Bulletin of Atomic Scientists,* April 1985, p. 19.

32. "Mr. Nixon underscored his determination to pound away at the same deceptive code words by inveighing against 'an arbitrary racial balance' in a Michigan antibusing stronghold Thursday." "Distortions on Busing," editorial, *New York Times,* Aug. 29, 1972.

33. "Captured Viet Cong documents have set forth a new and frightening enemy timetable for the war in Vietnam: 'Bloodbath in May, Victory in June.'" "Reds Predict June Victory in Vietnam," *Philadelphia Bulletin,* March 11, 1968.

34. "Now, in Guatemala in 1954, what Wisner and the CIA needed was someone to serve as a leader of the coup and a focal point around which anti-Arbenz Guatemalans could rally. The man chosen was Colonel Carlos Castillo-Armas, a dapper, dedicated and ascetic-looking career officer who had tunneled his way out of prison to freedom after leading an unsuccessful revolt against Arbenz in 1950." David Wise and Thomas B. Ross, *The Invisible Government,* New York:

Random House, 1964, p. 183. Immediately on assuming power, in order to crush internal opposition, "Castillo Armas picked José Bernabe Linares, who ran the secret police under the late dictator Ubico to perform this service for him. Linares was known to have submerged political enemies in electric-shock baths, and perfected a head-shrinking steel skull cap to pry loose secrets and crush improper thoughts." *Hispanic American Report,* Aug.-Sept., 1954, p. 10.

35. "The most obvious change in climate [following Castro's victory in Cuba] was the agreement of the Eisenhower administration in mid-1960, reversing long-established policy, to major economic support for Latin American social welfare projects designed to raise the living standards of the masses and to head off additional Castro-type revolutions." Edwin Lieuwen, *Arms and Politics in Latin America,* New York: Praeger, Revised ed., 1961, p. xi.

36. The *Philadelphia Inquirer* prides itself on balance in its regular Op. Ed. columnists, with David Broder and Jeff Greenfield on "the left," George Will and Charles Krauthammer on the right. Broder's and Greenfield's columns fit precisely the concept of celebratory liberal, neither of them ever making any waves that would upset anybody in the mainstream.

37. "It is easier for a camel to go through the eye of a needle, than for a rich man to enter into the kingdom of God." (Matthew, xix, 24.)

38. "According to officials here [Mochoa, South Vietnam], the peasants fear most the uniformed soldiers of the Civilian Irregular Defense groups—trained and paid for by the United States—who regularly rape, beat and rob the villagers they are supposed to protect." (R. W. Apple, "Saigon's Troops Plunder Hamlet," *New York Times,* Nov. 28, 1966.) The substitution of "Civilian Irregular" for "mercenary" was suggested in a vocabulary guideline for reporters issued by the U.S. authorities in Vietnam (see *Newsweek,* Oct. 20, 1969.)

39. The U.S. mass media have been very generous in finding civilian *rule* in countries like El Salvador, Guatemala, and the Southern Cone, where their government supports the regime (and supported the prior military leaders now in barracks retreat). Once again, they don't look below the surface when this is serviceable to the National Interest.

40. "Class warfare, it seems, is making a comeback." Alan Murray and Gerald Seib, "New Populism: Politicians Exploit Broad Public Support for Soaking the Rich," *Wall Street Journal,* Oct. 12, 1990.

41. Full accounts are given in Donner, *Age of Surveillance,* chapter 6; Blackstock, *Cointelpro;* Ward Churchill and Jim Vander Wall, *Agents of Repression* and *Cointelpro Papers;* Brian Glick, *War At Home.*

42. "Am I missing something, or is there some reason why Israeli assassination squads are called 'commandos,' while Arab (and, for that matter, IRA) squads are called 'terrorists'? Is it really just the pretty uniforms they wear?," Geoffrey Stokes, "Press Clips," *Village Voice,* April 26, 1988.

43. "Our present commitment to oppose force and terror by the National Liberation Front in South Vietnam is as solemn an engagement as any modern nation has made." (Herman Kahn, *Look Magazine,* Aug. 9, 1966.) Kahn never discussed when or where this commitment was entered into; nor did he discuss its possible conflict with other unmentioned but more explicit agreements, such as the U.N. Charter and the Geneva Accords, among other matters. See also, note 75 for a quote along the same lines by President Lyndon Johnson himself.

44. Marlene Cimons, "Bush Calls for Compassion, and Cure, for AIDS Victims," *Los Angeles Times,* March 30, 1990. This news report opens with the statement that Bush calls for compassion, and legislation to protect AIDS victims from discrimination. Eventually it quotes Jean McGuire, executive director of the AIDS Action Council, who "called Bush's speech 'long on compassion, but short on commitment.' " The quotes are from a speech by President Nixon explaining

why the social budget must be cut.

45. "Naturally, the common people don't want war; neither in Russia nor in England nor in America, nor for that matter in Germany. That is understood. But after all, it is the *leaders* of the country who determine the policy and it is always a simple matter to drag the people along, whether it is a democracy or a fascist dictatorship or a Parliament or a Communist dictatorship."

"'There is one difference,' I pointed out. 'In a democracy the people have some say in the matter through their representatives, and in the United States only Congress can declare war.' "

"'Oh, that is all well and good but, voice or no voice, the people can always be brought to the bidding of the leaders. That is easy. All you have to do is tell them they are being attacked and denounce the pacificists for lack of patriotism and exposing the country to danger. It works the same way in any country.'" Hermann Goering, from G. M. Gilbert, *Nuremberg Diary,* New York: New American Library, 1947, p. 278.

46. "Only one dollar out of every six of Representative Howard's 1986 campaign money came from his own constituents. The other five came from individuals and groups not qualified to vote in his district on election day." Stern, *Best Congress Money Can Buy,* p. 95. According to Mass. congressman James Shannon: "I'm no Common Causer, but this stuff has been bothering me... You go where the money is if you want to raise money, and its not going to be with the traditional Democratic constituencies. That's the problem." Quoted in Elizabeth Drew, *Politics and Money,* New York: Macmillan, 1983, p. 52.

47. "The former American ambassador to Moscow, Mr. George F. Kennan, who we knew in those years as the advocate of the containment policy, who was the chief policy planner of the State Department, declared recently in a lecture at Geneva University in Switzerland (I am quoting from the London *Times* of May 12, 1965), that 'after the Second World War, American policy makers could see Communism only in terms of a military threat. In creating NATO...they had drawn a line arbitrarily across Europe against an attack no one was planning.' Mr. Kennan, who in those years preached an containment policy, declares now (better late than never!) that the containment policy had nothing to contain." Isaac Deutscher, "Myths of the Cold War," in David Horowitz, ed., *Containment and Revolution,* Boston: Beacon Press, 1967, p. 14.

"As George F. Kennan, the author of the 'containment policy' has emphasized, American policy was 'by no means limited to holding the line.' And as Byrnes has repeatedly stressed, in 1945 and 1946 senior American officials were not primarily concerned with a Soviet political or military threat to Western Europe, their eyes were focused on conditions in the Soviet-occupied zone. Byrnes has been quite explicit; his policy always aimed at forcing the Russians to yield in Eastern Europe, and in mid-1947 he still continued to argue that the United States had it in its power to force the Russians to 'retire in a very decent manner.'" Gar Alperovitz, *Atomic Diplomacy: Hiroshima and Potsdam,* London: Secker & Warburg, 1966, p. 234.

48. On the contemporary use of "containment" as synonymous with "attack," Alfonso Chardy in the *Miami Herald* wrote that "Officials said that if Congress rejects the package [of aid to Contra armies], then Reagan may feel free to use other measures to *contain* Nicaragua." "Reagan Weighs Nicaragua Options," March 9, 1986.

49. "Under the present system of nonaccountability, it is possible for contractors to inflate costs by pricing changes, and to attribute cost overruns to contract changes. In the vernacular of the world of defense contracts, change notices are sometimes referred to as contract nourishment." Subcommittee on Economy in Government, *The Economics of Military Procurement,* 91st Congress, 1st Session, 1969, p. 12.

50. In speaking of Bernard Fall's evidence and conclusion that the Vietcong uprising was not externally originated, John Mecklin states: "Surely such a contention is debatable in view of its diametric contradiction of the official position of the U.S. government." *New York Times,* July 2, 1967.

51. This is the estimate given by Ingrid Palmer, for the corruption drain of aid programs to Indonesia in the decade following the 1965 coup. "The Economy, 1965-1975," in Malcolm Caldwell, ed., *Ten Years' Military Terror In Indonesia,* Nottingham: Spokesman Books, 1975, p. 148. For details on Indonesian shakedown state practices, see Chomsky and Herman, *The Washington Connection,* pp. 205-218.

52. "A memorandum [of] Nov. 26 by David Packard, Deputy Secretary of Defense, asked senior defense officials to consider using the term 'cost growth'... Mr. Packard wrote that 'cost over-run' was widely used by Government and public with 'imprecise meaning.'" *New York Times,* Dec. 11, 1969.

53. "Because Americans typically start from the previously described 'popular support' view, we frequently feel uncomfortable collaborating with established governments against insurgent movements... Castro, struggling in the Sierra Maestra, could be easily seen as a popular, Jacksonian crusader for the common man and against the entrenched interests; Batista fitted equally well the role of ruthless, exploitative tyrant. That there was a reality as well as appearance in this role-casting is not the point. The point is that the emotional reaction of Americans to insurgencies frequently interferes with a realistic assessment of alternatives..."

"Confiscation of chickens, razing of houses, or destruction of villages have a place in counterinsurgency efforts, but only if they are done for a strong reason: namely, to penalize those who have assisted the insurgents [presumably just plain stealing or completely random destruction would not be a 'strong reason' for this Rand Corporation economist]... Military discipline must be tightened and brought under firm control so that whatever harshness is meted out by government forces is unambiguously imposed because of behavior of the population that contributes to the insurgent movement." Charles Wolf, Jr., *United States Policy and the Third World,* Boston: Little, Brown, 1967, pp. 57-58, 66.

54. According to former Master Sergeant Donald Duncan, "One day I asked one of our Vietnamese helicopter pilots what he thought of the last bomb raid. 'I think maybe today we make many Vietcong.' " *Ramparts,* Feb. 1966, p. 24.

55. On December 19, 1965, U.N. Ambassador Arthur J. Goldberg stated that "We have had a great problem here maintaining our credibility with our own people." (*New York Times,* Dec. 20, 1965) This was followed almost immediately by a "peace offensive," described by Max Frankel as a "virtually public campaign of propaganda and psychological warfare to win support for the U.S. position and respect for its intentions." *New York Times,* Jan. 5, 1966.

56. "The order to eliminate 2,4,5-T left crop destruction—called 'crop denial' by the command—the major remaining part of the herbicide program." Ralph Blumenthal, "U.S. Says Division in Vietnam Used Banned Defoliant," *New York Times,* Oct. 24, 1970. For a more extensive discussion of the program, see William Buckingham, *Operation Ranch Hand: The Air Force and Herbicides in Southeast Asia, 1961-1971,* Washington, DC: U.S. Air Force, 1982.

57. See also, Peter Riddell, "Talks yes, but no deals, says Washington," *Financial Times,* Dec. 7, 1990.

58. "[In the language of deterrence theorists] a Soviet first-strike capability would suggest the possibility of a surprise attack, and so be terribly destabilizing, whereas an *American* first-strike capability exists only as a potential response to 'aggression,' and so is not destabilizing at all. In Wohlstetter's classic remark that 'When not coupled with the ability to strike in retaliation [a first-strike] ca-

pability might suggest—erroneously, to be sure, in the case of the democracies—an intention to strike first,' one is reminded of Lenin's dictum that a gun in the hands of a policeman is an instrument of capitalist oppression, but a gun in the hands of a worker is an instrument of liberation." Philip Green, *Deadly Logic, The Theory of Nuclear Deterrence*, Columbus: Ohio State University Press, 1966, p. 246.

59. For an excellent discussion of the application of the word to the Third World, see Chomsky, *Necessary Illusions*, pp. 106-09.

60. "Network executives now tended to survey their schedules in terms of demographic product demands. Negotiations resembled transactions to deliver blocs of people. An advertising agency would be telling a network, in effect: 'For Shampoo Y, our client is ready to invest $1,800,000 in women 18-49.'" Barnouw, *The Sponsor*, p. 71.

61. After pointing out that the Soviet Union is perceived as a threat by the U.S. mass media if it aids a victim of U.S. attack, Chomsky notes that: "Such actions prove that Soviet leaders are not serious about detente and cannot be trusted, statesmen and commentators soberly observe." *Necessary Illusions*, p. 26. It was never suggested in the mainstream media that U.S. attacks on Nicaragua or support of South African aggression and mass murder in El Salvador, raised any question about the U.S. commitment to detente.

62. "Shortly after the president [Kennedy] was inaugurated, CIA director Allen Dulles told Kennedy that he would face a 'disposal problem' should he not go ahead with the invasion of Cuba. What would the president do with the thousands of Cuban exiles that had been promised his support for the liberation of their island? They had been well trained in the arts of death and destruction." Landau, *Dangerous Doctrine*, p. 74.

63. "And I think the time's come when it would be good for all of us to take a new fresh look at dissent, and we welcome responsible dissent [see *Responsible*], but there's a great deal of difference between responsible dissent and some of the things that are taking place in this country which I consider to be extremely dangerous to our national interest, and I consider it not very helpful to the men that are fighting the war for us." Transcript of President Lyndon B. Johnson's News Conference, *New York Times*, Nov. 18, 1967.

64. "I'm amazed that the press in this country who insist on the right to live by the First Amendment and to be protected by it, doesn't insist that these storm trooper tactics live by the First Amendment, too, and that they be wiped out." Transcript of President's Press Conference, *New York Times*, Nov. 18, 1967.

65. "Ironically, the consultants being used to advise companies on destroying papers describe themselves as experts in 'document retention,' " Demac, *Liberty Denied*, p. 63.

66. For a summary of "dove" positions on Nicaragua, see Chomsky, *Necessary Illusions*, pp. 60-61.

67. This is a satirical rendering of the dove position during the Vietnam war, where the military enterprise was not challenged, only the next escalation.

68. "As 'downwinders,' born and raised downwind of the Hanford Nuclear Reservation in Washington, we learned several years ago that the government decided—with cold deliberation—to use us as guinea pigs by releasing radioactivity into our food, water, milk and air without our consent." Tom Bailie, "Growing Up as a Nuclear Guinea Pig," *New York Times*, Op. Ed., July 22, 1990.

69. This was a phrase used by Vice President Spiro Agnew during the Nixon Administration's assault on press and protesters.

70. "Adolph Eichmann was a thoroughly responsible person, according to his understanding of responsibility. For him it was clear that the heads of state set policy. His role was to implement, and fortunately, he felt, it was never part of his

job actually to have to kill anyone." Lisa Peattie, "Normalizing the unthinkable," *Bulletin of Atomic Scientists,* March 1984, p. 33.

71. "The emphasis of these so-called 'empowerment' proposals is on self-help, free-market enterprise and minimal cost to the government." Timothy Noah, "Bush 'Empowerment' Self-Help Plans for the Poor Could Prove as Costly as Any Proposals by Liberals," *Wall Street Journal,* Jan. 30, 1991. According to an analysis of the Center on Budget and Policy Priorities, "the proposed budget would mean a net loss of $600 million, after inflation, in nonentitlement spending for low income groups." Timothy Noam and Hilary Stout, "President's Plan Seeks 'Empowerment' of Poor Through Poverty-Fighting Plans," *Wall Street Journal,* Feb. 5, 1991.

72. In the summer of 1967, a senior U.S. officer responsible for policy-making reported: "We keep on destroying them; yet they always come back. And in the meantime, nothing changes in the enemy position amongst the population. That is why we are now at the grass roots... I didn't think...that the enemy was so deeply embedded in the fabric of the country." Peter Arnett, *Philadelphia Inquirer,* July 22, 1967.

73. "The [U.S.] planes were credited by military spokesmen with having destroyed or damaged 473 'enemy structures'...According to some American advisers to Vietnamese military units, 'enemy structures' sometimes includes civilian houses. Once destroyed, they are listed as 'enemy structures.'" Charles Mohr, *New York Times,* Aug. 9, 1966.

   "Each afternoon, in the air-conditioned press-briefing room in Saigon, the United States Military Command releases a communique reporting that 300 or more 'enemy structures' have been destroyed by American fighter-bombers or by the guns of Seventh Fleet warships that day. The statistics imply sound military progress until a visit to the countryside reveals that what is meant by an 'enemy structure' is usually a peasant hut in a hamlet the Communists control, or which the American and South Vietnamese authorities suspect the Communists control." Neil Sheehan, *New York Times Magazine,* Oct. 9, 1966.

74. "There is a common ground between all the various examples of systems analysis referred to in these essays... To put the case most broadly: the value of a given method of work is determined by asking the opinion of those who have hired it done." (Philip Green, *Deadly Logic,* pp. 18, 90.)

75. "It is not a commitment that I made, but a commitment that the United States made. That is a pretty big commitment—the United States' promise." L.B. Johnson, quoted by Max Frankel, *New York Times,* March 3, 1968.

76. Leslie Gelb refers to Bush as "far-sighted" in his *New York Times* column of April 21, 1991, with apparent reference solely to the political advantage of the war to Bush and his coterie.

77. See Barnouw, *The Sponsor;* Barry Cole and Mal Oettinger, *Reluctant Regulators,* Reading, MA: Addison-Wesley, 1978; James W. Baughman, *Television's Guardians: The FCC and the Politics of Programming,* Knoxville: University of Tennessee Press, 1985.

78. "The attached report contains studies of nine critical periods in the Vietnam war. In each of these periods the pattern of U.S. military escalation in the context of Vietnamese or international pressures for negotiations is shown to persist, despite the special characteristics of each episode. Although in the first two of these periods military involvement is less prominent than in the later periods, all serve as background for an understanding of the Administration's proclivity to see as threat rather than as promise the emergence of Vietnamese or neutral initiatives for compromise political solutions." (Franz Schurmann, Peter Dale Scott, Reginald Zelnik, *The Politics of Escalation in Vietnam,* New York: Fawcett, 1966, p. 14.) On the aggressive fending off of any diplomactic course

during the Gulf crisis beginning on August 2, 1990, see Chomsky, *Deterring Democracy,* pp. 203-210.

79. "At about 7:15 p.m. last Thursday President Nixon chose to tell the nation, in his televised press conference, that 'I believe that forced integration of the suburbs is not in the national interest.'" *Wall Street Journal,* Dec. 16, 1970.

80. "The G.A.O. report cited as one instance of abuse the provision by the Defense Department in 1961 of an 8,000-ton steel forge press...then used '78 per cent of the actual production time for commercial work...'" "Proxmire Links 23 Contractors to Defense Waste," *New York Times,* Jan. 6, 1968.

81. *Civilian Casualty, Social Welfare and Refugee Problems in South Vietnam,* Hearings before the Subcommittee on Refugees, 91st Congress, 1st Session, 1969, p. 27.

82. "Recognizing the importance of private investment from abroad, the [South] Koreans have set up a broad incentive program, offering up to five years of full tax exemption for approved projects, plus another three years of half exemption...There are direct U.S. investments in lines ranging from clocks to nylon yarn, knitwear, and oil refining. Recently, however, U.S. companies have made commitments for fertilizer, chemical, oil refining, and electronics ventures...[In mid-1965] there were 677 thousand workers known to be unemployed, and perhaps 2 million underemployed... Under Korean law, the standard work week for men is 48 hours, but it can be extended to 60 hours by agreement...A small minority of the labor force is represented by unions. Koreans cash wages are among the lowest anywhere, with manufacturing workers, skilled and unskilled, averaging $.77 a day." *Korea,* a report prepared by the Economic Research Division, The Chase Manhattan Bank, 1967.

   In Brazil, "To be sure the military regime...has been no model of democratic permissiveness. Brazilian journalists deemed to be unfriendly to the government may find themselves behind bars... But U.S. firms are leading the investment parade... Under a new investment guarantee agreement with the U.S., Brazil since 1965 [when the military took over] has approved more than $120 million worth of new projects by U.S. firms... Besides the rules limiting pay increases to percentages well below the rate at which the cost of living is rising, there is an almost total prohibition against strikes." *Wall Street Journal,* March 9, 1967.

83. For a systematic study of gap myths, see Gervasi, *The Myth of Soviet Military Supremacy.*

84. Peter Clausen, "Star warriors try again," Bulletin of Atomic Scientists, June 1991, p. 9.

85. According to one of his biographers, Henry Luce believed that "God had founded America as a global beacon of freedom." Swanberg, *Luce and His Empire,* p. 217, quoted in Landau, *Dangerous Doctrine,* p. 36.

86. This law was expounded in a speech given by Mr. Goldwater in New York City, January 15, 1964. Goldwater's Law is based on the following sociological analysis: (1) People are poor because they are stupid and/or lazy. (2) Money cannot overcome stupidity or laziness. (3) Money can make poverty more attractive. (4) Therefore increased subsidies to the poor will induce more people to opt for "poverty." Q.E.D.

87. "It was definitely a good night's work. I don't know how many gooks we got really, but we got plenty. We counted 140 on the ground this morning. An aerial observer reported 350. The North Vietnamese always drag a lot of their dead away." U.S. Marine Captain Andrew de Bona, *New York Times,* Sept. 12, 1967.

88. "Why, then, this restlessness? Because when a great ship cuts through the sea, the waters are always stirred and troubled. And our ship is moving—moving through new waters, toward new shores." L. B. Johnson, State of the Union Message, *New York Times,* Jan. 18, 1968. See the description of "Great Man" in

Henry Fielding, *The Life of Mr. Jonathan Wild the Great,* London: 1743, pp. 256-60.

89. On the centrality of growth in economic thinking and market practice, see E.J. Mishan, *The Costs of Economic Growth,* London: Staples Press, 1967; Fred Hirsch, *The Social Limits to Growth,* Cambridge: Harvard University Press, 1978; R.B. DuBoff, *Accumulation & Power: An Economic History of the United States,* Armonk, NY: M.E. Sharpe, 1989.

90. The Vietnam war spherical guavas, which were an advance over the previous "lazy dog" bomb, held up to 166,400 pellets, enclosed in small metal bomblets that also provided steel and other metal pieces that were thrown out with great force. According to Dr. Jean-Paul Vigier, a weapons expert, the guavas were "a new event in the annals of war. Like combat gas they are a weapon designed to harm noncombatants and civilian populations... the cluster bombs [guavas] have been developed for use in underdeveloped countries." (Quoted in Dave Dellinger, "Report from the Tribunal, *Liberation,* April, 1967.)

91. In 1962 a former FBI agent claimed that 1,500 of 8,500 members, or almost one-fifth of the Party, were FBI informants. "As a result of paying this small army of informants, the FBI had become the Communist Party's largest financial angel." (Fred J. Cook, *The FBI Nobody Knows,* New York: Macmillan, 1964, p. 33.)

92. The *New York Times,* editorializing on the World Court's "tendentious" and "predictable" decision that "found the United States guilty of violating international law by supporting the 'contra' war against Nicaragua," referred specifically to the Court as "a hostile forum." "America's Guilt—Or Default," July 1, 1986.

93. For a discussion and citations, see Chomsky, *Necessary Illusions.* pp. 95-96.

94. "As battle rages, we will continue as best we can to help the good people of South Vietnam enrich the condition of their life—to feed the hungry, to tend the sick—teach the young, shelter the homeless, and help the farmer increase his crops, and the workers to find a job." L.B. Johnson, Press Conference on July 28, 1965.

"The tactic is bomb, bomb, bomb—and U.S. planes are doing it over North and South Vietnam at the incredible rate of more than 3,000 pounds a minute around the clock." A.P. dispatch, *York Gazette,* May 1, 1967.

95. U.S. support of the military junta in South Vietnam against Buddhist agitation in 1966 was explained as follows: "American officials suggest that the strategy and aims of Thich Tri Quang [a leading Buddhist] are basically incompatible with the interests of the United States in Vietnam...and they do not feel that any government controlled by Thich Tri Quang would be amenable to U.S. influence." Neil Sheehan, *New York Times,* April 11, 1966.

96. "1969 Enemy Infiltration Into South Vietnam Is Estimated at 100,000 to 110,000," *New York Times,* Jan. 7, 1970.

97. "Interrogation is a kind of euphemism. What the overwhelming evidence we saw and heard demonstrated was that this interrogation process [employed by the Saigon government], the kinds of aids to interrogation and the methods used to get answers to questions amount to the most brutal of the methods of torture known to history." John Pemberton, in *Civilian Casualty, Social Welfare and Refugee Problems in South Vietnam,* Hearings before the Subcommittee on Refugees, 91st Congress, 1st Session, 1969, p. 114.

98. "I should like to state for the record as forcefully as I can that whatever may have been our mistakes in the past, it is the policy of this Government not to intervene in the domestic affairs of foreign countries... The particular form of government in any country and the particular persons who constitute that government are a matter of domestic concern to the peoples of that country. The fact that there may be American investments abroad in no way alters the

fact that this Government will not intervene in the affairs of other nations." (U.S. Undersecretary of State Webb, U.S. Congress, House of Representatives, Committee on Banking and Currency Hearings, *Export-Import Bank Loan Guarantee Authority*, Washington, 1949, p. 56.)

99. Thus James Reston describes, with deep emotion, the "propaganda of the most vicious nature" employed by opponents of the Johnson Administration: One peace group, "for example, circulated a leaflet with a photograph of a soldier plunging a knife into the stomach of a mutilated and half-naked man. The caption read: 'Getting the Point: South Vietnamese Rangers Interrogate a Prisoner.' It urged University of California students to 'join the march against the war in Vietnam.'" (James Reston, *New York Times,* April 21, 1965.)

100. In explaining his lobbying for S&L looters, Senator Dennis DeConcini "said his sole interest in American Continental Corp. and its Lincoln Savings & Loan Association subsidiary was whether federal bureaucratic actions would cause the loss of jobs." Paulette Thomas, "Sen. DeConcini Calls Lobbying Commonplace," *Wall Street Journal,* Nov. 20, 1990.

101. On departing from South Vietnam, Mr. Henry Cabot Lodge, Jr., presented the American philosophy of the military junta (and the case for retaining Marshal Ky and his associates):

Certainly the biggest nation-building entity is the military. Also, it has the reservoir of administrative talent. It's the most likely place where they can go to find people to do certain administrative jobs. I grant you, ideally speaking it is better for the community not to have the military do them.But in a country at this stage of development, they must do it... So, I believe the military must be a participant in the Government here in the future. *New York Times,* April 26, 1967.

102. "On the basis of Kahn's example, it seems reasonable to conclude that where so great a part of the area of investigation ...consists of political and other evaluative considerations, or is so far removed from practical human experience as to be insusceptible of 'hard' analysis that does not import the hidden judgments and guesses of the analyst, those who hope to find any especially believable answers to the intellectual problems of our age in the results of systems analysis are whistling in the dark." Green, *Deadly Logic,* p. 89.

103. "Air Vice Marshal Nguyen Cao Ky, the current Premier of South Vietnam, was a French pilot. On occasional visits to the countryside he appears before the peasants in a trim black flight suit with a lavender scarf around his neck and a pearl-handled pistol at his waist—a kind of Asian Captain Marvel.

"The Deputy Premier, Lieut. Gen. Nguyen Huu Co, and other generals in the Saigon military junta, were officers or sergeants in the French colonial forces. Their fondness for French cuisine, snappy uniforms, and cocktail parties and receptions creates a pale but faithful reflection of the social round of colonial days. They are the Vietnamese who have inherited the worst of two cultures—the pretentiousness of the native mandarins and the rigidity of the French colonial officers and administrators." Neil Sheehan, *New York Times Magazine,* Oct. 9, 1966.

104. "People ask me who my heroes are. I have only one—Hitler. I admire Hitler because he pulled his country together when it was in a terrible state in the early thirties. But the situation here is so desperate now that one man would not be enough. We need four or five Hitlers in Vietnam." (Marshall Ky, as quoted in an interview with Brian Moynihan, *Sunday Mirror* [London], July 4, 1965.) In a subsequent "clarification," Ky stated that "when I referred to Hitler incidentally during one of my conversations with journalists, I had in mind that Vietnam needed above all leadership and a sense of discipline..." *New York Times,* July 16, 1965. In a still further clarification in the summer of 1966, "Refer-

ring to earlier reports quoting him as saying Hitler was his idol, Premier Ky said this was not exactly what he meant. He said that when somebody asked him what South Vietnam needed to unify its people, he had answered a 'strong man' and had pointed out that Germany under Hitler was able to rise and grow strong. Besides, he said amid laughter, he did not like Hitler because 'he was not handsome and not a lady-killer.'" Reuters, covering Ky's press conference at Manila, *New York Times,* international edition, Aug. 13-14.

105. "Premier Ky...said in an interview that his regime was not yet ready to face the threat of Communist political agitation after a negotiated cease-fire because it had not had time to begin to overcome what he called the many social and economic injustices in South Vietnam." (Charles Mohr, *New York Times,* Sept. 1, 1965.) A year later, "One South Vietnamese official said recently: 'Frankly, we are not strong enough now to compete with the Communists on a purely political basis.'" Charles Mohr, *New York Times,* Oct. 24, 1966.

106. "Usually it is the tenants who are most eager for land reform and landlords who are reluctant. In the southern half of Vietnam, however, the landlords are accepting the Government's land reform more readily than the tenants." *New York Times,* April 5, 1955.

"The population has serious causes for complaint against the [Diem] regime. In the first place, there is the matter of land reform. The regime did carry out several years ago [a land reform] but it was infinitely more modest that the Vietminh's. The result is that landowners who were refugees in Saigon during the war reoccupied their farms in 1956-7 and demanded rent payment. The peasants did not like it." Max Clos, *Le Figaro,* Feb. 9, 1961.

"With only 25 per cent of the non-urban population under effective government control, a large mass of landless peasants stands to lose a great deal the day Saigon reestablishes control over the countryside and thus restores the old landlord-tenant relationship, as invariably happened in the past wherever government troops reoccupied a given area. (In fact, in some such areas the landlords arrived in the supply trucks of the troops and some unit commanders could be persuaded to launch a clearing operation in the area where the returning landlords promised to share the proceeds with them.)" Bernard Fall, *Foreign Affairs,* Oct. 1966.

In a study by Dr. Roy L. Prosterman for a Congressional subcommittee, it was stated that: "Virtually all land reform ceased in 1961, and the major new development in the law has been one prescribing in effect 'negative land reform,' or the return of the landlords to their former positions in areas that have been resecured." *New York Times,* March 6, 1968.

107. "One study found...that 53 percent of low-income defendants received prison sentences, compared to only 26 percent of high-income defendants....When time served is compared for similar offenses—including first-time offenders—African-Americans serve far longer sentences than whites. In the federal prison system, sentences for African-Americans are 20 percent longer for similar crimes." Alexander Lichtenstein and Michael Kroll, *The Fortress Economy,* Philadelphia: American Friends Service Committee, 1990, pp. 5-6. Judge Lois Forer writes that "The basic problem is that most poor people do not receive a due process trial in either civil or criminal courts. In civil matters, many who cannot afford the high costs of litigation simply forego their rights." *Money and Justice,* New York: W.W. Norton, 1984, p. 22.

108. Suharto, the dictator of Indonesia and manager of one of the great holocausts of the post-World War II era, having brought his country into alignment with us, has long been treated as both moderate and leader. Most recently, Argentina's president Menem, having accommodated completely to the U.S.-IMF rules for Argentina, and genuflecting to U.S. power in the manner of

Somoza on foreign policy issues, has also become a leader-moderate. On press treatment of Menem, see *Lies of Our Times,* Jan.-Feb. 1992, p. 17.

109. For an account of how Tony Coelho went after contributions of independent oil drillers, and fought hard for their interests on the tax front because "I just believe in the industry and I believe in independent oil," see Jackson, *Honest Graft,* pp. 118-121.

110. In fact, the prime role of the United States government in relation to the murderous behavior of amenable tyrants is protecting them and deflecting attention from their crimes, which may occasionally require insistence on the prosecution of some low-level personnel. For a discussion, see Edward S. Herman, "The United States Versus Human Rights in the Third World," pp. 92-96.

111. The phrase was used by Nixon and Agnew in their attacks on the Eastern liberal establishment in the media, allegedly subverting the National Interest.

112. Linkage was used by Kissinger and Reagan to stymie important foreign policy actions on arms limitations by tying them to extraneous issues, like Soviet "geopolitical conduct." As Gervasi notes, "'Linkage,' then, appears to be a term used only in the absence of real links, and only when it is convenient to create artificial ones. It means to invoke opposition to a policy that would otherwise stand unopposed, and to demand support for another policy which otherwise would gain little favor, by suggesting there ought to be a link between the two when otherwise no link would exist, and even when it might be unwise to create one." *Myth of Soviet Military Supremacy,* p. 223. On the other hand, when it was proposed in the Gulf crisis of 1990-91 that an Iraqi withdrawal from Kuwait should be linked to negotiations on Palestinian-Israeli relations, this was rejected with indignation by U.S. officials, although the connection between these sets of events was far closer than in the cases invoked by Kissinger and Reagan. See further, Chomsky, *Deterring Democracy,* pp. 208-10.

113. "'There just don't seem to be lucrative targets out on the trail anymore,' according to 1st Lt. John McNabb of San Antonio, Texas." "U.S. Fliers at Thailand Base Note Drop in Red Infiltration," *International Herald Tribune,* Oct. 24, 1972. The phrase was also commonly used during the Gulf war bombing of January and February 1991.

114. Michael Wines, "'Lynch Mob,' Reagan Says of Aides' Critics," *New York Times,* Feb. 2, 1988.

115. "And the best way for contractors to do that [maximize short-term profits] in our current system is to invest in 'market intelligence,' a euphemism for hiring consultants and lobbyists to intervene in the process in the executive branch and on Capitol Hill" (Secretary of Defense Frank Carlucci). Ralph Cipriano, "Carlucci faults Congress on procurement," *Philadelphia Inquirer,* July 10, 1988.

116. The fact that the two most powerful leaders of the Sandinistas, the Ortega brothers, could not reasonably be called Marxist-Leninists, never interfered with the designation in the Free Press. See Chomsky, *Culture of Terrorism,* p. 104, note 6.

117. "Rulers of most poor countries, by reason of that very poverty, can recruit mercenaries from among their own people. This method is less conspicuous than the Congolese method, but it is also less reliable because the danger of defection and mutiny is inescapable when national forces are used in a revolutionary situation. This danger, in turn, can give rise to a demand for extra-national, counterrevolutionary forces—Belgian regular troops in the nominally independent Congo, French regular troops in nominally independent Gabon, U.S. regular troops in nominally independent Santo Domingo and South Vietnam." Conor Cruise O'Brien, "The Counterrevolutionary Reflex," *The Columbia University Forum,* Spring 1966, p. 21.

118. "More than 70 former South African mercenaries from the Congo have signed contracts as 'combat experts' in the jungle with the American forces in Vietnam,

the *Sunday Times* of Johannesburg announces...Jan van Wijk, former lieutenant of the mercenaries in the Congo...and his fellows have been solicited by...the U.S. Embassy in Leopoldville to engage themselves in Vietnam." *Le Monde,* Jan. 6, 1966, quoted in *Viet Report,* March-April 1966, p. 15.

119. In the summer of 1966 President Ferdinand Marcos agreed to send 2,000 Filipinos to Vietnam. This represented a complete about face for Mr. Marcos: "As a candidate he opposed a suggestion for a similar force made by the then President, Diosdado Macapagal... The general assumption has been that, among other things, Mr. Marcos hoped the gesture would not go unnoticed in Washington when foreign economic and military aid was being allocated." William Beecher, *New York Times,* Aug. 2, 1966.

President Marcos' action did not go unnoticed. One month later it was announced that U.S. aid to the Philippines for agricultural improvement programs was being increased from $25 to $45 million, that $16 to $20 million was being allocated to help re-equip the Philippine army to meet the communist threat, and other programs of aid were being increased significantly. (Richard Eder, *New York Times,* Sept. 16, 1966.) The premium (brokerage commission) for the 2,000 man Filipino force appears to have been about $25,000 per member.

120. "Senate stuck in 1980s," *Bulletin of Atomic Scientists,* Oct. 1990, p. 3. See also, "Who's micromanaging the Pentagon?," *Bulletin of Atomic Scientists,* Oct. 1989, p. 6.

121. On Cambodia, the *New York Times* reported on Oct. 16, 1988 that the United States and its allies "have decided that without some sign of compromise by Vietnam toward a political settlement [i.e., agreeing to our terms], the Khmer Rouge forces must be allowed to serve as military pressure on Vietnam, despite their past." The *Times* has never to my knowledge suggested the usefulness of ANC or PLO "military pressure" for bringing South Africa or Israel to the bargaining table.

122. See "Rogers Rejects Pressure on Greece as 'Arrogance,' " *New York Times,* Aug. 25, 1972.

123. "The United States announced today that it had paid a 'missing person gratuity' of $6,472 to the wife of a Vietnamese man allegedly killed by American Green Beret soldiers because he was a double agent." B. Drummond Ayres, Jr., "Wife of Vietnamese Paid $6,472 by U.S.," *New York Times,* Oct. 6, 1969.

124. "The routine replacement of a battlefield nuclear missile five years from now hardly seems an issue to get very excited about. Yet what Secretary of State James A. Baker 3d has found as he visited NATO capitals is that 'modernization,' as the plan to upgrade the short-range Lance missile is known has emerged" as a serious issue, etc. Serge Schmemann, "NATO's German Woes," *New York Times,* Feb. 15, 1989.

125. "But true peace lies neither in bombs nor in truncheon. It lies in the pattern of mutual respect and mutual forbearance that is the essence of a civilized society" (Spiro Agnew). Richard Nixon also used the phrase in his 1973 State of the Union Message, *New York Times,* Feb. 3, 1973.

126. Writing of the primitive napalm of the early Vietnam war era, one expert described it as follows:

"Consisting of nine-two to ninety-six per cent aluminum napthenate and four to eight per cent aluminum palmitate, it burns at 800 to 1300 degrees centigrade and may continue to burn for fifteen minutes, causing deep, severe burns, with a very high death rate. The new 'supernapalm,' Napalm-2 has sodium, magnesium and phosphorus added. It burns at 1500 to 2000 degrees centigrade. Not satisfied with this, the United States has recently been using magnesium bombs, which consist of eighty-five to ninety-six per cent magnesium, with aluminum powder. This burns at a temperature of about 3500 degrees centigrade, or about three times the heat of the old-fashioned, pre-Vietnam napalm...

"Dr. Behar testified that about half of those wounded by napalm die from the burns. Among those suffering phosphorus burns from napalm, about three fourths die: 'These burns are of an atrocious nature, in the sense that the phosphorus fragments continue to burn inside the body for eight to ten days. A number of different complications are to be found...due to the chemical nature of the phosphorus itself.'" Dave Dellinger, "Report From the Tribunal," *Liberation,* April 1967.

127. "If we take up arms...it is to help the nation-builders" (Lyndon B.Johnson, speaking to the Veterans of Foreign Wars, *New York Times,* March 14, 1968). See also note 101.

128. "NED has acted as an international political action committee (PAC) dispensing U.S. government funds to further certain partisan political projects around the world... Despite its mandate to strengthen the indigenous democratic process, NED often interferes with that process by creating or supporting organizations which conform to a narrow, interventionist U.S. political agenda. In doing so, NED bolsters elite organizations while undercutting broad-based movements and fostering dependency of foreign private groups on U.S. largesse." Council on Hemispheric Affairs and Inter-Hemispheric Education Resource Center, *National Endowment for Democracy (NED): A Foreign Policy Branch Gone Awry,* March 1990, p. 4.

129. The historian John Lewis Gaddis explains and justifies western intervention against the Bolsheviks from 1917 and thereafter on the ground that "the most profound revolutionary challenge of the century was mounted against the West"—as Chomsky notes, not by actions but merely "by changing the social order of Russia and proclaiming revolutionary intentions." Chomsky,*Necessary Illusions,* pp. 181-83.

130. "Many observers and diplomats here and abroad...have misinterpreted the Administration's offer to negotiate as an offer to compromise with the Vietcong in South Vietnam. General Taylor's testimony should have made it clear that such a compromise is not anticipated here... Washington's purpose at such negotiations would be to ratify the end of the Communist threat to South Vietnam and not to compromise on the basis of the existing military balance... They believe the Communists would now negotiate *or give up* [emphasis added] only if they were prepared to honor the potential force that the United States can bring to bear." Max Frankel, *New York Times,* Feb. 18, 1966.

For James Reston, on the other hand, "The enduring mystery of the war in Vietnam is why the Communists have not accepted the American offers of unconditional peace talks." *New York Times,* Dec. 31, 1965.

131. Jonathan Marshall. Peter Dale Scott and Jane Hunter, *The Iran-Contra Connection: Secret Teams and Covert Operations in the Reagan Era,* Boston: South End Press, 1987, pp. 36-37.

132. See note 58 for the dichotomous treatment of defense-offensive, stabilizing-destabilizing in nuclear deterrence theory.

133. "...there is a huge irony in our obsession with foreign influence in view of the fact that for three decades the CIA has played the foreign agent's role *par excellence* on political stages all over the world. In the same way, the Army's enormous computerized domestic intelligence filing operation at Fort Holabird with its 100,000 subjects was called the 'Counterintelligence Analysis Branch,' on the theory [better: claim or rationalization] that it was merely monitoring the activities of foreign intelligence agents." Donner, *Age of Surveillance,* p. 20.

134. Holly Sklar, *Washington's War on Nicaragua,* Boston: South End Press, 1988, p. 17.

135. "The CIA knew about Operation Condor, the Argentine [military intelligence officer] explained, and indeed had played a key part in setting up the compu-

terized links between the intelligence and operational units of the six military regimes: Chile, Argentina, Uruguay, Brazil, Paraguay, and Bolivia." Landau, *Dangerous Doctrine,* p. 119.

136. The phrase is used in explaining the rise of abuses of inside information in Tim Carrington and Edward T. Pound, "War Games: Pushing Defense Firms To Compete, Pentagon Harms Buying System," *Wall Street Journal,* June 27, 1988.

137. On the assassination efforts, see the Senate Intelligence Committee report,*Alleged Assassination Plots Involving Foreign Leaders,* pp. 79-180; on Mongoose more generally, Hinckle and Turner,*The Fish is Red.*

138. See Linda Hunt, "U.S. coverup of Nazi scientists," *Bulletin of Atomic Scientists,* April 1985, pp. 16-24; also, Chistopher Simpson, *Blowback.*

139. For discussion of the estimated killings and the background and character of the Phoenix program, see Chomsky and Herman, *The Washington Connection,* pp. 322-28.

140. "At first, the people who get paid to think up catchy military code names toyed with the idea of calling the operation Poised Hammer." But deciding that that phrase was too "bellicose," they settled on Provide Comfort II. Clyde Haberman, "Allied Strike Force Forms in Turkey," *New York Times* July 25, 1991.

141. See the discussion of this and other anti-guerrilla and anti-civilian campaigns in Halliday and Cumings, *Korea: The Unknown War,* pp. 146-50.

142. Describing the "meat market" established by Tony Coelho to sell Democratic candidates, Brooks Jackson says, "it paid to put the best merchandise up front." Coelho's PAC director, Tom Nides, "subtly tried to steer the candidates with the best prospects to donors with money to give." Earlier, "He forced candidates to stand behind tables, each with a name card and a place to display his or her literature." PAC managers could pick and choose among those displayed. Coelho's staff "made sales calls, pushing candidates who could claim business credentials."*Honest Graft,* pp. 69, 91-92.

143. According to high U.S. officials in South Vietnam, commenting on the lock-stock-and-barrel transfer of the pacification program to the military in May 1967, "The big problem in pacification is local security, and that's the military's job. Who's got the clout with the South Vietnamese forces? Westmoreland... We've been playing the be-nice-to-Asia game for 10 years, and it's been a flop. We can't afford it any longer." (Quoted in Jonathan Randal, *New York Times,* May 13, 1967.)

"Soon the Government will have no need to win the hearts and minds of Bensuc. There will be no Bensuc." (*New York Times,* Jan. 11, 1967.) "Four villages—Bensuc, Rachap, Bungcong, and Rachkeim—have in fact already ceased to exist. As they left, many of the women saw their homes put to the torch or bulldozed flat. 'I was very poor in my village, but I didn't mind that. I wanted to stay. Last week the fish-shaped planes flew over our fields. My husband didn't know what they were. He stood up and they shot him down and killed him. I wish I had stayed and got killed too.'" (*New York Times,* Jan. 15, 1967).

"Col. Marvin Fuller, commander of a brigade in the operation [scorching the earth over a 100-square-mile area in South Vietnam] said anyone living in the operational area is presumed to be an enemy. Inhabitants were being evacuated to government controlled areas.

"Fuller said water buffalo, ducks, chickens and pigs were being slaughtered to deny fresh meat to enemy battalions. Dogs were killed because in a pinch the guerillas slaughter them for food, he said.

"...fires dotted the countryside as U.S.infantrymen set the torch to home, farm wagons and piles of rice straw. Hundreds of tons of rice have been destroyed or removed." (A.P. dispatch from Saigon, *York Gazette,* March 14, 1967.)

144. "The PAC managers told him 'the problem was not partisanship, but our fail-

ure to adequately market candidates,' Coelho wrote. So he set out to market Democratic House candidates in the increasingly crowded bazaar of special interest money managers." Jackson, *Honest Graft*, p. 69.

145. Quoted in "Kicking the Chemical Habit," *Conservation 89*, National Wildlife Federation, June 30, 1989.

146. "The doctrine of plausible deniability has been ridiculed, but in one important respect it has worked as intended: It is the C.I.A. we have been investigating and criticizing rather than the men who gave it marching orders, or the undebated policies they pursued." Thomas Powers, "The C.I.A., and Honor," *New York Times*, Op. Ed., July 27, 1980.

147. "Coelho believed he had turned aside a right-wing Republican revolution, fighting money with money." Jackson, *Honest Graft*, p. 19.

148. The establishment experts on "terrorism," for example, all agree that Soviet bloc countries have been free from this scourge. The attacks on Cuba by the United States and its proxies, or on Nicaragua 1981-89, are simply ignored by these experts under Preferential Method principles. For a summary discussion of U.S.-sponsored terrorism against Cuba, see Chomsky, *Necessary Illusions*, pp. 274-75.

149. "Defense Secretary Melvin Laird outlined a U.S. military strategy of 'realistic deterrence' that's designed to 'prevent wars' rather than merely 'manage crises'...the Secretary said there is a pressing need to modernize conventional weapons and to step up development of new offensive nuclear weapons." ("Laird Outlines Strategy to 'Prevent Wars' But Discloses a Go-Slow ABM Approach," *Wall Street Journal*, March 10, 1971.)

150. For a study showing that, for the members of the Pennsylvania legislature in the 1971-1972 session, there was a statistically significant relationship between votes against abortion rights and votes for capital punishment and other things deleterious to post-fetal life, see Robert Edelstein, Edward S. Herman, and Mary W. Herman, "Moral Consistency and the Abortion Issue," *Commonweal*, March 22, 1974.

151. The phrase was coined by Defense Secretary Melvin Laird at a news conference on Oct. 9, 1969, describing a policy of bombing "targets of opportunity as they present themselves." Terence Smith, "Concepts of 'Protective Reaction,' " *New York Times*, Sept. 24, 1971.

152. "They [the protestors] are not promoting peace but postponing it. They are not persuading the President or Congress to end the war, but deceiving Ho Chi Minh and General Giap into prolonging it." (James Reston, "The Stupidity of Intelligence," *New York Times*, Oct. 17, 1965.) This column was reproduced by A. N. Spanel, Founder-Chairman of International Latex Corporation, with the following comment: "We recommend that it be read and pondered especially by the honest, well-meaning Americans drawn into the swamp of confusion staged by the familiar communist conspiracy."

In April 1967 Mr. Reston referred to the idea that "the doves are deceiving the enemy into prolonging the killing" as "the new gospel according to our embattled masters..." ("Washington: Blessed Are The War Makers?" *New York Times*, April 28, 1967.)

153. Navy fliers on defoliation missions are reported to have as their motto: "Only you can prevent a forest." The slogan of the Psi-War pilots, dropping leaflets from DC-3's is: "Every litterbit helps." Harvey, *Air War—Vietnam*, pp. 39, 51. These drolleries remind us of the persistence, even in times of adversity, of the great tradition of native U.S. humor (*cf.* Mark Twain).

154. For an excellent discussion, see Kornbluh, *Nicaragua: The Price of Intervention*, chapter 4.

155. For some perspective on the scale of public information and propaganda pro-

grams of the government, see Herman and Chomsky, *Manufacturing Consent*, pp. 18-21.

156. "You know the endless attempts I made for a peaceful clarification and understanding of the problem of Austria, and later of the problem of the Sudetenland, Bohemia and Moravia. It was all in vain...In my talks with Polish statesmen...I formulated at last the German proposals and...there is nothing more modest or loyal than these proposals. I should like to say this to the world. I alone was in the position to make such proposals, for I know very well that in doing so I brought myself into opposition to millions of Germans. These proposals have been refused...I am wrongly judged if my love of peace and my patience are mistaken for weakness or even cowardice." (Adolf Hitler, Sept. 1, 1939, the morning of the attack on Poland, quoted in William Shirer, *The Rise and Fall of the Third Reich*, New York: Simon and Schuster, 1959, p. 793.)

"I have stated publicly and many times, again and again, America's willingness to begin unconditional discussions with any government at any place at any time... Fifteen efforts have been made to start these discussions, with the help of 40 nations throughout the world. But there has been no answer. But we are going to continue to persist, if persist we must, until death and desolation have led to the same conference table where others could now join us at a much smaller cost." (L. B. Johnson, *New York Times*, July 29, 1965.)

157. The classic statement, made in 1960 by the president of CBS, is that: "I suggest that a program in which a large part of the audience is interested is by that very fact a program in the public interest." Quoted in Barnouw, *Sponsor*, p. 123. Barnouw has an excellent account of the gradual attrition of "public interest" programs in the traditional sense of the term.

158. In testimony before Congress on South Africa's invasions of Angola and the issues involved in settling the war in Angola and occupation of Namibia, U.S. official Chester Crocker made a very special point of the importance of considering South Africa's "security problems" in any settlement. *Namibia and Regional Destabilization in Southern Africa*, Hearing before Subcommittee on Africa, House Committee on Foreign Affairs, 98th Cong., 1st sess., Feb. 15, 1983, pp. 13-14.

159. "'Radical nationalism' is another of those curious terms of US political theology—like 'Communism,' 'stability,' 'containment,'...—with technical meanings only dimly related to their normal sense: in this case, the reference is to nationalist movements that do not obey orders, whatever their political complexion may be, as opposed to 'moderate nationalists,' properly obedient." Chomsky, *Turning The Tide*, p. 173.

160. Silvia Nasar, "Third World Embracing Reforms to Encourage Economic Growth," *New York Times*, July 8, 1991. Nasar identifies reforms strictly as changes facilitating market expansion, including the liquidation of government support programs for the weak enacted in earlier "reform" periods. For a critical analysis, see Arthur McEwan, "The 'Success' of Free Market Reforms," *Lies of Our Times*, Sept. 1991, pp. 21-22.

161. The term is used in Richard Dale, "International Banking Is Out of Control," *Challenge*, January-February 1983.

162. "The first of the five massive raids, which the Pentagon later called 'reinforced protective reaction strikes,' came on March 27, 1970. The most intensive strikes were conducted between May 1 and May 4, 1970, when more than 500 aircraft took part in response to what Mr. Laird described as 'attacks on our unarmed reconnaissance aircraft.'" Terence Smith, "Concepts of 'Protective Reaction,'" *New York Times*, Sept. 24, 1971.

163. For an excellent background discussion, Chomsky, *The Fateful Triangle*, Boston: South End Press, 1983, chap. 3. For rejectionism in the post-Gulf War con-

text, Chomsky, "Letter from Lexington," *Lies of Our Times,* May 1991.

164. Thus economist Walter Heller wrote that "As a statesman, a President has a vital, not to say vested, interest, on behalf of the nation, in prosperity and rapid growth. They put at his disposal, as nothing else can, the resources needed to achieve great societies at home and grand designs abroad." (*New Dimensions of Political Economy,* Cambridge, MA: Harvard University Press, 1967, pp. 10-11. See Robert A. Brady, *The Spirit and Structure of German Fascism,* New York: Citadel Press, 1937, esp. chapter II, "Science, Handmaiden of Inspired Truth.")

165. As Professor Robert Scalapino explained to David Schoenbrun on National Educational Television, our restraint is shown by the fact that "We have the power, you know, to eradicate that country [Vietnam]."

166. See Robert S. McIntyre, "Are the Democrats Really So Stupid?" *New York Times,* Op. Ed., May 14, 1990.

167. "Nixon gave us revenue sharing, and Reagan gave us revenue bleeding" (Michigan Governor James Blanchard, quoted in the *New York Times,* May 21, 1990).

168. On the Reaganite fabrication and use of this concept, Morley and Petras, *The Reagan Administration and Nicaragua,* pp. 1-13, 33ff.

169. "Bush has repeatedly insisted on the restoration of Kuwait's 'rightful leaders to their place.' " *Bulletin of Atomic Scientists,* editorial, Oct. 1990.

170. Statement of Vice President Spiro T. Agnew. See also note 125 above.

171. "Mr. Humphrey told newsmen the administration had no choice but to send troops to the Dominican Republic 'because of the safety of our nationals.' " *New York Times,* May 18, 1965.

172. "The statements made by John Foster Dulles and General Navarre [during the French-Indochinese war] about *Chinese technicians* were inspired by their desire to explain away their failures by attributing them to extraneous causes." Jules Roy, *The Battle of Dienbienphu,* New York: Harper & Row, 1965, p. 203 (emphasis added).

173. A U.S. major, quoted in an AP dispatch from the destroyed town Bentre in Vietnam, *New York Times,* Feb. 8, 1968.

174. After describing the indignation of the U.S. press over Nicaraguan hot pursuit of contra terrorists into Honduras, Noam Chomsky then shows the complete press nonchalance over Israeli attacks on Lebanon, including those not even pretended to be in response to attacks, but merely to prove that "the iron fist is in full working order" (quoting the London *Guardian*). "The U.S. government is happy to explain why it supports Israeli violence deep inside Lebanon: the grounds are the sacred inherent right of self-defense, which may legitimately be invoked by the United States and its clients, under quite a broad interpretation—thought not, of course, by others, in particular, by victims of U.S. terror." *Necessary Illusions,* pp. 52-53.

175. Mr. Henry Cabot Lodge, Jr., stated before a Congressional Committee in the summer of 1965 that the U.S. would not withdraw from South Vietnam even if the government of that country asked us to. This was shortly thereafter amplified by an anonymous "high official" in Washington, who explained that Mr. Lodge meant that we would not leave if asked to do so "by a left-wing or even neutralist government that, in the U.S. view, did not reflect the true feelings of the South Vietnamese people or military leaders." (*New York Times,* Aug. 13, 1965.)

176. "The Johnson Administration has tried with the *utmost sincerity* [emphasis added; Reston had apparently developed a finely calibrated sinceriometer] to get Moscow to limit the arms race, to stop building an anti-ballistic missile system, to keep weapons out of space, to help end the war in Vietnam, and to cooperate in reducing tensions in Europe and the under-developed world—but Moscow has refused." (James Reston, *New York Times,* Nov. 5, 1967.)

177. Jack Raymond, *New York Times,* June 28, 1965:

As the helicopter nears guerilla territory, it draws ground fire, usually from machine guns near Vietcong bases. The helicopter drops a flare and scoops out of harm's way. The forward air controller in his observation plane drops sulphur and smoke bombs into the vicinity of the ground fire.

At the same time, the forward air controller, in radio contact with the helicopter and the waiting "killer planes," orders the lurking fighters to attack.

The fighter-bombers swoop into the target zone and bomb and strafe the base.

We also call it "skunk hunting," said Capt. John S. Lynch, an Air Force officer from Norfolk, VA... He added: "Day in and day out, whenever the weather permits—and sometimes even when the weather is foul—we go skunk hunting. 'We are going on a skunk hunt' the squadron leader will say, and everyone answers, 'Roger.'"

178. The State Department plan for China during World War II was "that we assume the leadership in assisting China to develop a strong, stable, and unified government in order that she may also become the principal stabilizing factor in the Far East." (Quoted from the Yalta Papers, p. 353, by Gabriel, Kolko, *The Politics of War,* New York: Random House, 1968, p. 221.) The Communist victory in China was deemed to be destabilizing in the Far East, despite the fact that it resulted in the establishment of a strong and unified state. Similarly, President Truman's decision to send military aid to the French in Indochina in 1950 was "to assist them in restoring stability."

179. Referring to the destruction of Bensuc and the resettlement of its 3,800 inabitants, the *New York Times* reported that most of the residents were "considered to be passive Vietcong" (Jan. 11, 1967). One officer stated,in reference to the relocation of Iron Triangle civilians, "Your heart goes out to them...but these are not innocent civilians, these are 100 per cent Viet Cong families, an enemy population..." (U.S. Army Major Robert Schweitzer to a *Baltimore Sun* correspondent, quoted in the *New Republic,* Jan. 28, 1967.)

180. "[U.S. officials] object if you call Phu Cuong a concentration camp, though that is what it is: these people have been arbitrarily rounded up and detained there, behind barbed wire, subjected to interrogation, and informers have been placed among them...The barbed wire is there, they explain patiently, to protect the camp from the Vietcong, but if the 'refugees' are Viet Cong dependents, it is hard to imagine why their husbands and fathers would attack them with mortars and hand grenades." McCarthy, *Vietnam,* pp. 41-42.

181. "By the Alice-in-Wonderland logic of the Nixon camp, *Plessy v. Ferguson,* which added a racial qualification to the 14th Amendment's 'equal protection' clause, was strict construction, while *Brown v. Topeka,* which extirpated that gratuitous qualification (and finally made our construction color-blind) was a case of loose construction!" Francis Wilhoit, *Commonweal,* May 1970, pp. 183-84.

182. Sir Frank Kitson's definition of subversion includes "the use of political and economic pressure, strikes, protest marches, and propaganda" designed to force the governing class "to do things which they do not want to do." *Low Intensity Operations,* London: Faber & Faber, 1972, p. 3.

183. For good analyses of Reaganite tax policy, see Frank Ackerman, *Reaganomics: Rhetoric and Reality,* Boston: South End Press, 1982, chapter 3; and Ackerman, *Hazardous to Our Wealth: Economic Policies in the 1980s,* Boston: South End Press, 1984, chapter 3.

184. "One cannot avoid concluding that this whole notion [by nuclear deterrence theorists] of threats, commitments, etc., depends on an asymmetrical evaluation of the world in which behavior that is reasonable and even educational when done by us is offensive sabre rattling when done by our opponents." Green, *Deadly Logic,* p. 152.

185. In speaking of jobs in the new Reagan administration, Kenneth Bacon noted

that "Indeed, toughness is one of the five criteria" Reagan and Meese have set for appointees. ("In Sub-Cabinet Jobs, Reaganites Stress the S.O.B. Factor," *Wall Street Journal,* Dec. 24, 1980.) An undated 1991 ad for *The New Republic* is addressed to "Liberals with guts," and stresses the magazine's providing "a special kind of tough, unflinching politics" (see *Mere gook rule).*

186. "The Soviet leaders are not apparently trying to revive the most dangerous phase of the cold war, but they seem determined to go into the second half century of their revolution by creating as much michief as they can, in Vietnam and elsewhere." James Reston, *New York Times,* Nov. 5, 1967.

187. John Gerassi, *The Great Fear in Latin America,* New York: Collier Books, 1965, pp. 195-6:

Trujillo's policy, like that of most Latin American dictators, was "Anti-communism," a catchword he used so well that he caught numerous admirers in Washington, especialy among State Department officials, senators and congressmen. Under the anti-communist slogan, Trujillo executed his opponents, an estimated 500,000 over 32 years, counting the Dominican exiles his henchmen sought out and murdered in New York, Mexico, Caracas, and Paris...

But Trujillo was "anti-communist," and thus was our friend. He had more apologists in Washington than any other strong man in the continent or even, except Formosa's Chiang Kai-shek, in the world. One United States economist sent there to help the Dominican Republic's finances, reacted: "Let's face it: this was a government of gangsters. And anyone who did business with them knew it." Yet plenty of businessmen did business with Trujillo, and so did our government, giving Trujillo millions of dollars with which he supported a huge lobby in Washington—to sell his sugar to our country's housewives.

188. "The agreement...calls for Boeing to plead guilty to two felony charges of 'unauthorized conveyance' of a pair of sensitive Defense Department budget documents in 1984,..." Andy Pasztor, "Boeing Is Said Ready to Accept Felony Charges," *Wall Street Journal,* Nov. 6, 1989.

189. "[W]e have fewer warheads than we had in 1967...over recent years we've followed a policy of kind of unilaterally disarming and the idea that maybe the others would follow suit" (Reagan in 1985). Chomsky notes that this is in reference to a period "When US strategic weapons more than doubled to over 9000 with constant technological improvements, a novel form of unilateral disarmament." *Turning The Tide,* p. 174.

190. The Big PX was a phrase used in Vietnam by GI's thinking nostalgically of home, where the consumer opportunities were greater.

191. This was a Gulf war reporters' phrase, not necessarily ironical, referring to government handouts passed along by the media without evaluation or verification.

192. When the President of Nicaragua in 1909 refused U.S. orders, and negotiated for a loan in Great Britain instead of granting the United States a monopoly on lending, U.S. Secretary of State Philander Knox accused the Nicaraguan government of "keeping Central America in tension of turmoil," i.e., provoking the United States to destabilize and attack Nicaragua, which it did. See Landau, *Dangerous Doctrine,* p. 18.

193. "More new ground was broken when LDF complaints were filed with the Department of Housing and Urban Development challenging urban renewal practices in Baltimore, Md., and Pulaski County, Tenn. Both urge cut-off of federal funds to projects that amount to Negro removal, with illegally inadequate relocation. In the latter case, project boundaries were so drawn that white-owned houses in the renewal area would escape the bulldozers." (Legal Defense Fund Report for 1966, p. 17.)

"At a cost of more than three billion dollars the Urban Renewal Agency

(URA) has succeeded in materially reducing the supply of low-cost housing in American cities." (Scott Greer, *Urban Renewal and American Cities,* Indianapolis: Bobbs-Merrill, 1965, p. 3)

194. On "coopting the experts" as a business policy in the field of business regulation, see Bruce Owen and Ronald Braeutigam, *The Regulation Game,* Cambridge, MA: Ballinger, 1978, p. 7. On the system whereby sound experts on terrorism are funded, housed, and pushed, Herman and O'Sullivan, *The "Terrorism" Industry,* chaps. 4-6.

195. When asked by journalist Robert Guillain what proportion of the reported 700 "Vietcong" killed in Operation Masher were civilians, a U.S. military officer replied: "In a Vietcong area like that one, civilians and military are all the same." (*Le Monde,* Feb. 24-March 2, 1966.) In a letter from one combat soldier cited by Drew Pearson and Jack Anderson: "'The daily enemy-killed-in-action figures,' he charged, 'can be trusted as much as a paper bag can be trusted to store water. Everyone who is not in a friendly uniform is counted as an enemy KIA.'" (*York Gazette,* May 12, 1967.) According to one Marine 2nd Lieutenant, following an air attack on a Vietnamese village, "We never found any dead soldiers but, as is the custom in Viet Cong controlled areas, all the dead found in the area were listed as Viet Cong killed in action in the official battle reports." Letter in *Cong. Rec.,* June 16, 1967.

196. The quoted phrase is the DOD's definition of the act of war. Lewis Lapham, *Money and Class in America,* New York: Weidenfield and Nicholson, 1998, p. 127.

197. "Behind a facade of photographs, flags and slogans there is a grim structure of decrees, political prisons, concentration camps, milder 're-education centers,' secret police....The whole machinery of security has been used to discourage active opposition of any kind from any source." (*Life Magazine,* describing the Diem government of South Vietnam, May 13, 1957.)

"Instead of uniting it, Diem has divided the South. Instead of crushing merely his legitimate enemies, the Communists, he has crushed all opposition of every kind, however anti-Communist it might be. In doing so, he has destroyed the very basis on which his regime should be founded. He has been able to do this, simply and solely because of the massive dollar aid he has had from across the Pacific, which kept in power a man who, by all the laws of human and political affairs,would long ago have fallen. Diem's main supporters are to be found in North America, not in Free Vietnam..." (David Hotham, in R. Lindholm, ed., *Viet-Nam: The First Five Years,* Lansing: Michigan State University Press, 1959, p. 346.)

198. "We have chosen to fight a limited war in Vietnam in an attempt to prevent a larger war—a war that's almost certain to follow..." (Lyndon B. Johnson, State of the Union Message, *New York Times,* Jan. 11, 1967).

199. A phrase used by U.S. military personnel in Vietnam to describe their role. "With the 'widow-makers' in A-Shau valley," *Le Monde,* Aug. 11-12, 1968.

200. See Gervasi, *Myth of Soviet Military Supremacy,* pp. 11-12, 227-28.

Index

This index does *not* include the words in the alphabetized Doublespeak Dictionary.

About South End Press

South End Press is a nonprofit, collectively-run book publisher with over 150 titles in print. Since our founding in 1977, we have tried to meet the needs of readers who are exploring, or are already committed to, the politics of radical social change.

Our goal is to publish books that encourage critical thinking and constructive action on the key political, cultural, social, economic, and ecological issues shaping life in the United States and in the world. In this way, we hope to give expression to a wide diversity of democratic social movements and to provide an alternative to the products of corporate publishing.

If you would like a free catalog of South End Press books or information about our membership program—which offers two free books and a 40% discount on all titles—please call 1-800-533-8478, or write us at South End Press, 116 Saint Botolph Street, Boston, MA 02115.

Other titles of interest from South End Press:

The Real Terror Network: Terrorism in Fact and Propaganda
Edward S. Herman

Necessary Illusions: Thought Control in Democratic Societies
Noam Chomsky

Turning the Tide: U.S. Intervention in Central America and the Struggle for Peace
Noam Chomsky

On Power and Ideology: The Managua Lectures
Noam Chomsky

After the Cataclysm: Postwar Indochina and the Reconstruction of Imperial Ideology
Noam Chomsky and Edward S. Herman

The Washington Connection and Third World Fascism
Noam Chomsky and Edward S. Herman

The Iran-Contra Connection: Secret Teams and Covert Operations in the Reagan Era
Jonathan Marshall, Peter Dale Scott, and Jane Hunter